Raising Kids
& Tomatoes

amusing tales and appetizing recipes

Other Books from *The Baltimore Sun*:

Gaining A Yard: The Building of Baltimore's Football Stadium

Motherhood is a Contact Sport

The Wild Side of Maryland: An Outdoor Guide

The 1996-1997 Maryland Business Almanac

Cal Touches Home

The Great Game of Maryland Politics

This *Baltimore Sun* book was published by SunSource, the information service of the *Sun*. To order any of the above titles, or for information on research, reprints and information from the paper's archives, please call 410.332.6800.

Raising Kids
& Tomatoes

amusing tales and appetizing recipes

Happy Eating,

Rob Kasper

Rob Kasper

THE BALTIMORE SUN

Published by
The Baltimore Sun
A Times-Mirror company
501 N. Calvert Street
Baltimore, MD 21278

Edited by Catherine Cook
Layout and design by Jennifer Halbert
Photographs of Rob Kasper by Jim Burger

ISBN – 0-9649819-8-X

Raising Kids and Tomatoes: amusing tales and appetizing recipes: a publication of the Baltimore Sun Company - 1998 - Baltimore, MD: Baltimore Sun Co.: 1998

*To my mother and father, who taught me to
appreciate good food and good writing.*

Contents:

Acknowledgements

MANY PEOPLE HAVE HELPED ME IN MY CAREER AND I WANT TO ACKNOWLEDGE some of them. I will start with my mother, Mary Ellen Kasper. In addition to providing me with a deep appreciation of good food, Mom planted the idea of a career in journalism. Being a newspaper reporter would be interesting work, my mom told me one day when I was about 12 years old, when we were sitting at the kitchen table. And, she added, you could ask people all kinds of personal questions, like how old they are.

My dad, Harry Kasper, was my first editor. When I was a kid in school, I would present my carefully crafted compositions to him and he would take out his black pen and slice them to ribbons. In these sessions, Dad taught me the value of using short sentences and strong verbs.

My brothers — Dan, Mark and Dick — my sisters-in-law — Sherry, Kathy and Jeanne — my nephews and niece, my countless cousins, and my uncles and aunts, have, whether they knew it or not, provided me with a great amount of material for my columns. I thank them, and hope that they repress any urge to set the record straight.

I want to thank Steve Parks and Kathy Lally, my first editors at *The Sun*, who hired me in 1978 to write features for a weekly section of the paper covering Anne Arundel County. Over the years, a variety of top *Sun* editors — the late Paul Banker, Hal Williams, Jim Houck, Kathy Christensen, and now John Carroll and Bill Marimow — have allowed me to write a free-ranging column. I thank them for the freedom.

I also am grateful to *The Sun's* publisher, Mike Waller, for helping me get this book off the ground.

Legions of editors at *The Sun* have straightened out my copy, but I want to acknowledge Catherine Cook, an editor of immense skill and unfailing good humor. In addition to shepherding most of my newspaper columns into print, she has also served as editor of this book and, along with copy editor Bruce Friedland, helped me to bring old work up to date.

I would also like to acknowledge two former *Sun* colleagues, copy editor Mal Allen who died in 1988, and fashion editor Vida Roberts who died in 1998. In addition to helping me with my craft, they regularly made me laugh, and that made showing up for work much easier.

I want to thank Jim Burns, an editor of the *Los Angeles Times* FoodStyles syndicate, for sending my column to subscribing newspapers in the United States and Canada. My co-workers at *The Sun* have given me many tips and much support. I thank them. Similarly, I thank the newspaper readers and serious eaters who over the years have written, telephoned or stopped me on the street to give me story ideas.

I want to thank the staff of SunSource for producing this book.

Finally, I owe a great deal of thanks to my family. My wife, Judy, and our sons, Matthew and Michael, have put up with my habit of turning events in their lives into fodder for my columns. I thank them for their tolerance and remind them that in my work and in my life, they are my inspiration.

Rob Kasper
Baltimore, Maryland
August 1998

Introduction

WHEN FORCED TO EXPLAIN HOW I LANDED A JOB THAT PAYS ME TO EAT, I CREDIT the kitchen table of my youth. Events that took place around that oak table in the middle of my family's kitchen got me interested in the wider world.

The kitchen table was where meals were served, where tales were told, where opinions were offered. As a kid, I quickly learned that if I sat quietly in a corner, listening to the adult conversations spilling out from the kitchen table, I could hear things you weren't supposed to — gossip about grown-ups behaving badly, table-pounding arguments about Democrats and Republicans, debates about which aunt makes the better roast beef gravy. Interesting stuff. After being trained as a kitchen-table eavesdropper, pursuing a career in journalism — a craft that encouraged quiet listening and vivid storytelling — seemed logical.

Shortly after arriving in Baltimore and going to work at *The Sun* in 1978, I volunteered to write a column about eating. Most editors were skeptical of the idea, saying readers wanted a column on the mechanics of cooking, not the free-ranging one I was proposing. My idea, as I confessed later to a colleague, was to use food as an opening to write about anything that came to mind. As long as something happened at the kitchen table, it was fair game for me.

My primary qualification to write about food was that I was an enthusiastic eater. I grew up in the Midwest, a region known for big eaters, in a household of four boys. During my teen-age years in St. Joseph, Mo., virtually all conversations with my parents began with them telling me to "close the refrigerator door." After picking up an undergraduate degree at the University of Kansas in American Studies and a master's degree in journalism from Northwestern University, I landed my first full-time newspaper job, as bowling editor and sports reporter at the *Hammond (Ind.) Times*. From there I moved on to the *Louisville Times*, the sister paper, now defunct, of the *Courier-Journal*. There I covered a variety of beats, from following Hubert Humphrey's 1972 presidential primary campaign around Indiana, to covering the local planning and zoning board, to writing feature stories for the paper's weekend magazine.

By the time I got to Baltimore I knew what I liked to write about, and it was not planning and zoning. It was food.

The column called "The Happy Eater" first appeared in 1981. It got off the ground for two reasons. First of all, it was championed by then-features editor Kathy Lally. Secondly, I agreed to write the column, in addition to performing my other writing assignments, for no extra pay. Generally speaking, if a newspaper reporter volunteers to do extra work for no extra pay, few bosses will object.

Eventually the column evolved from a once-a-week offering to a twice-a-week assignment. Down the road I began writing a third weekly column, on family life.

My interest in food deepened along the way. Instead of merely sitting at the table shoveling down the fare, I began spending more time at the stove. Through trial, error and with the help of my wife, Judy, I learned to cook. When a loaf of homemade bread rises, or a slab of ribs comes off the grill in a near nirvana state, I feel as if I am making some progress on the road of life.

My belief in the powers of the kitchen table to nurture good and strong thought permeates this collections of essays.

Sorting through almost 20 years of food columns to include in this book, I saw that whether I was writing about rockfish pulled from the Chesapeake Bay, or about the similarities of raising kids and tomatoes, or sermonizing about what is wrong with America today — not enough homemade pies — I was, in the end, addressing something that happened at the kitchen table.

The kitchen table I grew up with in St. Joseph was oval. The one my family sits at in Baltimore is rectangular. Nonetheless, the kitchen-table dynamic has remained the same over the years. The kitchen table is the Ellis Island of family life, the place where new arrivals — groceries, newspapers, a baseball bat — make their first stop. It is a reference station, a repository of schoolbooks, dictionaries and newspapers, a place where facts — from Cal Ripken's batting average to the names of the Greek gods — are verified. It is where house rules — from how late a teen-ager stays out, to what kind of milk to buy — are vigorously debated. It is a place to chew on what life has to offer.

As a reporter, whenever I interview writers I admire, I ask them about the kitchen tables of their pasts. Both Russell Baker and Garrison Keillor told me the family dinner table was a source of inspiration for their literary careers. Both recalled sitting at tables — Baker in West Baltimore, Keillor in Anoka, Minn. — listening to relatives telling tales. Both said these kitchen-table experiences made them want to become good yarn spinners.

Which proves, I guess, that the literary life can start with supper; that good eating can nourish good writing; in short, that many of life's better moments happen at a kitchen table.

Chapter 1

Fall

National salvation is in the oven

RECENTLY IT HIT ME WHAT IS WRONG WITH OUR COUNTRY TODAY. FEWER PIES are being baked in America's kitchens.

At a Washington gathering that I would describe as a "deep background lunch," I was handed a sheet of paper saying the number of pies baked from scratch fell 48 percent from 1979 to 1989. This statistic came from researchers for Crisco. They keep track of such things because shortening is an essential ingredient in a flaky pie crust.

It was grim news because a homemade pie with a flaky crust is one of life's great joys. Such a crust is airy, yet has texture. It makes its presence known without being assertive. It displays one of the great struggles of the universe, the tension between being and nothingness, right there in a 9-inch pie pan.

I did a little research and found that during the same period that pie baking slumped, faith in institutions declined. Fewer people said they could trust their fellow men, and the divorce rate increased. In short, the social fabric of America fell apart.

A source, whom I will call Deep Dish, told me that baking-industry probes have uncovered three reasons behind the drop in pie baking. First, Americans feel they don't have enough time to bake a pie. Secondly, pies suffer because, unlike "portable" foods such as cookies, pies are difficult to cart around. Thirdly, there is a widespread belief that the only time to bake pies is during the holidays.

I take issue with these reasons, not on statistical grounds, but on high moral ground, the place where all questions involving dessert and the meaning of life end up.

First, the time issue. It takes about an hour to an hour and a half to bake a pie. This is a significant chunk of the day, especially when, according to one survey I found, 38 percent of Americans already feel rushed.

But it seems to me the larger question is, What do you get for your trouble? The answer is satisfaction, in many forms. Making a pie, for instance, is a good way to cope with what appears to be a major source of trouble in America, the lack of communication between people living under the same roof.

For years now the best-seller list has been clogged with books about how men and women don't speak the same language. Meanwhile, columns offering advice on how parents and kids can talk to each other have popped up faster than new flavors of yogurt.

I say, put a homemade pie into this void and you will plug up the problem. Pull a pie out of the oven and you will find your family. In the presence of a homemade pie, warring parties talk to each other, even if they are different genders or from different generations. Pies can make tight-lipped teenagers chattier than Phil Donahue. Pies can inspire new forms of interfamily communication, like a note placed on a leftover piece of pie reading "Touch this and you die."

On the second anti-pie point, that pies are immobile, I say that what this country needs is not more get-up-and-go but more sitting still. Ever since expressways entered our lives, we have equated movement with progress, even though we ended up in fast-food restaurants. I say the time has come to sit down, drink a cup of coffee and have a slab of homemade pie. If we as a people would spend 30 minutes or so sitting at the kitchen table eating a piece of homemade pie and letting our minds float, our sense of purpose would return. Who knows — maybe even serendipity, something last experienced back in 1970, would make a return appearance.

The third point is tricky. There is no disputing that the urge to eat pies runs strong on holidays. For instance, at Thanksgiving, the high holy day of pies, four pies — a pumpkin, a mince, a peanut butter and a sour cream and raisin — appear at my family's feast. Fall is the prime pie baking season in America, with winter, which plays host to such holidays as Christmas, Hanukkah and the birthday of George "Love-Those-Cherries" Washington, coming in second.

It is fitting to bake on special occasions. But I believe special occasions should not be restricted to state-recognized holidays. Most Sundays, for instance, merit consideration as occasions worthy of homemade pie. A Sunday-night pie is a great antidote to Monday-morning dread. Eating pie fights depression, which, as we all know, is a growing problem in America today.

No matter how much things change...

ONE COOL AUTUMN EVENING WE HAD ROAST CHICKEN AND STATE CAPITALS for supper. It gave me an insight into how much things have changed on the food scene, and how much they have remained the same.

The roasted chicken was virtually the same dish I had eaten many years ago when I was a kid. And the routine of a parent simultaneously fixing supper and asking a kid to name the capital of Indiana brought back memories of when I was the fifth-grader scribbling down answers at the kitchen table, not the adult standing at the stove.

But there were also changes. The chicken was seasoned with rosemary and garlic the other night, not the salt and celery of chickens gone by. The side dish was rice, flavored with chicken juice, replacing the mashed potatoes and creamy gravy of my youth.

And while Indianapolis is still the state capital, "Ind.," I learned, is no longer the correct abbreviation for Indiana. Now it is "IN." Topeka is the capital of modern day KS, not the "Kans." of my past. Hawaii has kept its difficult-to-spell capital, Honolulu, but picked up an easy-to-remember abbreviation, "HI."

The reluctance to begin doing homework carries over from generation to generation. The other night while quizzing my son, there was much squirming. So when the opportunity presented itself to delay the inquisition and rub a raw chicken with oil, the kid leaped at it.

We coated the chicken with garlic and olive oil, one of the arsenal of oils we now stockpile in our kitchen. We have two types of olive oil, extra-virgin and regular. There is peanut oil for wok work. An occasional sunflower oil, and some corn oil.

When I was the kid doing homework, there were only two types of cooking oil, liquid and solid. The liquid was vegetable oil in a bottle. The solid was Crisco or some related globular substance that my mom mixed with flour to make pie crusts, and that I melted in a pan to pop popcorn.

My mom used to rub the chicken with butter, at least we called it butter. I think it was really margarine. My mom was a major fan of margarine — it was cheaper than butter, and with four kids, price mattered. Butter was a rare adult treat.

The chicken neck has an ageless audience appeal. As do the other parts — the gizzard and the heart — that are stored in the interior of the chicken carcass.

As always there was and is great interest in ogling, but not eating, these exotic parts. At least among the kids.

My dad used to eat the chicken heart, often pushing it in front of me and my brothers, asking if we wanted a taste. We recoiled in horror.

It was an effective display of courage. Alas, it is a measure I cannot meet. Now my wife is the chicken-innards eater of the household. I still recoil in horror.

When my mom handled them, the neck, gizzard and liver became broth, which eventually played a role in my mother's magnificent chicken gravy. It was smooth, milky, a gravy unsurpassed by any gravy I have tasted. The chicken gravy regularly rested in the middle of a ring of mashed potatoes.

We still have mashed potatoes and gravy, but not as often as we have rice and chicken juice. When I was a kid, rice was the occasional dish, not potatoes. Now it is the other way around. As the chicken cooked in the oven, my son and I finished off the remaining state capitals in the homework. I found some of the correct answers alarming. Springfield, which I used to remember as the stomping ground of Abraham Lincoln, is now remembered as the town where Bart Simpson lives. It is also the capital of "IL," not Ill.

The homework was cleared away, and the rest of the family joined us. There was the same eating, much concern about the chicken touching the rice, and questions about the mysterious specks — the rosemary — that appeared on the plate. Claims were made about being "full," which quickly dissolved at the mention of dessert. It turned out there wasn't any dessert because somebody had eaten all the cookies. Nobody confessed.

The kids were shooed away from the table so the adults could enjoy some wine and a moment of peace. The chicken carcass sat before us, battered but with a sandwich or two left in it, a testimony to the timelessness of a roast chicken supper.

Frying the flowers

I WAS FRYING FLOWERS. THAT'S RIGHT, FLOWERS, BLOSSOMS OF SUMMER squash, stuffed with fontina cheese and garlic, were crackling in the frying pan.

As the stuffed flowers moved around in the hot oil, I thought they looked like little footballs. Both the frying flowers and flying footballs were brown and wobbly. My imagery was probably influenced by the fact that, like many American males, I spend a lot of time in the fall either tossing a football around or watching other guys toss it.

For example, just before I fried the flowers, I had spent part of the afternoon watching one of my kids play in a football game between two middle schools, a real game as the kids would say, one with uniforms and referees. On the way home from the game, the sweat-soaked football player helped me pick the blossoms from the squash plants in our community garden plot. When we arrived home, my other son wanted to play catch with the football in the alley. So I played a little football and then I fried a few flowers.

I did it because I had a surplus of summer squash blossoms. Long yellow squash, which is what unpicked squash blossoms become when they grow up, had been piling up on our kitchen counter, like a yellow wall, substantial and unmoving. One way to slow down the influx, was, I figured, to nip the squash blossoms in the bud.

I also did it because I was curious. I had read about people eating fried blossoms, and I wanted to try it. I guess you could say I was curious yellow.

I wanted to try it in the summer, the height of the squash season, but I didn't have the courage. I struggled with the question, "Do real men eat flowers?" Basically I came up with the answer that real men eat anything that is deep-fried.

Besides, I was running out of time to try. I knew that pretty soon the production from the garden would wind down, even from the notoriously prolific squash. So after my son's football game, I stopped by the garden, scared off the rabbits and grabbed a handful of blossoms. These plants had not been sprayed with any chemicals. The bugs, the rabbits and the mice seem to like them that way.

I searched cookbooks for a fried flower recipe. I found one in the paperback version of Alice Waters' "Chez Panisse Menu Cookbook" (Random

House, 1995). Waters is a big fan of edible flowers.

A few years ago, after making several smart-aleck remarks about flowers as food, I finally visited her restaurant, Chez Panisse, in Berkeley, Calif. Once I tasted the nasturtiums, I changed my tune. The bugs were right. Flowers that are free of pesticides can taste pretty good.

The flower-stuffing maneuver did require some talent. So as I pushed cheese and garlic into each blossom, I told myself I was learning a new skill.

Once a blossom was stuffed, I twisted its ends and dropped it in a wash made of eggs and milk. Next I rolled it in cornmeal, and dropped it in bubbling olive oil.

I cooked the blossoms for about three minutes, turning them with a pair of tongs. They cooled off on paper towels and I sprinkled them with salt and pepper.

I tried two different stuffings for the blossoms. One was made of garlic, parsley and cheese. Another was made of pesto sauce and cheese. I preferred the pesto sauce version, it had more pizazz.

Both versions were pretty good. They had a flavor that was a pleasant cross of french fries and raw vegetables. And frying them was a hoot.

Once the squash in the garden are kaput, I doubt that I will be able to get my hands on any blossoms in the grocery store. They are not an everyday item. But as long as the squash keeps budding, I will keep frying flowers.

They make good hors d'oeuvres. Even football players eat them. The recipe on the following page is from Alice Waters' "Chez Panisse Menu Cookbook."

Fried Squash Blossoms

Serves 6

¼ cup Italian parsley leaves and 12 sprigs Italian parsley
4 to 5 cloves garlic
12 fresh open squash blossoms
½ pound fontina cheese
2 eggs
¼ cup milk
1 cup fine cornmeal
½ cup black olives

Mince ¼ cup Italian parsley with garlic. Open individual blossoms wide enough to insert small piece of cheese. Add a pinch of the garlic and parsley mixture and gently twist ends of blossom together.

Beat eggs with milk. Dip each blossom into this mixture, then roll quickly and evenly in cornmeal. Refrigerate for a few minutes.

Deep-fry blossoms in a skillet half full of oil of your choice at 350 to 400 degrees for about three minutes or until they brown and cheese is melted. Drain on paper towels and serve immediately, garnished with lots of Italian parsley and black olives.

From "Chez Panisse Menu Cookbook"
by Alice Waters (Random House, 1995)

Going whole-hog for good bacon

A WHIFF OF BACON MAKES ME WEAK. THE PERFUME OF SIZZLING PORK NEVER fails to turn my head. It can even wake me from a nap.

Bacon has this power over other folks as well. Put a baking sheet loaded with strips of bacon under the broiler and members of your household, as well as any nearby mice, will show up in front of your stove. It you cook it, they will come.

Both the two-legged and four-legged creatures want the same thing, to eat the stuff that smells so good. I try to deal with all comers by feeding strips of cooked bacon to the humans, and by putting a piece of raw bacon rind in mousetraps. Bacon rind is, in my experience, a more effective mouse bait than peanut butter or cheese.

For eating I prefer husky bacon, the thick slices and slabs sold in butcher shops and some farmers' markets. But I won't turn down strips of the skinny supermarket bacon.

For a treat, I decided to order a $20, 2½-pound slab of smoked bacon shipped from Roy L. Hoffman and Son Meats in Hagerstown. This is the body beautiful of bacon. It doesn't shrink when you cook it. The meat comes from select Maryland, grain-fed hogs. The smoke comes from white hickory. The procedure is supervised by the Hoffman family, whose members have been smoking meat in Western Maryland for more than 70 years.

Years ago, fall was the traditional season for bacon-making. With winter approaching, a farmer butchered his hogs and made bacon by slowly curing meat with salt, spices and wood smoke. Nowadays, most big meatpacking plants cure pork year-round by injecting the meat with solutions. This "wet curing" method produces bacon faster and less expensively than the old style, but it shrinks the meat.

Various groups have objections to eating the fatty meat of a pig, but I am not a member of these groups. I come from a long line of devoted bacon eaters. For example, at a recent gathering of our clan, family members spent many hours debating the question of how to make the perfect bacon, lettuce and tomato sandwich.

As is true with most family discussions, there was little agreement in this one. On one side were the strict sandwich constructionists, who argued that only the ingredients that should be placed between two slices of mayonnaise-covered bread were those mentioned in the sandwich title. Namely bacon, lettuce and tomato.

Then there were the loose constructionists, who held that the sandwich could contain a variety of ingredients and still be considered a bona fide BLT.

One member of this faction said she adds slices of raw onion and sprinkles of black pepper to her bacon, lettuce and tomato. Still another told of a BLT recipe that called for adding slices of chicken breasts spiced with cumin, peppers and thyme, and sauted in a bit of bacon fat.

I was appalled by such talk. I stayed appalled after polishing off three sandwiches made only with the title ingredients. Then, I weakened and began taking small bites of one of the rebel BLTs. I liked the flavor of the raw onions, but didn't care for the taste of pepper.

Soon I was experimenting with sandwich breads. I had a wild ride with pumpernickel. But I refused, under heavy pressure, to try toasted white bread. I have my standards.

On the cooking front, an effort was made with beeping bacon in the microwave, but it could not produce bacon fast enough for the lunch crowd. Beeping was replaced by the bulk-cooking method of sticking metal baking sheets loaded with bacon under the broiler. This method produced vast amounts of sandwich-ready material as well as lots of hot bacon grease, and a grease fire.

I was nodding off on the front porch when I heard the commotion in the kitchen. The pool of grease that had collected in the bottom of one of the baking sheets had caught fire. When I arrived on the scene, the fiery pan had been removed from the oven and was sitting on top of the stove, kicking up pretty mean-looking flames.

I reached into a kitchen cabinet, pulled out a box of baking soda, and poured it on the fire. The baking soda knocked out the flames faster than Mike Tyson finished off Peter McNeeley.

A couple of kids standing in the kitchen were impressed that I knew baking soda would kill the fire. "These are things," I told them with a straight face, "that bacon-eaters know."

The kids quickly moved from being impressed to being grossed out by the cup of "white stuff" that sat on the nearby counter top. It was a cup of bacon grease, runoff collected from previous, less-fiery bacon-cooking sessions.

When I was a kid, my mother had a custom-made container for bacon grease. It was stainless steel and had a filter. From time to time, she would use spoonfuls of the bacon drippings to season green beans, or sunny-side-up eggs, or fried chicken.

Rather than being impressed by the wisdom of their elders, the modern-day kids were repelled by the "gross" appearance of the grease cup. They couldn't wait to throw the container of congealed bacon drippings into the trash.

And that is why they never got to try another one of the world's greatest sandwiches, one that ranks right up there in delight with the BLT. A soft crab cooked in bacon drippings.

The meat of the issue

ONE ORDINARY OCTOBER NIGHT DAVID GILLISS, A BALTIMORE-AREA LAWYER, devoured a steak, the first meat he had eaten in 20 years. As a sizzling New York strip was placed in front of him at Ruth's Chris Steak House, a downtown Baltimore restaurant, Gilliss picked up his knife and fork and announced, "My hands are shaking."

A collection of guys in suits — one of Gilliss' friends, several of his colleagues, his older brother, Ed, and I — had gathered to witness Gilliss' return to the ranks of the carnivores after two decades as a vegetarian.

When Henry Kass, a colleague of Gilliss' and an acquaintance of mine, told me about the meat-eating event, I wanted to attend for two reasons. First, it is rare these days to find somebody giving up vegetarianism. Usually, it is the other way around. Second, the dinner seemed like a good excuse to eat steak.

After sitting down at the table, Gilliss' fellow diners had debated which cut of meat — a 9-ounce petit filet mignon or the 16-ounce New York strip — Gilliss should order for the occasion. The filet mignon contingent had argued theirs was a "good transition steak," but the New York strip forces, rallied by the words of Gilliss' friend Ray Peroutka — "Go large or go home!" — had prevailed.

Now the moment and the New York strip had arrived. The roomful of flesh eaters paused to watch Gilliss. He sliced, he chewed, the onlookers applauded. "Boy, that's good," Gilliss said. "It is all coming back to me. It tastes even better than 20 years ago."

Soon Gilliss was the recipient of cigars and wisecracks. He was asked if his lower intestine was "doing the Macarena." He was queried on whether he was contemplating any other big changes, such as switching from a gas to a charcoal grill, or trying a new career.

A few days after the feed, I reached Gilliss by phone at his office in the law firm of Niles, Barton and Wilmer. He reported no changes in digestion or lifestyle.

Bringing meat back into his diet was a matter of personal taste, not ideology, he said. "I have shown myself that I could do it," he said of his 20 years of vegetarianism. "Now it is time to move on and try other experiences."

Gilliss said he still has fond feelings for vegetables and vegetarians, especially the vegetarian who is his wife, Karen Gilliss Wilson. She is also the chief cook in his family.

When I spoke with Gilliss' wife by phone, she seemed to be taking the switch in her husband's diet with a mixture of amusement and common sense.

"There aren't going to be many changes in the way things are around here because I'm still the only one who cooks," she said from their Towson home.

She said the couple's two children, Lauren, 5, and Ryan, 18 months, have been raised in a permissive vegetarian environment. "They eat a surprising amount of black beans and tofu," she said, and they like "chicken and dumplings at Grandma's."

Thinking aloud, she pondered the potential drawbacks and benefits of her husband's new meat-eating ways. On the downside, she said, when they dine at restaurants there will be fewer of her husband's selections that she will be interested in tasting.

But on the upside, she said, if her husband really craves meat, maybe he will start cooking. "He can develop a whole new series of cooking skills," she said, her voice rising with enthusiasm as she considered the prospect.

When I asked her what the household was going to have for dinner that night, she laughed and said she had no idea. She was going to be teaching a course in business ethics at the University of Baltimore and her husband was in charge of dinner. Rumor had it, she said, that he was considering a visit to a rotisserie chicken joint.

Ironically, it was her husband who introduced her to vegetarianism. It was in the late '70s when they were students at the College of Wooster, in Ohio, she said.

Gilliss confirmed his wife's recollection, saying that at the time he met her, he had been a vegetarian for several years. His vegetarian days got started, he said, because of doughnuts.

Gilliss and his freshman college roommate, Adam Grossberg, were planning to have a doughnut-eating contest. Then "we thought better of it," he said. "We started thinking about what was good for us and for the world. We were young and idealistic." The two college guys became vegetarians.

"For some reason we chose not to abuse our bodies," recalled Grossberg, now an associate professor of economics at Trinity College in Hartford, Conn. "Which is unusual for 18-year-old boys."

Grossberg said he stayed on a vegetarian diet for about 10 years. When he and his wife, Amy, had children, the family began eating meat. It was more a matter of convenience than philosophy, he said.

Now, however, Grossberg is thinking of going back to his vegetarian ways. "I don't think meat is doing anything good for my body," he said.

Meanwhile, Gilliss is taking a different dietary journey.

After two decades of abstinence from meat, Gilliss followed up the boisterous steak rendezvous with a quieter reunion. A few days later he had a hot dog for lunch.

Go ahead, enjoy the candy

HALLOWEEN IS ONE OF MY FAVORITE EVENTS. IT REWARDS PRETENDING, OFTEN with chocolate. Talk about a great deal. You act out a fantasy and in return people give you candy.

As a big fan of Halloween, I am on the lookout for threats to the celebration. Lately, I think I have found two.

The first is excessive worry about kids eating Halloween candy. Researchers have proven that there is no scientific basis to the idea that when kids eat candy they become hyperactive monsters. Nonetheless, folks continue to believe the candy-makes-monsters story.

I suppose there are a number of explanations for this. Often this belief is part of a family's culinary lore. It has been passed down from parent to parent. And, of course, it is easier to believe than an alternative explanation. Namely, that the kid was a monster long before he ate any candy.

Don't get me wrong. I am not trying to control what people think about Halloween candy. I believe that in America it is OK for some people to harbor such anti-candy sentiments, as long as they keep them confined to the kitchen. But if they try to put anti-candy sentiments into practice at the front door, there is trouble. For example, when people start giving out boxes of raisins or rice cakes to Halloween callers, I get riled.

The way I see it, when these pernicious purveyors of purity are handing out their so-called healthy treats, they are attacking the essence of Halloween. Halloween is supposed to be a time of revelry. It is supposed to give its participants a feeling that not only is there evil in the great wide world, there is also some in their little loot bag, usually in the form of a dozen candy bars.

By contrast, it is hard to revel in the company of a rice cake, to sin while toting a box of raisins.

Those of us who treasure the decadent nature of Halloween must take action to stop the dispersal of healthy treats. Parents must examine the loot their kids bring home on Halloween. For instance, if while sifting through his kid's loot, a dad finds a healthy treat, he should act quickly. First, he should quiz his kid until he finds out which quirky neighbor is passing out the contraband. Secondly, he should expose the offender to community scorn.

Only by taking this kind of decisive action can these anti-candy types and what they stand for be stomped into the ground. Think about it! One year your kid will come home with a couple of rice cakes. And unless you act, the next Halloween the kid could come home toting pamphlets on the many benefits of eating beans.

The other threat to Halloween is the increasing tendency to feed people pumpkin seeds. Each Halloween, more pumpkin-seed recipes appear in newspapers and magazines.

The trouble with most of these pumpkin-seed dishes is that they taste like pulp. Moreover, they don't inspire any bad behavior.

They do, however, get rid of those seeds that you scooped out of the pumpkin to make a jack-o'-lantern. And so I often fall victim to the very temptation I warn others against. I make pumpkin seeds and serve them to others. Here is my favorite pumpkin seed recipe. To fully appreciate the flavor of the seeds, you should first eat a couple of candy bars.

Pumpkin Seeds

The seeds:
½ cup pumpkin seeds
1 teaspoon olive oil
1 teaspoon Creole seasoning (see below)

The seasoning (makes about ⅔ cup)
2½ tablespoons paprika
2 tablespoons salt
2 tablespoons garlic powder
1 tablespoon black pepper
1 tablespoon onion powder
1 tablespoon cayenne pepper
1 tablespoon dried leaf oregano
1 tablespoon dried leaf thyme

Combine all seasoning ingredients thoroughly and store in an airtight container. Heat oven to 350 degrees. Rinse pumpkin seeds, combine them with olive oil and a teaspoon of seasoning. Place on baking sheet and bake until brown and crisp, about 15 minutes. (Remaining seasoning can be saved for additional pumpkin seeds or for Creole dishes.)

From "Emeril's New Orleans Cooking"
by Emeril Lagasse & Jessie Tirsch (Morrow, 1993)

A toast to cider

"COLD SWEET CIDER," READ THE SIGN OUTSIDE THE FRUIT STAND. I PULLED OVER. I was on a cider run, driving up and over the Western Maryland mountains on a glorious fall day. When I turned off Interstate 70 and onto Maryland Route 66 the scenery began to resemble a landscape painting. The silver waters of Beaver Creek ran alongside the road, pausing now and then to circle a fading field of beans or visit a trout hatchery. Near Cavetown, the road skirted an apple orchard, and intersected Route 64. I turned right and a few hundred yards up the road, stopped at the Lewis family's fruit stand for two jugs of their dark apple cider.

The Lewis family has been growing apples and pressing cider for two generations. One of the current cider makers, Nevin Lewis, recalled that 35 years ago his father, Keller, would haul apples to the Grossnickle cider press. This was a community cider press, and farmers around Smithsburg paid a small per-gallon fee for use of the press.

It was a massive old press, with a big wooden tank to catch freshly pressed juice. It made good cider, Lewis said. But it never would pass a modern health inspection, he added.

These days the Lewis family makes cider in its own press, using gleaming stainless-steel tanks, clear plastic hoses and other devices that health inspectors smile upon. The cider is put in 1-gallon plastic jugs, kept cold, and sold at the family's Washington County fruit stand and at farmers' markets in Baltimore, Columbia and Hagerstown.

The cider press sits in a building about halfway between the roadside stand — watched over by Nevin Lewis' sister, Jane Huff, and her husband, Bill — and an apple orchard, part of the 150 acres of apples that the family works.

In the orchard, it was harvest time. The air was crisp. The trees were laden with fruit. Lewis, along with some of his relatives and a handful of hired workers, was loading bulk bins, 25-bushel containers, with freshly picked apples. Jumping off a tractor, Lewis hopped into his truck and drove me over to the cider press. He gave me a quick tour and talked about what makes a good cider.

He started with the apples. Cider apples don't have to be pretty, but they do have to be clean, he said. "You use your cull apples," Lewis said, using the growers' term for fruit that is not good-looking enough to be sold in markets. Before these less-than-stunning-looking apples roll into the cider press, they are washed in water to remove any dirt.

You use a blend of at least two and sometimes three different types of apples, he said, to balance the acid and sweet flavors of the cider. He ticked off the list of the Lewis family's approved cider apples. "We use reds (Red Delicious), Jonathan, York, Winesap, Grimes and Lowery." Rome and McIntosh apples are not used for their cider, he said.

Out in the apple orchard, Lewis showed me a few of the devices farmers use to measure the pressure and sugar content of apples and thereby figure out when to pick the crop. Using a sugar tester, a device that winemakers use to test the sugar content of their grapes, Lewis examined a slice of a Jonathan apple and reported it had a sugar content of "15-bricks." This meant the apple was "great for cider."

When discussing the McIntosh and Rome apples, Lewis cited years of cider-making experience rather than scientific data as the reason these varieties are kept out of the press. "For us, they just don't make good cider," he said.

Another key to cider-making is the press used to crush the fruit, Lewis said. Some cider-makers use air bags or belts to force the juice from the pumice, or ground-up fruit, he said. Lewis prefers the old-style rack press which, working something like an olive oil press, uses hydraulic pressure to squeeze juice out of apple pumice that has been placed in cloth-bottom trays.

Using a rack press requires a lot of cleanup work, he said. So he has an industrial-strength washing machine just to wash the cloth used in the trays. Moreover, cider made on a rack press usually leaves a few tiny pieces of fruit in the bottom of the jugs.

But for Lewis, the superior flavor of the cider made on a rack press is worth the extra work the press requires. Besides, he said, a few pieces of apple in your cider is a sign that you are drinking the real stuff, not some apple-flavored liquid made from concentrate.

Usually, the Lewis family makes cider in 65- to 80-gallon batches, Lewis said. The cider season peaks around Halloween, when the family sells about 1,000 gallons a week.

The walkie-talkie radio in Lewis' truck crackled. He was needed in the orchard. If the weather cooperates, he said, the apple-picking season can stretch into November. A stretch of warm days and cool nights was ideal weather for the apple crop. But farmers know the weather can be fickle. And since the sun was shining, Lewis hurried back to the apples.

I took two gallons of the Lewis family's "cold sweet cider" back home over the mountains with me. It was gone in four days.

On the bourbon beat

ON A DARK AND HOWLING NIGHT I SAT IN A FRIEND'S HOME, PENCIL IN ONE hand, glass in the other, and took notes on six premium bourbons.

These were among the slew of better bourbons that have arrived on the market recently. Sometimes called "single-barrel" or "small batch" bourbons, these are the corn whiskeys that distillers have taken extra care in producing, drawing them from selected barrels that have spent years in the middle rows of the rackhouse, the spot according to lore, where temperatures remain moderate and bourbon ages gracefully.

These pick-of-the-litter bourbons generally carry higher proofs, that is more alcohol, and more distinctive flavors than their fellow bourbons. They also carry bigger price tags, selling in the $30- to $40-a-bottle range.

Rather than a definitive sampling of every premium bourbon on the market, this was a small excursion into the land of better bourbon. My fellow taster was a colleague from *The Sun*, Fred Rasmussen, who like me, regards himself as a friend of well-made whiskey. We poured a sample of each of the six bourbons in glasses and examined their copper colors. We sniffed their aromas. Then we sipped, noting the flavor and finish of each sample, and scribbled comments. No ice. No mixers. No singing. A passer-by would have thought we were two thirsty auditors.

When we tallied our results we had come to virtually opposite conclusions. His favorite of the six was Booker's, named after Booker Noe, the reigning whiskey maker at Jim Beam. This was whiskey Rasmussen found "Rolls-Royce smooth." I rated it fifth, saying its high-octane 124 proof could "knock your gums out." My favorite was Blanton's. Drinking this silky smooth bourbon, I wrote, "must be what it feels like to be rich." Rasmussen, on the other hand, thought Blanton's was "a little shy" in aroma, and rated it third among six.

His favorites were Booker's, then Baker's, Blanton's, Basil Hayden's, Wild Turkey Kentucky Spirit and Knob Creek. My rankings were Blanton's, Basil Hayden's, Wild Turkey Kentucky Spirit, Knob Creek, Booker's and Baker's.

Besides tasting bourbon, I learned a bit about its Maryland roots. Ed O'Daniel, president of the Kentucky Distillers Association, told me his theory that the original bourbon makers came to Kentucky by way of Southern Maryland.

Years ago, immigrants from Scotland and Ireland made their way to St. Mary's and Charles counties, he said, but were lured to the Kentucky territory by "corn grants." The grants, dispensed by the governor of Virginia, who then presided over the Kentucky territory, gave land to settlers who promised to grow corn.

The Kentucky settlers ended up growing much more corn than they needed. And so, these Scotch-Irish folks "did what they knew how to do," O'Daniel said. "They made whiskey."

The whiskey makers did have to change an ingredient. Before they came "west," the whiskey makers made their liquor with another readily available grain, rye. But once they got past the Cumberland Gap, they made their whiskey from the abundant supplies of corn. Then they shipped the whiskey in barrels made from the native white oak trees, down the Ohio and Mississippi rivers to New Orleans, and the American bourbon industry was born.

This theory of the Maryland heritage of Kentucky bourbon makers is strengthened, O'Daniel said, when he visits Southern Maryland and reads the names in small-town telephone books.

"When I read the names in the Leonardtown phone book, it is like reading the names in the phone book of Lebanon, Ky. There are all those Scotch-Irish names . . . like Mattingly and O'Daniel," suggesting, he said, that the families are linked. O'Daniel added that his own family hailed from Charles and St. Mary's counties.

Nowadays, the buzz in the bourbon industry is the willingness of some consumers to pay more for a better bourbon.

"If you are the kind of person who is into appreciating locally made beers, or single-malt Scotch, then premium bourbon is right in there," Chuck Cowdery told me.

Cowdery is a bourbon enthusiast. He worked in the industry for 15 years, and he wrote, produced and directed a public-television documentary about bourbon called "Made and Bottled in Kentucky." He also writes for special-interest publications. For instance, in the *Malt Advocate*, a magazine from Emmaus, Pa., sold in Baltimore-area liquor stores and "dedicated to the discerning consumption of beer and whiskey," Cowdery explained how Jim Beam uses two formulas, or mash bills — one using 77 percent corn and 13 percent rye, another using 63 percent corn and 27 percent rye — plus 10 percent malt to make its various whiskeys.

When I talked to him, Cowdery said the interest in premium bourbons was one of the few bright spots in the otherwise drab bourbon industry. Overall, Americans are drinking about half as much bourbon as they drank about 20 years ago, he said. But sales of the better bourbons are increasing.

Cowdery views the industry commotion over the high-end bourbons as a mixed blessing. He points out, for instance, that a number of the bourbons are made from the same recipe. Differences in their flavors could come from the way these bourbons are filtered, proofed or aged.

At the end of our tasting, Rasmussen and I decided that while the chemistry of the better bourbons was daunting, we were not discouraged. We liked the taste of the good stuff. We added the names of several top-dollar bourbons to a couple of Christmas lists — ours.

Emptying the keg

WHEN IT CAME TIME TO RETURN THE KEG OF BEER, I COULDN'T DO IT. THERE was still beer left in it. Lots of beer.

It was tough to tell exactly how much was left over, but using the old-knock-on-the-side-of-the-barrel routine, my guess was that the keg was half full. This was embarrassing to me, for several reasons.

First of all it meant that I had bought too much beer for the gathering of about 60 co-workers held at a colleague's lovely — at least before we descended upon it — Mount Washington home. Instead of the 13.2 gallon college-boy size barrel of beer that I took to the party, I should have bought the more sensible, mid-life size, the 2.75 gallon mini-keg.

Secondly, it meant that all those trend stories about people drinking less and going to bed early no longer referred to other people. They were now hitting close to home. The party was a roaring success. I was among the last to leave. And I was home and in bed by around midnight.

Finally, just as I try to eat every morsel prepared by a four-star chef, I felt an obligation to make sure that a keg of well-made beer is emptied.

The beer in the keg was good stuff, a lager called Marzen. It was brewed by Theo DeGroen's Baltimore Brewing Company, a brewery that had just won medals at the 1994 Great American Beer Festival in Denver.

DeGroen's Doppelbock beer won a silver medal in the competition for best bock beer in America. First place went to Samuel Adams Double Bock, made by the Boston Beer Company. Another DeGroen beer, its Weizen Bock, won second place in competition for best German Wheat Ale. First place went to a wheat beer made by Denver's Tabernash Brewing Company.

I worried that if I went back to the Baltimore Brewing Company, a nationally acclaimed outfit, with a half-full keg, my reputation as a beer drinker would suffer.

Suppose one of the brewery crew picked up the keg and heard beer sloshing around inside it. They might ask me, "Why did you leave half of this wonderful beer untouched? What kind of person are you? What kind of people do you socialize with?"

So to save face, I had to empty the keg. The morning after the shindig I retrieved the keg from the party house and lugged it to my back yard. I kept the beer cold and spent most of that day stretched out on the sofa, thinking of keg-emptying schemes. I thought about giving the backyard plants and the resident slugs a beer shower. Slugs love beer, even though it ends up killing them. There might be a message there.

This beer, however, was too good to use on the shrubbery. So I started asking acquaintances if they wanted some free beer. Most said "Yes!" That presented me with the problem of how to get the beer out of the keg and into my friends' homes.

I found the answer in the kitchen recycling bin, empty plastic milk jugs. My kids guzzle gallons of milk and toss the empty containers in a recycling bin. I pulled several jugs from the bin, washed them, and carried them out in the back yard to the keg.

The jugs filled up with beer and with lots of foam. I quickly perfected a foam-removal technique — squeezing the sides of the plastic jug. This sent beer foam squirting out of the jug and on the plants. The foam also hit a slug that was lounging on the bricks. After squirting out foam, I filled the empty space in the jugs with more beer.

It was tempting, but I did not, repeat not, dump any milk out of plastic jugs in the family fridge to make room for beer. I did, however, borrow several lids from full milk jugs. I covered these topless milk jugs with little plastic bags and put their lids on the beer jugs.

Even after filling the milk jugs the keg still had some life in it. I resorted to giving away pitchers of beer to neighbors.

It took me several days, but eventually I got the keg down to a level of respectable emptiness. When the keg was light and I could pick it up without groaning, I felt it was safe to return it.

Under sail

THE 5 A.M. STARS HUNG SO LOW OVER TILGHMAN ISLAND THEY SEEMED TO BE resting on the Lady Katie's rigging.

This predawn vision of cooperation between nature and a skipjack was a fitting beginning to a day of oystering. It was a day skipper Stanley Larrimore later gave his highest compliment: "a good drudgin' day."

Dredging is one kind of oystering. A dredge, or "drudge," is a sack made of rope with metal edges. As it is pulled across the bottom of a river or the Chesapeake Bay, the bag fills up with oysters.

Tonging is another kind of oystering. Some tongers use only their own strength to operate the rakes that scoop oysters from the bottom. Other use machines to operate the tongs.

And there are divers. They prowl the bottom and send up baskets full of oysters to their accompanying boats. Divers need tanks of air and dry suits to keep the cold bay water out. All the Lady Katie needs is wind.

For generations these magnificent wooden boats have asked only for a breeze and some seamanship to bring home a catch.

Some days the wind is too strong for the skipjacks to sail. As compensation for this uncooperative weather, Maryland law permits skipjack captains to rely on engines rather than sails to power their boats two days a week – Monday and Tuesday.

For the rest of the working week, Wednesday through Saturday, skipjacks must rely on sails. As their sails fill, the skipjack's momentum pulls the drudges over the bottom.

November to mid-March is skipjack season in Maryland. So on this star-studded morning, the Lady Katie's crew, and those of other skipjacks, were getting ready for a day's work.

"It is what you're used to," said Larrimore of the difference between drudgers and tongers. He was at the wheel and the Lady Katie was under way. "It is how you were brought up. My family were drudgers."

Of divers Larrimore had little to say. He told a story of how one tonger friend had encountered a diver on "his" sandbar. The tonger told the diver he had about five minutes to clear out or risk getting mistaken for an oyster. The diver left.

Down in the galley, the Lady Katie's crew of six huddled around a small table. The cabin was snug. Breakfast was eggs, bacon, toast and coffee served in thick white cups. It looked like a scene from a Winslow Homer painting.

Up top, Larrimore stood at the wheel easing the Lady Katie out to Easter Hill bar, the spot in the Choptank River near the bay that he and a few other skippers thought would yield a day's catch. Behind him an outdoor motor hummed on a small dinghy. The motor was legal. Skipjacks can use a motor to get to and from the drudging spot. But once the drudges go into the water, the motor has to be turned off.

A Maryland Marine Police boat was nearby to make sure that the Lady Katie and the dozen or so other skipjacks out that day abided by the rules.

Darkness was giving way to daylight. The wind was coming up. The water looked like dark silk rippling in the breeze.

The mainsail went. Larrimore kept an eye on his watch and the other boats. No drudging was allowed until sunrise.

Suddenly Larrimore yelled, "Ho," and the two dredges splashed into the water.

Then the ballet began. The Lady Katie's sails filled with wind. The crew sprang to work. Boats 50 feet long moved around each other with the ease of dancers.

When the dredges hit bottom, the Lady Katie slowed, then regained its pace.

After a few minutes of scraping, Larrimore signaled the crew to hoist the dredges. A gasoline-powered winch groaned as it reeled up the dark cargo, which was dumped onto the deck. The crewmen pounced on the new arrivals. Some crewmen knelt on knee pads. Others squatted. They all pawed though the catch.

What looked liked dark, muddy rocks were oysters. A crab or two, awakened from a winter slumber, waved blue claws in protest, but were paid little heed.

The crew culled the catch. Oysters that were too small, less than 3 inches in diameter, were tossed overboard. Acceptable oysters were flicked between a crewman's legs or over his shoulder, onto the deck.

With the empty dredges aboard, Larrimore turned the Lady Katie around and headed back toward the bed of oysters he "knew" was there.

When his boat neared the oysters, Larrimore hollered.

"Ho." The crew tossed the two dredges back to the bottom. The routine started again.

"Finding oysters is really guesswork," said Larrimore after he snapped on a device that showed the bottom was 13 feet down. "You know where the bars are, but you can't see the bottom."

Each time the Lady Katie turned around, the thick wooden boom swung across the deck. Members of the crew, feeling the boat change directions, would nonchalantly duck under the head-hammering boom.

No warnings were shouted. No one looked up. The crew simply knew when to duck.

In addition to the Lady Katie, five or so other skipjacks were working this section of water, which Larrimore said was the Easter Hill oyster bar.

It was close quarters. So close that occasionally a crew member from one boat would reach out and touch the boom of a passing boat. The day before, Larrimore said, the boats had worked even closer. A few boats had collided. There were some hard feelings about that, he said.

But today the sun was shining, the breeze benign, the mood jovial. A boat would slide within 5 feet of the Lady Katie and its skipper would ask Larrimore, "What time is it, Stanley?"

Rising to the moment, Larrimore would then ask one crew member, who happened to be carrying a woman's watch, what time it was.

"Your boat has the ugliest crew," a voice from a passing skipjack yelled at Larrimore.

"I don't know about that," Larrimore replied. "But we got one guy who is wearing his wife's watch."

"Damn, Stanley," said Tony Worm, the offending watch-wearer. "You don't have to go tellin' everybody."

With each lick across the bottom, the piles of oysters on the Lady Katie would grow. The six-man crew had divided into two teams, one tending each drudge. Periodically, one man would shovel the oysters back farther on the deck to make room for more.

Maryland oysters, Louisiana recipe

THERE WAS JUST ME, MY SPOUSE AND THE OYSTERS. IT TURNED OUT TO BE A delicious Saturday night.

The oysters, plump mollusks, came from Nick's Inner Harbor Seafood in Baltimore's Cross Street Market. The oyster knife to pry them open came from neighbors. How embarrassing to be caught at home on a Saturday night with no oyster knife.

The recipe for this dish, skillet oysters, came from Emeril Lagasse's cookbook "Louisiana Real & Rustic," (Morrow, 1996). Folks who live around the Chesapeake Bay are usually wary of taking any advice from an "outsider" on how to cook oysters. But I am here to tell you, this New Orleans chef can be trusted with the beloved bivalve.

He makes you work. When you prepare one of his dishes, there is a whole lot of chopping going on. You also have to mix a variety of peppery spices to make a jarful of the required rub. You apply a teaspoonful or two and then save the rest for another of his recipes. Sometimes you take shortcuts. For example, for the skillet oyster dish, my wife and I made the required rub, but we didn't make our own chicken broth from browned bones. Instead, we used canned broth. Still, the dish was wonderful. Even though the oysters were swimming in spices, garlic and chopped onions, their distinct flavor didn't get lost.

Ordinarily, I'm a proponent of having our family eat Saturday night supper together. The kids, teen-agers, rail against this notion. They believe the most boring spot in the world on a Saturday night is at home with their parents. But on this evening I was glad there were only two of us, not four of us, at the table. The recipe for skillet oysters said it would feed four, but by the time my wife and I finished eating, there was nothing left in the skillet but memories. A few hours later, when I sailed out to the cinema to pick up the young social butterflies, I was the picture of contentment, even though it was almost past my bedtime.

Skillet Oysters

Serves 4 as first course

½ stick butter
1 tablespoon flour
2 cups thinly sliced onions
¾ teaspoon salt
¾ teaspoon freshly ground black pepper
2 tablespoons chopped garlic
3 tablespoons plus 2 teaspoons chopped parsley
¼ cup chopped green onions
1 cup chicken broth
1 teaspoon Worcestershire sauce
¼ teaspoon Tabasco sauce
1 teaspoon lemon zest
2 tablespoons fresh lemon juice
2 dozen shucked oysters, with their liquor
¾ cup dried fine bread crumbs
½ cup freshly grated Parmesan cheese
1 teaspoon Rustic Rub (see next page)
1 teaspoon dried oregano
½ teaspoon dried thyme
1 teaspoon dried basil
2 tablespoons olive oil

Preheat oven to 450 degrees.

Melt the butter over medium high heat in a large skillet with oven-proof handle. Add the flour and blend. Cook on stove top for 2 to 3 minutes, stirring constantly, until the roux is light brown, the color of sandpaper.

Add the onions, salt and black pepper. Cook, stirring often, for 6 to 8 minutes, or until the onions are golden. Add the garlic, the 3 tablespoons of parsley and the green onions. Cook for about 2 minutes, stirring constantly. Add the broth, Worcestershire and Tabasco. Stir and bring to a boil. Reduce the heat to medium and cook for 4 to 5 minutes. Add the lemon zest and 1 tablespoon of the lemon juice. Remove from heat and add the oysters. Mix well and set aside.

In a mixing bowl, combine the bread crumbs, cheese and the remaining 2 teaspoons of parsley, the rub, oregano, thyme, basil, olive oil and the remaining 1 tablespoon of lemon juice. Mix well. Spread this mixture over the oyster mixture in the skillet.

Bake for 15 minutes, or until the mixture is bubbly. Serve hot.

Rustic Rub

Makes 2 cups

8 tablespoons paprika
3 tablespoons cayenne
5 tablespoons freshly ground black pepper
6 tablespoons garlic powder
3 tablespoons onion powder
6 tablespoons salt
2½ tablespoons dried oregano
2½ tablespoons dried thyme

Combine all ingredients in mixing bowl. Mix well.
The mixture can be stored in an airtight container in the spice cabinet for up to 3 months.

From "Louisiana Real & Rustic"
by Emeril Lagasse (Morrow, 1996)

Oyster cooking contest produces gems

JUST WHEN YOU THINK YOU HAVE TASTED EVERY POSSIBLE OYSTER DISH, NEW ones come along and blow you away.

That happened to me in the fall of 1997 while I was serving on a panel of judges at the National Oyster Cook-Off in Leonardtown. The winning dish combined oyster stew and mashed potatoes. When I first saw oyster stew swimming in a bowl of mashed potatoes, I told myself, "This is either going to be horrible or wonderful." It was the latter.

The curried stew had rich, warm flavors and the mashed potatoes thickened the mixture and gave it a pleasing texture.

This dish came from Sally Brassfield, who lives in California, a Southern Maryland community of about 8,000 that sits at the foot of the Thomas Johnson Bridge on the banks of the Patuxent River. By winning both the soups and stews category and the grand prize of the cook-off, Brassfield picked up $1,000 in prize money and a silver tray.

Kenneth R. Ward of Hulmeville, Pa., finished second in soups and stews and won $150 with an oyster leek chowder dish. Dorrie Mednick of Baltimore made an oyster chowder with smoked salmon and finished third, picking up $100.

The contest is sponsored by the Maryland Department of Agriculture Seafood Marketing Program, the Rotary Club of St. Mary's and the St. Mary's County Department of Economic and Community Development.

There were other unusual yet successful pairings with oysters. Matching cheese and oysters, for instance, can be tricky. It is easy for the flavor of the cheese to swallow that of the mollusk. But Joyce M. Johnson of Chevy Chase matched some broiled oysters with a spread of goat cheese and herbs. The result was a dish that, rather than muting the oysters, encouraged them to stand up and say hallelujah. This dish, served on toast atop a bed of greens, finished first in the outdoor cookery and salads section of the contest.

The dish that finished second in this category called for massaging the oysters with a barbecue rub, frying them and then serving them in endive leaves. It was made by Mark Mayers of Ocean City. The third-place finisher was last year's grand-prize winner, Marty Hyson of Baltimore. Hyson covered oysters with a mixture of garlic, basil and chopped walnuts, then grilled them over a fire topped with hickory chips.

Southern Maryland is famous for stuffing its hams with a spicy mixture of kale, and Sallie Bilko of Lexington Park won first place in the main-dish category by treating oysters as if they were hams. She stuffed them with seasoned greens and baked them.

Second place in the main-dish category went to Robert R. Vining of Metairie, La., who combined oysters, angel-hair pasta and Tasso, a seasoned smoked ham popular in Cajun country. Debra Wheat of Terrell, Texas, finished third with an oyster and shrimp quiche.

The winning hors d'oeuvre paired breaded oysters with a sprightly jalapeno mayonnaise. It was whipped up by Richard M. Rizzio Jr. of Troy, Mich. Thomas G. Fitzmorris of Covington, La., finished second in the category with a peppery oysters au poivre. Shirely DeSantis of Bethlehem, Pa., came in third with a dish that covered oysters with a mixture of ginger, black bean and hoisin sauces and chili paste.

Following is the recipe for the overall winner.

Sally Brassfield's Curried Oyster Stew

Serves 6

1 pint Maryland oysters with liquor
¼ cup butter
1 small onion, minced
1 tablespoon flour
½ teaspoon salt
½ teaspoon curry powder
1 pint milk
½ cup fresh or frozen corn
1 tablespoon dry sherry
mashed potatoes
parsley

Drain oysters, reserving liquor. In 2-quart pan, melt butter. Stir in onion, flour, curry powder and salt. Cook for 5 minutes over low to medium heat, stirring frequently.

Add oyster liquid and milk, simmer for 2 to 3 minutes. Add corn and oysters, cook until the edges of the oysters curl. Add sherry and salt and pepper to taste. Place a scoop of mashed potatoes in the center of a large soup bowl and spoon stew over potatoes. Garnish with parsley and serve.

Serving you right

WHAT DOES IT TAKE TO BE A GREAT WAITER?
"Pure charm," says Rerta Dobbie, a waitress at the Pizza Hut in Mount Airy. "I smile a lot."

No wasted steps, says Peggy Schaefer, a waitress at Baltimore's Polo Grill. "When you go in the back [the kitchen], you calculate what each table needs and you take it with you. You never make an empty trip."

An even temperament, says Wendy Anuszewski, a waitress at the Crab Shanty in Ellicott City. "When the chef yells at you or if your table yells at you, you can't go cry in the back."

Timing is crucial, says Seamus Fogarty, a waiter at the Hyatt Regency Inner Harbor in downtown Baltimore. When customers sit down, a waiter should be at their table within a minute. "Half the battle is the early groundwork," he says. "Greeting them, getting them something to drink."

I asked these four waiters and waitresses to analyze their craft because they had been declared the best in the state. They won the 1994 Servers Classic, an annual contest sponsored by the Restaurant Association of Maryland. They passed written and oral exams. At the finals they were among 30 waiters and waitresses who were graded as they served a four-course meal to the big cheeses of the state's restaurant industry at the Holiday Inn Timonium Plaza.

Curious about what distinguishes great waiters from the mere mediocre, I first telephoned Vivienne Wildes. Wildes is a one-time Capitol Hill waitress who later became director of personnel at the highly regarded Inn at Little Washington in Virginia. She, along with three veterans of the restaurant business, have formed the Waiters Association, a professional society for waiters. The association, which has 1,500 members, is based in State College, Pa., where Wildes is doing graduate work at Penn State University.

One sign of superior service, Wildes said, is when the waiter anticipates the unspoken needs of the customer. "It is called 'reading the guests,'" she said, and offered an example. If a guest is sitting in front of his food with his arms crossed, a good waiter will take that as a sign that something is wrong.

When I quizzed the prize-winning Maryland servers about the distinguishing characteristics of waiters who had the right stuff, all of them mentioned attitude. You have to be accommodating, yet still keep your sense of self-respect, they said.

"You do whatever it takes," said Dobbie, who has been a Pizza Hut waitress for eight years. "But you don't give away the store." And, she added, "you smile through it all."

"What it is really about," said Schaefer, is "spoiling your customers." In her 23-year waitressing career, she has worked at "the Polo Grill, Peerce's Plantation, Velleggia's in Towson, Cacao Lane in Ellicott City and . . . an ice cream place in Catonsville called Father's Gay 90s."

Anuszewski, who has worked at the Crab Shanty since 1981, summarized the basics of good service. "You make sure the meal comes out of the kitchen quickly. You make sure that there are no big nuisances near the table. You sway them away from a dish that isn't looking like it should."

But she said, a good waitress goes beyond these basics. You do things that make the customer come back, such as holding your tongue when a customer says you have served him the wrong dish. "You don't say, 'I know you ordered the fried seafood.' " Instead, she said, you apologize for the "mistake" and get the customer what he now says he wants. "Ninety-five percent of the time," Anuszewski said, "the customer knows what the restaurant has done for him and he feels grateful."

Fogarty said thorough training is crucial to success. In waiter's argot, Fogarty, in his 60s, is "a lifer." He started his career as a lad working in a bar and general store in his hometown of Thurles in Ireland's Tipperary County. He was an apprentice in restaurants in London and Dublin before graduating to the rank of waiter. He worked as a waiter on cruise ships, and came to America in 1961.

He came to Baltimore in 1980 to work at Cafe des Artistes, then situated in downtown Baltimore. He has since worked at the Waterfront Hotel in Fells Point, Miller Brothers restaurant, the Center Club, Carolyn's Cafe and the John Eager Howard Room in the Belvedere Hotel.

His training, Fogarty said, has given him confidence, something all good waiters need to make it through the inevitable rough spots, such as the night at Carolyn's Cafe that he got "slammed." Slammed is a waiter's term for the situation when there are too many customers and too few waiters.

"One night a customer told me, 'You are the best waiter I have ever had, anywhere,'" Fogarty said. "Well, the next night, nobody was in the restaurant. So one of the waiters went home early. And later a crowd came in and I got slammed. And a man told me, 'You are the worst waiter I have had anywhere, anytime.'

"And I said to him, 'You're right: Last night I was the best, and tonight I am the worst.'"

Hard-to-beat biscuits

BEFORE EATING ORRELL'S MARYLAND BEATEN BISCUITS, I HAD NOT BEEN A fan of the genre. Most of the beaten biscuits I had tried to bite into had been tough enough to crack a molar. While the crust of Orrell's biscuits has what biscuit makers like to call a good "surface tension," the interior is tender.

They also have good flavor. Many beaten biscuits I have encountered seemed to rely on what was stuffed in them — a slice of country ham, a mound of chicken salad or a dollop of homemade jelly — to carry the taste along. But Orrell's beaten biscuits tasted good when simply served at room temperature with a cup of coffee.

These strangely shaped morsels — they look like golf balls with one flat side — are historic. They have been made on the Eastern Shore and in Southern Maryland since the days when Maryland was a British colony. The "beating" part of the process — a technique of putting air in dough that doesn't contain yeast — probably got passed down from Native Americans.

Now the clobbering of Orrell's dough is presided over by Ruth Orrell, who has been making the biscuits for more than 60 years. Orrell is described by her daughter-in-law, Peggy Orrell, as an "authoritative thinker" who "keeps us stepping."

The biscuits, a mixture of flour, lard, salt, sugar, baking powder and water, are made Tuesday, Wednesday and Thursday mornings in an addition on the back of Orrell's big yellow house. The house is in the middle of Wye Mills, at Routes 50 and 662, right on the line of Talbot and Queen Anne's counties.

Orrell and her daughter-in-law are among several Orrell family members who co-own the biscuit-making operation. The business also has a manager, Trygve Lund, six women who shape the biscuits, a man who beats the dough, and two delivery men. The bags of 12 biscuits — regular, cheese or honey — are sold for about $4 a bag in stores throughout the Eastern Shore, in Graul's markets around Baltimore and Annapolis, and the Chevy Chase Supermarket. The business also mails biscuits at about $7 a dozen, plus postage, to eaters around the United States.

The biscuit makers welcome visitors but ask that large groups give them some notice before showing up. School kids, a group Orrell feels comfortable addressing, are frequent visitors. For 24 years she taught school, in the one-room Little Red School House in the nearby town of Longwoods. Back then she made biscuit dough before school started, and while she was teaching, other women would form the biscuits.

The afternoon I visited Orrell's, the biscuit-making had stopped. Orrell led me through the kitchen, sold me a bag of biscuits and then hunted around until she found an old "biscuit beater," a hammer that was once used to pound the dough.

These days the dough is pounded by a custom-made stainless-steel device that looks like a punch-packing pasta maker. The crew of "biscuit ladies" form the dough into the traditional lumps, and the biscuits are baked at about 500 degrees for about 20 minutes. Over the years various machines have attempted to shape the biscuits, but none, according to Peggy Orrell, has done the job as well as the biscuit ladies.

I had arrived at Orrell's (about 70 miles east of Baltimore) late in the afternoon. Orrell and her daughter-in-law were about to leave. After giving me the tour, Orrell walked me out the door and offered me some yellow tomatoes she had grown in her garden. I was touched by the gesture. Later, Peggy Orrell told me that her mother-in-law had been trying to get rid of those tomatoes for days.

Left on my own, I took in the pleasant small-town sights. There was the 400-year-old Wye Oak, the largest white oak in the United States. Its crown was almost higher than the tops of the grain bins that stood on the grounds of the nearby grain mill. Down the road was the Old Wye Episcopal Church, built in 1721 with funds that came in part from the sale of a gift of 60,000 pounds of tobacco.

There was a small grocery store and a post office. In the middle of town a stream had been dammed as it meandered toward the Wye River, forming a picturesque lake. According to a couple of fellows who worked at a nearby Department of Natural Resources outpost, the lake was full of perch and crappie. I was sorry I did not have my fishing pole. I ate a few biscuits as I walked around the lake and carried the rest back to Baltimore.

Beaten biscuits, I learned, do not go "stale." Instead, they "dry up," a process that takes about 10 days. Even then the biscuits are said to have several culinary lives left. They can be pulverized in a food processor and put in a meatloaf, or used as breading for pork chops or chicken. Peggy Orrell said her mother-in-law makes pancakes by mixing a cup of the ground-up biscuit crumbs with an egg, milk, oil and baking powder. "They are very good pancakes," she said.

I did not make pancakes with leftover beaten biscuits because there were no leftovers. Instead, the next morning I ate a day-old biscuit and enjoyed its doughy flavor with a cup of black coffee. Then I wrapped two more biscuits in a paper towel and warmed them for about 15 seconds in the microwave, and topped them with butter. Buttered beaten biscuits for breakfast. Nothing better.

A few words about horseradish

FULL OF ANTICIPATION, I DUG UP THE HORSERADISH. I HAD BEEN ACCUSTOMED to dealing with ground horseradish in jar, but now I was going to get the herb in its primal form, horseradish roots.

I'm talking grind-your-own horseradish. Common-sense sorts might ask why anyone would want to dig up and grind his own horseradish. This has little to do with common sense. This has to do with gardening.

Gardening is a leisure-time activity that involves lots of time and not much leisure. In the spring, when enthusiasm and the barometer are surging, you plant every kind of plant you can get your hands on. In the fall, when enthusiasm is dropping faster than your frost-bitten tomatoes, you look over in the corner of the garden at one of the few surviving species, and ask, "Is that a plant or a weed?"

In the case of the horseradish plant, the answer varies. Some folks regard it as a pungent gift of nature. Others regard it as a nuisance. Right now, I'd have to say I'm uncommitted.

When I dug up the horseradish roots in my garden, they looked ugly. That, of course, is how roots are supposed to look. Try to name a good-looking root. Can't do it. Even ginger root looks as if it might have come from a mastodon.

Another drawback of roots is that they are dirty. They can't help that, either. They are products of the soil. Soil is gardeners' talk for dirt.

So I dug up these horseradish roots and washed them off in the kitchen sink, then wrapped them in a plastic bag and put them in the refrigerator.

I forgot about them until my wife screamed. It wasn't a terror-filled scream. It was more of a "what-in-the-world-is-this?" scream. Those might have been her exact words when she opened the fridge.

Like any veteran husband, I reassured my wife, without getting out of the kitchen chair I was sitting in. "Don't worry, dear," I said. "It is horseradish, and I have plans for it."

Like most statements made by husbands who don't want to get out of their chairs, this statement was, if not an outright lie, then definitely "a stretcher."

My plans for what to do with the horseradish roots could be described as "in development," or "awaiting inspiration." I know that fans of the root claim fresh horseradish is more versatile and pungent than the kind that comes in a jar. But I wasn't sure how to cash in on these advantages.

I recalled reading how chef Spike Gjerde of Spike & Charlie's restaurant and Pauli Santi, then the chef of the restaurants in the Belvedere, did inventive things with horseradish. They coated pieces of salmon and rockfish with mixtures made of horseradish, orange zest and turnips. "Encrusting" was what the chefs called their technique of coating fish with a horseradish batter and then cooking it.

I didn't feel ready to "encrust." But I could handle a hot dog. So I heated a pot of water until it boiled. Then I turned off the heat, tossed an all-beef dog in the hot water, and put the lid on the pot. In my kitchen this technique is called "steaming the dog."

As the dog steamed, I made a sauce for it. I grabbed one of the ugly horseradish roots. I peeled and grated it. When I had built a mound of shredded root in a bowl, I added a tablespoon of mayonnaise and stirred the mixture together.

I found a heel of homemade bread, split it open, and arranged the steaming dog and freshly made sauce on the crusty bread. I paused to admire my creation, a horseradish-rooted hot dog. As I took my first bite, I anticipated tasting bliss. Instead, I got bland. The horseradish sauce didn't have any kick. I added more grated root, but still got a mild-mannered sauce.

I had grown roots as blah as Melba toast. I didn't know where I had gone wrong.

Bill Mercier, a master horseradish grater, told me it wasn't my fault. Some roots, he said, are hot, and some aren't. The heat can vary from root to root.

Mercier regularly grates horseradish roots at his business, Coney Island, in Baltimore's Lexington Market. He sells grated horseradish in 4-ounce and 8-ounce jars for $1.75 and $3. Old-timers who visit his stand have told him tales about the glory days when there was a horseradish grater on every corner. Now Mercier is one of the few small-scale horseradish graters left in the Baltimore area.

Mercier said his business is brisk from Thanksgiving to New Year's, when people want fresh horseradish to put in the cocktail sauces they serve at holiday parties. And there is a surge of horseradish sales around Passover because it is a Jewish custom to serve the bitter herb at the Seder as a reminder of the hardships the Hebrews suffered in Egypt.

During the rest of the year, sales of horseradish are steady, but not overwhelming, Mercier said.

Baltimore is home to one of the nation's largest commercial horseradish packers, Tulkoff Products Co. In a telephone conversation, Lee Rome, the CEO of Tulkoff's, agreed that some roots are hotter than others and said it was common to make horseradish from a variety of roots. At Tulkoff's East Baltimore plant, the fiery roots of horseradish plants grown in Northern California are sometimes blended with the sweeter roots of Southern Illinois horseradish plants, he said. Rome, the horseradish hotshot, told me that if I wanted to make a good sauce, I needed some spicier roots.

Mercier, in the Lexington Market, told me not to be discouraged with my bland harvest. The horseradish plants will be back next year, he said. As a matter of fact, it is very hard to get rid of them, he added.

A few years ago, he put some horseradish plants in the back yard of his Catonsville home. He, like I, got a disappointing harvest. He thought he might grate those home-grown roots at his Lexington Market business. But they were so mild, and so skinny, that he decided to stick to his old supplier, who ships him fat, fiery roots grown in the Midwest.

Mercier dug up all the horseradish plants from his back yard and tossed them in a wooded area behind his house. The horseradish took root back there, and came back, year after year after year, Mercier said.

The only thing that could stop them was a subdivision. "They built some houses in those woods," Mercier said. "And that was the end of the horse-radish."

Dipping into doughnuts

IF THERE IS AN OPPORTUNE TIME TO MAKE DOUGHNUTS, IT WOULD BE AN autumn weekend, when you have plenty of time on your hands. That is not all you will end up having on your hands. There will be flour, powdered sugar and maybe little burn marks from hot oil. Doughnut-making is an aromatic, sensual and delicious mess. It is worth it, I think.

One weekend, members of my family made doughnuts. We used a yeast dough, which required a lot of punching. It also required much table-top space and patience. After the dough had risen, and been punched down, and shaped into doughnuts, it was time for the cooking process.

The doughnuts, like the heretics of old, were supposed to be cooked in very hot oil. It was quite a spectacle. The oil was about 375 degrees. When we dropped in a piece of dough, it was supposed to float. If it didn't, it meant the oil wasn't hot enough.

After bubbling away in the oil for about two minutes a side, the brown doughnuts were fetched from the oily caldron, then dropped on paper towels to cool. Quickly more dough was dropped into the oil. The aroma of the bubbling oil, the transformation of the doughnuts from white dough to crisp brown goodness and the peril of it all made for a dramatic day in the kitchen. I could see why communities used to get together for a heretic fry.

While they cooled, the doughnuts were covered either with powdered sugar or a topping made of orange juice. The orange topping was there for its flavor, not its vitamin C. As for the nutritional value of dough cooked in hot oil, let's just say doughnuts are terrific mental-health food.

Flour, sugar and orange peels were everywhere. From time to time, the pot of oil would send up a geyser. This was not an experience control freaks would enjoy. But, man, did it produce good doughnuts!

As soon as the doughnuts cooled, they disappeared. My kids, who consider themselves aficionados of various forms of fried dough, said that these homemade doughnuts were the best food they had ever gobbled. We cooked until we ran out of dough.

Such stories of the appeal of fresh doughnuts are old news to veteran bakers like John M. Fisher. He and his wife, Linda, operate Fishers' Bakery in Ellicott City. Fisher told me he learned the doughnut-making craft from

Norm Leidig, who back in 1948 opened Leidig's Bakery at 8143 Main St., the same spot where Fisher now operates his business.

Fisher said Leidig taught him that making doughnuts requires using quality ingredients and putting in long hours. "Norm said that if you are going to put vanilla in your doughnuts, you use real vanilla, not imitation," Fisher said. "And you don't use cheap flour."

Then there is the work. To get a yeast doughnut that gets in a hungry customer's hand by 7 o'clock in the morning, you have to start mixing ingredients at 3 or 4 o'clock, Fisher said. Cake doughnuts, which do not use yeast dough, are faster to make, he said. But doughnuts of either kind are the most labor-intensive item his bakery produces, Fisher said.

However, if you make fresh doughnuts, the customers will come, Fisher said. These days some fiber-conscious customers ask for muffins or bagels for breakfast at Fisher's shop, but on most mornings, doughnuts are in great demand. The colder the weather, Fisher said, the greater the hunger for doughnuts, especially among early-risers.

"The doughnut business is an a.m. business," Fisher said. "Sunday mornings, after church — and we are surrounded by churches — people want doughnuts."

Fisher's comments got me thinking about the link between church-going and doughnut-eating. Why, I wondered, are doughnut shops so busy after church lets out? Is it because after a morning spent worrying about the hereafter folks are ready to allow themselves a little pleasure in the here and now? Is it because after being virtuous for a few hours in church, folks are willing to cut themselves a little moral slack and wolf down something "sinful"? Or is it that doughnut-eating is part of the whole Sunday-morning experience? I suspect the answer is a mixture of all three reasons.

I have also found plenty of evidence from the secular side of life of the powerful appeal of doughnuts. For example, as a regular reader of crime stories in the newspaper, I have noticed that the thugs who rob convenience stores often can't resist taking a few doughnuts with them as they flee. One robber swiped some doughnuts and a bottle of spring water from a store in Anne Arundel County. Talk about conflicted.

I have also read that the director of a smell-and-taste research center on the West Coast has reported that most men find the aroma of homemade doughnuts and black licorice to be erotically stimulating.

I don't know about that. Licorice has never done anything for me. But on one of these long fall weekends, I might just cook some doughnuts in hot oil and let nature take its course.

Time to make the bagels

I THOUGHT I COULD HEAR THE VOICES OF NEW YORK'S OLD BAGEL MAKERS as I worked in my Baltimore kitchen, rolling strips of dough into a bagel. They were not pleased that a fella born in Dodge City, Kan., was attempting to make a New York bagel, the manna of Gotham. The old bagel guys were saying things like "Geddouta here!" and "Forgetaboutit!"

But like a hardened cabbie, I pushed ahead, ignoring the clamor around me. Besides, I had help, an inside source, a guy who knew a guy who had kibitzed with the old bagel guys.

My source was Charlie van Over, who attended Johns Hopkins University in the mid-'60s and who now is a baker and food consultant in Chester, Conn. The bagel recipe was in his new book, "The Best Bread Ever" (Broadway Books, 1997). I trust Charlie. He happens to be the guy who gave me the recipe for one of the best breads I have ever tasted. It's a baguette whose dough is mixed in a food processor fitted with a metal blade. I got Charlie's recipe about two years ago and have been using it to bake my family's weekly supply of bread ever since.

This trust was important, because if you are going to tackle something as daunting as bagel making — the recipe runs two pages in the book and takes two days to complete — you'd better have confidence in the guy giving you directions. Charlie knows his dough.

Moreover, Charlie's got connections. He got help on the bagel recipe from a buddy, Ray Frosti, a home baker who had made it his mission to conquer the bagel. Ray, Charlie told me, spent a lot of time talking with old bagel makers. He paid them respect, got them talking and got some of their secrets. The recipes and techniques were modified for home use and put in Charlie's book.

I got a copy of Charlie's book on a Monday morning. That night I started making the bagels. The work isn't especially hard, but the process of letting the dough sit, then waiting for it to proof is long. It took me two days to make six bagels.

On Wednesday morning, I fed them to my family. They were pretty good. They didn't have that rock-hard crust that you get in the big city. But they weren't those soft, suburban bagels that are sold in malls. My bagels had texture, a salty flavor and a good "bite."

They needed a little more attitude, a little flavor push, something to justify all the work.

The old bagel guys would probably say these bagels were not terrible. To which I would respond, "I work two days, and that's the thanks I get?"

New York Bagels

Makes 6 bagels

1 pound (3⅓ – 4 cups) unbleached bread flour
4 teaspoons brown sugar
2 teaspoons fine sea salt
1 teaspoon instant yeast or (1¼ teaspoons active dry yeast)
1 cup plus 3 tablespoons water
1 teaspoon baking soda
1 tablespoon white sugar
cornmeal for baking sheets
Note: You will also need an instant-read thermometer. A baking stone is optional

Generously sprinkle baking sheet with cornmeal and set aside.

Place the flour, brown sugar, salt and yeast in a food processor fitted with a metal blade. Using an instant-read thermometer, first measure the temperature of the flour mixture, then the water. Their combined temperatures should add up to 130 degrees if you are using a Cuisinart or KitchenAid food processor and 150 if you are using a Braun. Adjust the temperature of the water until you reach this sum.

With the machine running, pour all but 2 tablespoons of the water through the feed tube. Process for 20 seconds, adding the remaining water if the dough seems dry and does not form a ball.

Stop the machine and let the dough rest in the processor for 5 minutes. It will noticeably soften as it rests. Then process for 25 seconds longer, for a total mixing time of 45 seconds.

Stop the machine and take the temperature of the dough with the thermometer. It should be between 75 and 80 degrees. If lower than 75 degrees, process the dough once or twice for an additional 5 seconds each time, until the dough reaches the desired temperature. If higher than 80 degrees, scrape the dough from food processor into an ungreased bowl and refrigerate for 5 to 10 minutes, or until it reaches 80.

Scrape the dough onto a lightly floured work surface. Dough will be relatively firm. Divide the dough with knife or dough scraper into 6 equal pieces.

To form bagels, take each piece of dough and roll it into a ball. Flatten the ball, then fold it in half, sealing edges with your fingertips. Then fold again to form a tight cylinder. Roll dough into a tube about 9 inches long. Wrap the dough around the palm of your hand, overlapping the dough about 2 inches. Pinch the ends together to form a ring. Repeat with remaining balls, and transfer bagels to the baking sheet.

Rub a bit of flour on top of each bagel, then cover the bagels loosely with plastic wrap. Place bagels in refrigerator for 12 to 16 hours, preferably overnight.

The next day, an hour before baking, put the oven rack on the second shelf from the bottom of the oven and place a baking stone (if you have one) on the rack. Preheat oven to 450 degrees.

Take the bagels from the refrigerator. Remove plastic wrap and let them proof at room temperature, 70-72 degrees, for 20 to 25 minutes.

While bagels are proofing, bring a 4-quart pot of water to boil. Add the baking soda and white sugar. Sprinkle another baking sheet with cornmeal.

Insert thermometer in center of bagel dough; internal temperature should be between 55 and 60 degrees.

Set a colander in the sink. Drop one bagel in the boiling water. If it floats, it means bagels are proofed and ready to be boiled and baked. Boil the bagel for 5 to 10 seconds, then, using a slotted spoon, turn it over and boil it for another 5 to 10 seconds (sometimes bagels flip themselves). Boil remaining bagels for no more than 10 seconds a side and drain them in colander. Do not be concerned if bagels sit on top of each other; they are resilient and will regain their shape when baked.

Transfer the drained bagels to baking sheet, spaced 2 inches apart.

Place the baking sheet in the oven. Reduce the heat to 425 degrees and bake for about 10 minutes. Open the oven and rotate the tray of bagels so they brown evenly. Continue baking for 10 to 15 minutes longer, until bagels are uniformly browned.

Remove baking sheet from oven and transfer the bagels to a wire rack to cool. Serve them warm or let them cool completely before storing.

From "The Best Bread Ever"
by Charlie van Over (Broadway Books, 1997)

How to cook a duck

DUCKS HAVE A LOT OF DEFENDERS IN MARYLAND.

In inland states, a duck is often thought of as a wet and dirty critter best left on a farm pond. But in much of Maryland and the Delmarva Peninsula, ducks show up at the best of gatherings.

Ducks appear on men's ties, usually green ties. Duck decoys get the prime display windows at men's stores. There is duck china. Ducks get royal treatment at the Maryland Club, the bastion of Baltimore's establishment, where a duck sculpture shares a sitting room with portraits of state heroes.

But the real source of power for the duck in Maryland is the dinner table. It is the taste of cooked duck, not the duck's appearance, or its lifestyle, that gives the fowl its powerful hold on the state's citizens.

It is a taste that natives of other states – Kansas, for example – often find repelling or, at best, mystifying.

Several years ago, for example, a group of Kansas Farm Bureau presidents came to the East Coast to meet with the big wheels of agriculture in Washington. The Kansans got the royal treatment – personal tours of the White House, private meetings with their congressmen, an audience with the secretary of agriculture, and dinner at a dimly lighted Washington hotel.

Now, the dominant memory the Kansans have of that trip is not who they met, but what they were fed.

"Duck! They fed us duck with rice," recalled the Kansan this summer, two years after the dinner. Since the dinner, the man, who grew up eating beef and growing wheat, has refused both to hold office in the farm bureau and to return to Washington.

When duck defenders hear such stories they quickly shift the blame from the waterfowl to the chef.

"That duck wasn't cooked correctly," they say.

That, of course, leads to the question of how to cook duck. At an annual business meeting and duck dinner of the Eastern Shore Society of Baltimore City, several answers were offered.

Basically the three dominant theories of cooking duck were:
• Soak the wild out of the duck;
• Cook it fast, serve it pink, and;

• Sauce it up.

These theories came from men who should know. The Eastern Shore Society is a social organization, but it is difficult to belong to. Members must hail from the counties on Maryland's Eastern Shore, must know their family history (including the maiden names of all married women relatives), and must be willing to eat Eastern Shore delicacies such as oysters, muskrat and duck.

Moreover, the society keeps its members on their toes by changing the location of its yearly meetings. One year, the duck dinner was held at the Mount Washington Club, which is hidden under the Jones Falls expressway in a spot about as easy to find as a duck blind.

The "soak-the-wild-out-of-it" theory of duck cooking came from Everett Tolley, a native of Hoopers Island in Dorchester County.

"On Hoopers Island my mother used to soak the duck overnight in fresh water to take the wild taste out of it," said Tolley.

Next, Tolley said, the duck was basted with a flour and water mixture and then put in a hot oven and cooked for several hours.

The flour and water shell allowed the duck to cook without drying out, said Tolley. "Hoopers Island ducks always kept their juices," he said.

The "cook-it-fast-and-serve-it-pink-theory" was a conglomerate theory spun by natives of Queen Annes and Somerset counties.

Since wild duck doesn't have much fat, it shouldn't be cooked very long, the theorists said. The duck should be popped in a hot oven and kept there no longer than 45 minutes. The duck is served with its meat moist, and a little pink.

The 90 ducks served at the Eastern Shore Society dinner were not wild. They hailed from a farm in Long Island and were cooked by local caterers.

These suburban ducks were prepared following the sauce-it-up-theory. It was a theory advocated by Thomas Michael Green, the general manager and chef of Atlantic Caterers, Inc., and watched over by Fred T. Kirsch, an Eastern Shore Society member and a former Baltimore restaurateur.

Back in the kitchen, Green discounted the importance of a duck's wild heritage.

"It doesn't matter to a duck where he grows up," said Green.

"The only difference that matters is how you prepare it," he said.

He advocated cooking the duck in "high-sided pans because duck is very greasy," and basting it with a sauce.

"The sauce has orange marmalade, salt and pepper," said Green.

Out at the dinner table, Kirsch added a few, but not many, details to the correct preparation of duck sauce. A good sauce, he said, doesn't need much.

"Some people make a big deal out of sauce," said Kirsch, "but what it boils down to is orange peel and corn starch."

When it came time to eat the duck, divisions between counties healed.

"Peel back the skip," said Thomas E. Sommers, from Somserset County.

Representatives from other Eastern Shore counties nodded in agreement.

One novice duck eater who followed the sans-skin approach was Maj. Gen. Warren D. Hodges, the adjutant general of the Maryland National Guard and the featured speaker of the night.

General Hodges hailed from Lawrence, Kan., a state where "Eat More Beef" bumper stickers are as common as ducks in Maryland.

Where he grew up the steer is sacred. But like any good general, he recognized power when he saw it in front of him. He made a valiant attempt at cleaning his plate.

Later, when a skeptical waitress stared at the general's plate and asked if he wanted to take any of the leftover duck home with him, the general gave an answer that would have pleased any of Maryland's many duck defenders.

"No," he said, pushing, his plate to the center of table.

"I gave that bird my best."

A sauerkraut saga

LATELY, I'VE BEEN ON THE SAUERKRAUT TRAIL.

I've been working on the continuing investigation of who is responsible for the practice of serving sauerkraut with turkey.

Previously, I pointed out that you can't automatically blame, or credit, German immigrants for this practice. Germans in Baltimore serve kraut with turkey. But by now a lot of plain ol' Baltimoreans serve turkey that way as well. Germans in Pittsburgh and other German pockets of Pennsylvania don't. Nor do Germans in Germany.

Recently, I came upon some more sources of sauerkraut lore. Readers had sent me letters telling me to check out Missouri and Yugoslavia as places that matched the kraut with the bird.

And I talked with a scholar who has studied German migration patterns in America. He suggested that one answer to the turkey and kraut quandary lay with the geese.

The letter that told me to search for sauerkraut in Missouri came from Deborah Williams. Williams works in Baltimore, at the Health Care Financing Administration, but she grew up in Rolla, Mo.

She said folks who live in the nearby small central Missouri towns of Loose Creek, Frankenstein, Vienna and Vichy serve turkey with sauerkraut and white beans. She gave me the phone number of a Missouri sauerkraut source, Norma Helmig.

When I called Helmig, she said, of course, she served sauerkraut as a side dish with turkey. In Loose Creek, Helmig's hometown, folks "serve sauerkraut with everything," she said.

In addition to being served on holidays such as Thanksgiving and Christmas, sauerkraut is served year-round in these Missouri towns, she said.

"You'll find sauerkraut and beans at all the parish picnics," she said. The parishes she was referring to were Catholic. Almost all the 300 residents of Loose Creek eat sauerkraut, and almost everyone is Catholic, she said.

She added, however, that while kraut reigns in Loose Creek, its sphere of influence is limited.

"You go to Jeff City and ask for sauerkraut and people look at you strange," she said, referring to Jefferson City, the state capital, about 15 miles away from Loose Creek.

Next I checked a tip from another reader. Gloria Soto of Baltimore wrote saying the pairing of kraut and turkey might come from Yugoslavia. She sent me a recipe that she found in a cookbook called "Embassy Fare – a Guide to International Cooking." Under the heading of Yugoslavia, there was a recipe for turkey with sauerkraut.

Sure enough, when I called the Yugoslav National Tourist office in New York, Mira Macura, office manager there, confirmed the tip. Macura said that in her hometown of Belgrade on the feast of St. Nicholas, turkey and sauerkraut are served.

Finally, the German scholar I spoke with gave me another idea. George F. Jones, a retired professor of Medieval German literature at the University of Maryland didn't claim to be an expert in sauerkraut. But his knowledge of the German language did offer me some insights into the turkey and sauerkraut issue.

In Germany the turkey is not the bird of choice, he said. The goose is. A rough translation of the German word for turkey is "foreign chicken," he said.

As for the status of the goose, he quoted a German expression that "a roasted goose is a gift of God."

Traditionally the Germans serve their prized goose with sauerkraut, Jones said.

Putting all this together, I came up with my own kraut and bird theory.

It goes like this: When the folks from Southern Germany came to America they found a land with great opportunities, but lousy geese.

And so they substituted turkey for goose. And of course they kept the kraut.

Giving thanks for Thanksgiving

THANKSGIVING IS THE BEST HOLIDAY OF THE YEAR. HERE ARE 10 REASONS WHY.

First, it is the right length — a three-day celebration. I count the three days of the holiday as Thursday, Friday and Saturday. Wednesday and Sunday, the days devoted to holiday travel, are bummers, so I toss them out.

The big problem with other holidays is that they last too long. For example, we may start off the Christmas season all cheery and bright, but after weeks of shopping, we begin considering tying folks to the Christmas tree and having a big bonfire.

Thanksgiving avoids this problem. You can get along with anybody for three days, even most of your relatives. Besides, if you should have trouble mixing with the kinfolk, you can always run to work on Friday and blame your boss. Thanksgiving has a built-in pressure-relief day.

Second, during the Thanksgiving proceedings the kitchen table gets the respect it deserves. I believe most of life's significant events either happen at the kitchen table or are discussed there. This is especially true during this holiday season. The table is where potatoes are peeled, coffee consumed, leftovers eaten, and stories told. The heavy-duty holiday work may be done at the sink and stove, but the kitchen table provides crucial entertainment.

Third, Thanksgiving is a full-employment holiday. There is enough work for everyone, regardless of skill. If you don't cook, you can fetch forgotten ingredients. Or you can take the little kids for long walks. Or wash dishes. About the only way to be left out of the proceedings is to hide in the basement.

Fourth, at Thanksgiving we do something our moms have been trying to get us to do for years: We get passionate about vegetables. People who normally don't give a hoot about vegetables suddenly become adamant that certain vegetables — creamed onions, for instance, or, in my case, hominy — appear on the Thanksgiving table. The turkey may get the media attention, but it is these vegetable side dishes, these "gotta haves," that inspire loyalty among the masses.

Fifth, Thanksgiving is the only major holiday where jelly has to be served at the main meal. I am talking about cranberry jelly, that dark red stuff that jiggles as it sits on the table. Like a lot of families, ours has tried out fancier versions of the berry. The all-powerful committee of cooks — my mother, my wife and my sister-in-law — will soon rule, for example, on whether last year's garlicky cranberry chutney will merit a reappearance this year. But there will be no question about the appearance of the jiggling jelly. It is a fixture.

The sixth reason Thanksgiving is the greatest holiday is the way its disputes are settled. The question, for example, of whether mashed potatoes or sweet potatoes should win a spot on the menu is resolved by serving both.

The seventh reason Thanksgiving is the best is that it is the nation's premier pie-friendly holiday. Thanksgiving is one of the few bright spots in an otherwise grim national outlook on dessert making. At Thanksgiving, not only do most proper American households serve a homemade pumpkin pie, they also serve companion pies: mincemeat, apple or coconut cream. Making multiple pies is good for the nation. Show me somebody who loves his homemade pies, and I will show you a patriot.

Thanksgiving falls in oyster season, and that is the eighth reason it is the best holiday. In Maryland, folks tend to take fresh, juicy oysters for granted. In the Midwestern town where I grew up, oysters were a rarity. They showed up only at special events, such as Thanksgiving dinner, and then only in a few households, like that of my Uncle Charlie. One year, Uncle Charlie ate Thanksgiving dinner at our house, and a bowl of oyster stuffing showed up on our table. I have had fond feelings for Uncle Charlie and the holiday ever since.

The ninth reason Thanksgiving is the best holiday is that it marks the end of high school football season and the beginning of basketball season. I played high school football out of a sense of duty; the team needed bodies. By the time Thanksgiving rolled around I sighed with relief. I had made it through football season without serious injury and I could start playing basketball, the sport I played for fun. Now I'm more often a spectator than a participant in these sports. But I still feel good when I hear basketballs bouncing in school gyms. It means the season of duty has given way to the season of joy.

Finally, Thanksgiving does the best job of what a holiday is supposed to do. It brings us together. It reminds us of where we came from. It helps fill the emptiness inside us. Pass the pie.

'Grandma-cooked'

BOSTON CALLED BALTIMORE TO TALK ABOUT DEVELOPMENTS IN MEMPHIS that could change the agenda for the meeting in Kansas City.

The issue being discussed was how the turkey was going to be cooked at our family's Thanksgiving gathering.

This exchange was symptomatic, I think, of the kind of discussions that occur among families in the days leading up to Thanksgiving. Members of the family often have varying ideas of what should be on the table. So in the days leading up to the feast, phone calls are made, letters are written, pitches are made. The nation talks turkey.

The other day, for instance, my older brother, representing the Boston branch of the tribe, called me, the Baltimore representative, to pitch a turkey-cooking idea he got from our aunt in Memphis.

It seems that the Memphis contingent — our aunt, our uncle and a batch of cousins — have adopted the practice of deep-fat frying the turkey. This process involves injecting the bird with seasoning, then deep-fat frying the turkey in a vat of bubbling oil. Members of the Memphis contingent engage in this practice so frequently that they have purchased a deep-fat fryer. Reports had reached Boston that the deep-fat-fried turkey had moist meat, terrific skin and an overall pleasing flavor.

So Boston was pitching Baltimore to go along with the notion of giving the Thanksgiving turkey served in Kansas City the Memphis treatment.

Baltimore balked, for several reasons.

First, there was the equipment issue. The Kansas City kitchen didn't have a deep-fat fryer.

No problem, replied Boston, there are fryers for hire — businessmen in Kansas City who fry fowl for money. But, Baltimore countered, fetching the bird on Thanksgiving would require getting up early, getting into a car and driving to the site of the bubbling oil. All this driving could cut into the time set aside, by family tradition, for sitting in soft chairs and watching televised football games.

This point gave Boston pause. Baltimore quickly brought out its big arguments — stuffing and aroma. Baltimore noted that fried turkeys don't have stuffing inside them. And Boston had to agree with Baltimore that eating the stuffing from inside a turkey delivers inner peace.

Moreover, Baltimore said, if the turkey were cooked off the premises, the homestead wouldn't smell right. Everyone knows that on Thanksgiving a home is supposed to be filled with the aroma of turkey roasting in the oven.

Baltimore's objections seemed to cool the Boston proposal. But Boston can be persistent. It could call the delegations flying into Kansas City from San Francisco and Portland, Ore., and encourage them to push for a fried bird.

But Baltimore is ready for this possibility. To make sure that the turkey at this year's family gathering is roasted in the oven, a style once described as "Grandma-cooked," the Baltimore office called headquarters in Kansas City, the site of the feast.

Boston, Memphis, San Francisco, Portland and Baltimore may have theories about how the family turkey should be prepared, but Kansas City has the cook. After all the talking has stopped, chances are real good that this year's bird, like those in years past, will be "Grandma-cooked."

The guys get dish duty

BIG FEEDS LIKE THANKSGIVING PRODUCE IMMENSE AMOUNTS OF PLEASURE and great stacks of dirty dishes.

I don't enjoy doing the dishes, but a man's gotta do what a man's gotta do. And in our family, the menfolk do the Thanksgiving dishes. It is not as much an assignment based on gender as it is on talent.

In our tribe, the folks who bake the pies, roast the bird, stuff the stuffing, create the jalapeno and hominy casserole, serve the four kinds of cranberry relish, mash the potatoes and do something exotic — I'm still not sure what — to the squash, are of the female persuasion. The fetchers and scrubbers, the folks who make trips to the stores and restore order to the kitchen are of the guy persuasion. (Roles may vary from tribe to tribe, consult your local anthropologist for details.)

Like many guys, I cope in two ways when I'm stuck with an unpleasant job, such as washing dishes. First, I exaggerate the importance of the task. Second, I inject competition into the experience.

On the exaggeration front, I tell myself that doing the dishes proves you are a stand-up guy, and a valued member of the eating community. I might argue, without really believing it, that you can't get to heaven without putting your hands in soapy water. But I do believe that doing the dishes makes a guy a saint in the eyes of the cooks.

On the competition front, there is the tit-for-tat aspect of dish-washing. Put bluntly it is, "Them that works, eats." This is a message I grew up with. It was emblazoned on one of the towels that my three brothers and I used when we dried the family's dishes.

Like kids everywhere, we undertook this job with a great deal of complaining and competitiveness. And as with siblings everywhere, some of those feelings carry over to this day.

Take, for instance, the task of putting the dishes in the dishwasher on Thanksgiving. This job has been assumed by the oldest and the youngest of my brothers, who believe they are superior dishwasher-loaders. After the big Thanksgiving meal, my other brother and I, the middle children, let our siblings load the dishwasher. Then, in the spirit of brotherly love, we second-guess them, indicating in a not-so-subtle style that we could probably get more glasses in the upper rack.

To get some second-guessing ammunition for our annual gathering at our parents' house in Kansas City, I called an expert in dishwasher-loading, Julie Bundy. Bundy is manager of consumer information for Maytag Appliances in Newton, Iowa. Her company also makes Admiral, Jenn-Air and Magic Chef dishwashers. She pointed to a couple of mistakes that people, including my brothers, might make when loading a dishwasher.

One is allowing the silverware to "nest," or stick together, in the basket that holds dirty utensils. To ensure that spoons don't cling together and miss the dishwasher's cleansing spray, the artful loader puts some spoons in the basket with their handles facing up, some with their handles down, she said.

Another faux pas is loading glasses on top of the tines, the plastic dividers inside the dishwasher. The proper place for glasses is between the tines, she said. When you put a glass on top of a tine, you "restrict the water action," which results in inferior rinsing action.

I can't wait to catch my brothers in a nesting or rinsing-action mistake.

On the other hand, Bundy reinforced a point made by my know-it-all brothers. Namely, that people familiar with the features of a dishwasher end up doing the most efficient job of loading it. Examples of such features, she said, are the "convertible bowl tines" in the bottom rack of some dishwashers. They can be flipped over to accommodate either a big bowl or a series of dirty plates.

My mother has this feature on her dishwasher, and I hate it when my brothers knowingly flip those tines. They behave as if they read the owner's manual, which, come to think of it, they probably did.

A full dishwasher hardly makes a dent in the stack of dirty dishes generated by our Thanksgiving feast. There are still plenty of dishes that need to be washed by hand and dried with towels. This is where my other brother, my brother-in-law, several shifts of sons and nephews, and I step in and soap up.

Our goals are simple. We want to get this dish-washing thing over with as quickly as possible without breaking anything. We want to have some fun. If we find evidence that a guy has made a mistake — left a spot on a plate or smudge on a glass, for example — we rib him mercilessly.

This combination of good- and bad-natured competition keeps us going. Before we know it, we have polished off the bowls and other small stuff, and are facing the pots and pans — the crud-covered bad boys of Thanksgiving. Veterans can make short work of them as well.

By this time in the dish-washing battle, the big pots have been subjected to some serious soaking in soapy water. The soaking starts the minute the dish-washing crew arrives in the kitchen. Into each pan goes a shot of detergent and a couple of cups of water — hot water in most pots, but cold water in the rice pot. (A housemate in my college days who had lived in Japan taught me the cold-water-frees-stuck-rice secret.)

The relentless soaking action loosens most of the baked-on food. Any hangers-on are removed by one of three methods. First, an attack with a plastic scrubber. Second, scraping with the edge of a metal spatula. Third, the ultimate weapon — an assault with a soapy steel wool pad.

When we are down to the last pot, I dismiss the other members of the dishwashing crew. I take on that final pot alone, showing that dirty hunk of metal who is boss.

By then my Thanksgiving is almost over. Almost, but not quite. I still have pie-pan duty. I pick up a knife, walk over to the leftover pies and "even off" their rough edges. Some people may regard this action as a flimsy excuse to steal an extra piece of pie. I regard it as an attempt to achieve artistic purity. After all, there is little that offends the eye more than the sight of a pie with jagged edges.

After striking a blow for art, I pick up the pie with my fingers and take in the scene. The kitchen is quiet. Soiled plates have been cleansed. Glasses that were smudged now sparkle. Spoons that were forced to ride upside down in the dishwasher are now allowed to nestle, side by side, in the silverware drawer. That sliver of pumpkin pie tastes especially good, even with the faint aftertaste of soapsuds.

Chapter 2

Winter

A fishing expedition to Lexington Market

FISH TASTE BETTER WHEN THE WEATHER TURNS COLDER. MAYBE THIS HAPPENS because the flavor of the fish improves if it has been swimming in very cold waters. Or maybe it is because on a cold night, a sizzling platter of fish seems especially appealing to a chilly eater.

Regardless of whose cold flesh is responsible, that of the fish or that of the eater, a baked fish makes a pleasing winter supper.

A good fish supper begins, of course, earlier in the day with a trip to a fish market. One Saturday, when the snow crunched under our feet and the air was so sharp it made our cheeks sting, my family and I piled in our station wagon and headed to the Lexington Market in downtown Baltimore. Our mission was twofold: to fetch a fish and to buy a warm lunch.

One of the benefits of living in the Baltimore area is that its indoor markets — Lexington, Cross Street, Broadway, Hollins, Belair, Northeast and Lafayette — are full of merchants selling both fresh seafood and hot carry-out dishes. For me this dual attraction of cold fish and hot lunch makes going to market an ideal way to while away part of a winter afternoon.

Our group had to make several stops in the market to satisfy our various appetites. A couple of us got the combination meat and bean burrito, with extra hot sauce, at Pancho's stand. Then there was a stop at Park's Fried Chicken stand for one order of wings and an order of thighs, both fried in bubbling oil. My wife was tempted by the chicken livers, a dish we will never let her fix at home, but ended up with a hot pastrami sandwich from the Mary Mervis counter, and a bag of potato chips from the Utz's counter.

The fish, a handsome 3-pound rockfish or striped bass, came from Faidley's Seafood. This was a wild, or "God-made" rockfish, as opposed to the farm-raised variety. Later, while walking through the market, I noticed there were plenty of wild rockfish for sale at various fish stands in the market.

How people in Baltimore choose their fish merchant is a fascinating subject to me. Some seem to choose a merchant based on the price of the fish. Some seem to base the decision on the location of the fish stand, that is, on how far they have to carry the fish home.

I hop around from city market to city market and make my fish purchases based on geographic loyalty. At the Lexington Market, for instance, I buy fish from Bill Devine, the crusty proprietor of Faidley's, because he and I hail from that stronghold of seafood connoisseurs — Kansas. I'm not sure if it is true that all the world's big seafood eaters grew up in the Midwest. But I do know that after years of eating frozen fish covered in batter, I moved out here and got a new understanding of why so many people are crammed into the East Coast cities. They want to be near the good fish markets.

We brought the rockfish home from the market and cooked it that night using a recipe that is one of our favorites, Pesce ai ferri alla moda dell'Adriatico. Loosely translated that means fish broiled the Adriatic way. It comes from Marcella Hazan's 1978 book, "The Classic Italian Cookbook." Hazan hails from Italy, near Bologna. Even though she missed growing up in the Midwest, or buying seafood in Baltimore, she too is a major fan of fresh fish.

When cooking fish, she advocates using fresh ingredients, and a very hot fire.

Over the years, we must have made her "pesce ai ferri alla moda dell'Adriatico" about two dozen times.

But it never came out better than it did the other night. Why the same recipe tastes better one time than another is a question cooks often debate. But in this case the answer was clear. The fish tasted better because the weather was colder.

Fish Broiled the Adriatic Way

Serves 4

3-pound fish, whole, with head on
2 teaspoons salt
¼ cup olive oil
2 tablespoons lemon juice
6 tablespoons fine, dry, unflavored bread crumbs

Have whole fish cleaned and scaled. Wash it in cold water, and dry thoroughly on paper towels.

Salt fish on both sides, put it on platter, add the olive oil and lemon juice. Turn fish two or three times, coating it well. Add the bread crumbs, turning fish to coat both sides. Marinate for 1 to 2 hours at room temperature.

Heat oven broiler to maximum at least 15 minutes before cooking.

Put fish in oven-proof dish and place 4 or 5 inches away from the source of the heat. Broil on both sides until done. (Cooking times vary greatly, but a 3-pound striped bass should be done in about 20-25 minutes. The flesh should come away easily from the bone and show no traces of raw, pink color.) Baste the fish occasionally with lemon juice and olive oil while it broils. Serve piping hot.

From "The Classic Italian Cookbook"
by Marcella Hazan (Knopf, 1978)

In praise of the homely rutabaga

IN THE SUPERMARKET IT LOOKS LIKE A PALE YELLOW STONE, SOMETHING YOU might heave as you storm a castle. But on your plate it looks like orange mashed potatoes. And when made with butter, salt and maybe some sugar, it has a winning flavor.

It is rutabaga, a root vegetable with a hard peel and a few hard-core supporters. I am one of them.

I confess that I had pretty much forgotten about it until a recent visit to my mother's house in Kansas City. I grew up eating rutabaga. I would like to report that in the nation's midland, rutabaga is a widely appreciated winter vegetable. But Mom said that isn't so. She reported that every time she rolls a rutabaga down the supermarket conveyor belt, the cashier gets quizzical. Usually, she said, a question-and-answer session follows. It goes something like this:

"What is this?" the cashier asks, peering down at the pale yellow lump.

"Rutabaga," Mom replies.

"Whaddya do with it?" the cashier asks.

"Peel it, boil it and make it into a sweet cousin of mashed potatoes," Mom replies.

The exchange ends with the cashier fingering the hard rutabaga and doubting that anything that tough could be transformed into something light and fluffy.

Rutabaga apparently suffers from widespread anonymity. A rutabaga-eating colleague of mine reported that it is difficult to find a good selection of rutabaga in Baltimore-area grocery stores. Here, it seems, few folks appreciate the root vegetable's charms.

This colleague hails from the Canadian province of Ontario, where, she said, rutabaga is highly regarded and widely referred to as a turnip.

In some other climes, rutabaga is called "Swede," an apparent reference to its heritage. According to Larousse Gastronomique, a well-respected culinary reference work, the vegetable was originally grown in Scandinavia, where it was called "rotabagge."

The Scottish have another name for it. In Scotland, according to Francis

Bissell, author of "The Book of Food," a dish of mashed rutabaga and turnips is called "bashed neeps." Bashed neeps is said to be the traditional accompaniment to haggis, a dish that starts with the stomach of a sheep and goes on from there.

In my world, rutabaga usually accompanies roast beef or maybe roast turkey. As part of my reintroduction to rutabaga, I helped Mom make some during a visit to Kansas City.

We started by chopping the rutabaga into chunks. This particular rutabaga weighed a little over 1 pound and resembled an old softball. We cut it into 2-inch chunks, pieces about the size of a quartered orange.

Then we removed the yellowish peel from each chunk. (I later learned that peeling techniques vary from cook to cook, but all agree the important thing is to peel all the thick yellow skin, leaving only the pale orange pulp.)

Next, Mom put the rutabaga chunks in a 2-quart pan, covered them with cold water, put a lid on the pan and boiled the chunks for about 20 minutes, or until they could be easily pierced with a fork.

The water was drained, and the rutabaga was allowed to dry off. This was accomplished by letting it sit on very low heat in the warm pan for a few minutes.

Then came the mashing. Mom used an old-fashioned hand-held masher, but said it was probably OK to use an electric mixer for the task. After mashing, she added about a quarter-teaspoon of salt, a quarter-cup of sugar and a tablespoon or two of butter. Using a spoon, she mixed these ingredients through the mashed rutabaga until the dish looked fluffy. Finally, Mom tasted, adding "smidgens" of sugar until the dish had "the right flavor."

My colleague doesn't use sugar in her family's rutabaga. For a while she used orange juice concentrate, about a quarter cup, to sweeten the mashed root. Later, she increased the amount of salt from a dash to about 1 teaspoon per large rutabaga, and found that this made the dish sweet enough. No orange juice was needed. (Salt has a way of pulling the bitterness out of certain foods.)

Perhaps the most amazing quality of rutabaga is that when you fluff and sweeten it, kids will eat it. It is fairly rich in minerals and vitamin A. Just don't call it "bashed neeps," or mention that it is regarded as a friend of a sheep's stomach.

Vegetables too good for kids

I CAME TO AN APPRECIATION OF CAULIFLOWER LATER IN LIFE.
When I was a kid, cauliflower was one of those foods I was "supposed to eat." My dad, in an effort to stir up interest in the winter vegetable, would recite a couple of lines of corny poetry — "See the little cauliflower, growing sweeter by the hour" — as the steamed forms were placed before our assembled clan. My brothers and I would push the dreaded florets of cauliflower to the edges of our plates, and roll our eyes at our dad's performance. Those winter weeknight cauliflower encounters were not happy ones for me.

I recall frost covering the kitchen windows and steam rising off the limp cauliflower. In our house, kids had to taste everything, even vegetables, before getting dessert. I remember feeling trapped, both by the pieces of uneaten cauliflower that kept me from feasting on dessert and by the mounds of homework that later that night would keep me from watching television. The world of winter evenings presided over by adults seemed so unfair.

Now that I am a father and my kids roll their eyes at my supper-table orations, my sympathies have shifted. I have become a believer in homework and cauliflower. Homework is a good thing; it can keep the kids in their rooms, away from their parents. Moreover, I have learned to cozy up to cauliflower.

Part of my fondness for cauliflower is that it no longer holds me hostage. Life as an adult has its drawbacks — all that responsibility — but there are benefits. You don't always have to plow through a plate of steamed vegetables to get to the sweet stuff.

I would like to think that the cauliflower's celebrated nutritional profile has nothing to do with my newfound fondness for it. But the truth is, after you have heard that cauliflower is a member of the cruciferous clan of crunchy vegetables, the one rumored to be a big cancer fighter, the connection lingers in your mind. It is like learning that a new neighbor is the sister of a movie star. You already thought she was swell, but now that you know the family background, you can't help but think she is even sweller.

A major component of cauliflower's allure is that I have found a better way to cook it. Rather than steaming it, I roast it. The other night, I covered cauliflower with crushed coriander seeds, then applied a paste made of garlic and salt, and roasted it in a hot oven. The result was a dish with concentrated nut and garlic flavors, much more appealing than the stern, steamed cauliflower of my youth.

I found this cauliflower treatment in "Delia Smith's Winter Collection: Comfort Food" (Random House, 1997). I was not familiar with Smith, but the publicity material that came with the cookbook described her as "a British phenomenon," food editor of *The Magazine* and hostess of a British Broadcasting Corp. cooking series. After tasting her cauliflower, I was anxious to try other recipes in her book.

The other night, when I pulled the dish of cauliflower and broccoli with garlic and coriander out of the oven, the kids were doing homework. I didn't interrupt them. Instead, I took the dish to my wife, and we quickly polished it off. This version was, I told myself, an adults-only cauliflower.

Oven-Roasted Cauliflower and Broccoli with Garlic and Coriander

Serves 4

8 ounces (about 1 cup) cauliflower
8 ounces (about 1 cup) broccoli
1 heaping teaspoon coriander seeds, coarsely crushed
2 cloves garlic
salt and freshly ground pepper
3 tablespoons olive oil

Preheat oven to 400 degrees. Trim the cauliflower and broccoli into florets about 1 inch in diameter and place them in a mixing bowl, then sprinkle in the crushed coriander seeds. Crush the cloves of garlic together with ¾ teaspoon salt with mortar and pestle until you have a paste. Whisk the oil into this, then pour the whole mixture over the broccoli and cauliflower. Use your hands to toss and mix everything together to get a nice coating of oil and coriander, then arrange the florets in a large, shallow baking dish, and season with salt and pepper. Bake at 400 for 20-25 minutes, or until the cauliflower is tender when tested with a skewer. Serve immediately.

From "Delia Smith's Winter Collection: Comfort Food"
(Random House, 1997)

'Them that works, eats'

I GOT SOME DISTURBING NEWS ONE WINTER DAY. I WAS TOLD THAT IF I WANTED any fruitcake this year I was going to have to make it myself. My wife, the usual fruitcake maker, had decided to pursue other areas of interest, specifically, baking Christmas cookies. There wasn't enough time to bake both, she said, so she was choosing cookies over cake.

I took the news like a man. I begged. I whined. I whimpered. I told her, "It just won't be Christmas without the fruitcake." She had seen this act before, and was unmoved.

Next I tried negotiating. I said I would make the fruitcake if she would candy the orange and lemon rinds. Candying the orange and lemon rinds is a nasty job. The mounds of rind that go into the fruitcake have to be free of any pulp. This means you have to spend a lot of time attacking oranges and lemons with tools called zesters, or with sharp vegetable peelers. Last year I helped with the zesting part of the process. However, most of my rinds were rejected as being too pulpy. A pulpy rind is a bitter rind, I was told, and bitter rinds would ruin the flavor of the fruitcake.

Most of the time my contribution to fruitcake making consists of fetching the 23 ingredients that go in this cake. The original version of this recipe, found in "Maida Heatter's New Book of Great Desserts" (Knopf, 1982) called for a few more ingredients. But over the years, my wife has tossed out some ingredients and increased the quantities of others.

To get the goods, I visit Jeppi Nut, a store that sits on a short stretch of North High Street between Fayette and Gay streets, behind the main post office. The store, filled with the aroma of roasted peanuts, is a pleasant place to visit. But I always feel guilty when I go there because, according to the timetable of veteran fruitcake makers, I am behind schedule. I usually end up buying fruitcake ingredients in late November or early December. The pros were in Jeppi Nut way back in October. The pros have their fruitcakes aging, while mine are still theories.

I shake off the guilt by remembering the remarkable taste of this fruitcake. It is a fruity, nutty and rich delight that is a stratosphere above the flavor of gummy, store-bought fruitcakes, the ones the disc jockeys and other would-be comedians make so much fun of.

Making it, however, is a ton of work. I got tuckered out just typing the recipe for this column. First, you have to chop the fruit, candy those rinds, and soak the fruit in booze for at least a week. Next you make the cake batter, mix it with the marinated fruit and bake the cakes for 5 hours. Then you age the cakes for weeks, letting them rest in a cool spot, absorbing brandy, and leading, in general, the good fruitcake life.

There is no instant gratification in making this fruitcake. Instead, it requires lots of long, slow labor. But as the old saying goes, "Them that works, eats." And when my fruitcake labors come to fruition several weeks from now, I will have a hard time sharing.

Rob Kasper's Fruitcake

Yield : 6 cakes baked in 8-inch diameter cake pans.

Fruit
1 pound raisins
1 pound currants
1 pound pitted dates, each cut into 2 or 3 pieces
½ pound dried apricots, each cut into 2 or 3 pieces
½ pound dried brown figs, each cut into 2 or 3 pieces
½ cup candied lemon rind, (see below) cut into ½ inch pieces
½ cup candied orange rind (see below), cut into ½ inch pieces
½ pound candied pineapple, cut into ½ inch pieces
1 cup brandy
½ cup Triple Sec
(To candy orange and lemon rinds, remove only orange and yellow part, not white, of the peels. Cover with water and simmer 10-12 minutes. Drain, refresh with cold water. In another pan, boil 1 cup sugar, and ⅓ cup water to 230 degrees. Remove sugar water from heat, stir in rinds, let stand 30 minutes or more.)

Place all ingredients in a large bowl. Stir to mix well. Then transfer to large jar with tight cover, or divide among two or three jars. Cover tightly. Let stand for a week or more, turning the jars from side to side and from top to bottom occasionally to marinate fruit thoroughly.

Cake
2½ cups sifted all-purpose flour
1 teaspoon double-acting baking powder
3 tablespoons unsweetened cocoa powder
1 teaspoon powdered cloves
1 teaspoon cinnamon
1 teaspoon mace
2 teaspoons powdered (not granular) instant coffee or instant espresso
1 pound unsalted butter
1 pound dark brown sugar
9 eggs (medium or large) or 8 extra large eggs
1¼ cups dark molasses
2 pounds pecan halves
2 pounds walnut halves
additional brandy to be used after cakes are baked.

Adjust two racks to divide the oven into thirds and preheat oven to 225 degrees (check temperature with thermometer; if oven is hotter, cakes will burn). Butter sides only of cake pans. Cut baking-pan liner paper or aluminum foil to fit the bottoms of the pans, butter one side of the paper or foil, and place buttered side up in the pans. Set aside. Sift together the flour, baking powder, cocoa, cloves, cinnamon, mace and powdered instant coffee and set aside.

In the large bowl of an electric mixer, cream the butter. Add the sugar and beat well until light in color. Add the eggs one at a time, beating well after each addition. (The mixture will appear curdled — that's OK.)

On low speed add the sifted dry ingredients in three batches, alternating with the molasses in two additions. (It still might look curdled.)

In a very large mixing bowl (or any large container) mix the fruit into the batter, include any liquor that has not been absorbed. Finally, mix in the nuts. Use a large spoon or spatula, or use your hands.

Divide the batter evenly among the prepared pans. It's OK to fill to the top; pat the tops to make smooth and level.

Bake for 5 hours, checking the oven temperature occasionally with a thermometer. Once or twice during the baking, reverse the position of the pans, top to bottom and front to back, to ensure even baking. Remove from oven and cool for half an hour in the pans on racks. Carefully, with a small, sharp knife, cut around the edges to release the cake. Then cover each pan with a rack, turn over the pan and rack, remove the lining, cover with another rack and turn over again, leaving the cakes right-side up.

When the cakes have cooled, or while they are cooling, brush them with a conservative amount of brandy. Then carefully wrap the cakes airtight in plastic wrap. (Until they are chilled, handle carefully; they are fragile. To guarantee cakes don't dry out, cover plastic wrap with layer of foil.) Store the cakes for at least a week in the refrigerator, uncovering them and brushing them once or twice again with more brandy, then wrapping them up again. They may remain in the refrigerator or may be frozen. If they are frozen, let them stand at room temperature for about an hour before brushing them with more liquor. They absorb more when they are thawed.

Cake should be very cold when it is sliced. Cut portions small; this is rich.

Adapted from "Maida Heatter's New Book of Great Desserts"
(Knopf, 1982)

Fogey eggnog

DOING THINGS THE "SAME OLD WAY" AT THIS TIME OF YEAR IS VALUED, AT least by some of us. Those of us who treasure the old ways might call ourselves traditionalists. Others refer to us as fogeys.

The first time I was called a fogey by one of my kids, I was offended. But now, rather than fight the characterization of being someone who is behind the times, I embrace it. If the world is divided between "cool" people who are "with-it" and "fogeys" who are "out-of-it," I am much more comfortable in the second group.

For example, when it comes to holiday music, I prefer to listen to the modulated tones of Bing Crosby rather than to the louder musical offerings of Sean "Puff Daddy" Combs. I made this discovery one winter night while driving my youngest son home from a birthday party for Carey, one of his teen-age buddies. When my kid got in the car Bing was warbling "Mele Kalikimaka" on the car sound system. But as soon as Bing finished the final notes of this 1960s Christmas melody, the kid ejected the CD and began working the car radio, searching for his favorite sounds of the season, the rap music of Puff Daddy.

I regard Bing's "Mele Kalikimaka" as a classic. The kid thinks it is fogey music. I am not going to change the kid's mind about Bing. But he is not going to change my listening habits.

I feel the same way about my holiday eggnog as I do about my holiday music. It may be scorned as old-fashioned, out-of-date or even unhealthy, but this fogey eggnog is part of my holiday tradition.

In the 20 years or so that I have been making this eggnog at Christmas, I have seen its ingredients — egg yolks, sugar, cream and bourbon — wander in and out of public favor.

Back in the days when cholesterol was regarded as the source of all evil, eggs were virtually outlawed. Since then the emphasis among healthy eaters has switched to watching total dietary fat, and eggs have rebounded in popularity.

Now, the American Heart Association recommends that adults who don't have elevated cholesterol limit their egg intake to four a week. Moreover, eggs are also praised as a source of protein and vitamin D. One study even hinted that eggs and other sources of vitamin D could help people suffering with painful knee arthritis. Fogeys took note.

The egg yolks in my recipe, however, are uncooked, which means they have a slight chance of carrying salmonella. This means that in the eyes of health officials the nog is still a forbidden elixir. (Those worried about the risk of salmonella could substitute pasteurized eggs, but I am uncertain what effect this switch has on flavor.)

Sugar and cream have taken their knocks as well. Both have been accused of making us fatter, a charge that in the case of this eggnog probably still sticks. But the claim that sugar leads to hyperactivity is certainly not the case here. After downing one cup of this nog, you become extremely inactive. About the only thing you want to do is to take a nap.

Bourbon has never been widely regarded as a health food, but it too has bounced in and out of fashion. Once scorned by marketing types as a lowly "brown good" that only appealed to old folks, bourbon has had an image makeover. Now expensive, single-barrel bourbons are touted as a beverage of cool and with-it adults.

Even though my eggnog calls for bourbon, it remains firmly in the fogey camp. Instead of using these "with-it" single-barrel bourbons, my nog uses the cheap stuff. Mixing fine bourbon with sugar, cream and egg yolks would, I think, be a waste of good bourbon.

So here it is, my annual offering, the recipe for my fogey eggnog. I would be hard-pressed to come up with any benign effects this nog has on the body. But it tastes wonderful. It is a holiday tradition. And it soothes the soul. And maybe, after two cups, Puff Daddy will begin to sound like Bing Crosby.

Rob Kasper's Eggnog

Makes 8 to 10 cups
2 cups bourbon
1⅛ cups sugar
6 egg yolks, beaten
4 cups whipping cream

Blend bourbon and sugar in large mixing bowl. Let sit overnight. Beat egg yolks until they turn pale yellow. Add to bourbon mixture. Mix well. Cover and let sit in refrigerator at least 2 hours. Whip cream, add to bourbon mixture. Nog starts off very creamy, becomes soupy the longer it survives.

Mousse and memories

CHOCOLATE MOUSSE WILL BE SERVED AT OUR HOUSE ON CHRISTMAS EVE. IT is a holiday tradition that got off to a shaky start 17 years ago.

The recipe, lifted from a cookbook written by Maida Heatter, is a two-step affair. First, you make the chocolate mousse, then you add the whipped-cream topping.

My wife started the holiday tradition on a cold December night. She finished the first step, the mousse, but then was interrupted. She had to go to the hospital and give birth.

Eventually I got around to completing the second step and carried the finished dessert to Johns Hopkins Hospital where we gazed at our first-born — a baby boy wearing a Santa cap — and spooned down chocolate mousse.

Now, when the rich flavor of the mousse hits my tongue, the memories of prior Christmas Eves start rolling back. Some memories, like the chocolate in the mousse, are bittersweet. These make the whipped cream moments, of life and of the dessert, that much sweeter.

Since entering the parent business on that Christmas Eve, I have learned what generations before me knew. Namely, that being a parent is one of life's more difficult, but rewarding undertakings; and that much of the experience involves on-the-job training.

During dessert, I reflect on how some things have changed over the past two decades, and how some things have not.

For instance, the color of the Christmas lights on the Washington Monument in downtown Baltimore has changed. Back in 1980, as I walked to the hospital parking lot, I saw in the distance the red and green lights of the monument leap to life. It was, I told myself, a multicolored tribute to the birth of our son. Now the monument lights still glow at Christmastime, but they are a modern, memory-empty white.

Other facets of Baltimore holiday life, however, remain unchanged. A day or two after our first son was born, a water pipe beneath Mount Royal Avenue and West Lanvale Street erupted in honor of the occasion. And as the kid's 17th birthday drew near, a crew wielding jackhammers returned to the neighborhood, this time to minister to gurgling pipes beneath Park Avenue and Mosher Street. To paraphrase a favorite Irish tune, Oh, sonny boy, the pipes, the pipes are calling.

My late-night Christmas season routine has changed over the years. Not so long ago I stayed up late to assemble a major Christmas gift, a wagon, for the kid. Now I sometimes find myself staying up late at night, making sure that the kid has returned home safely in a different kind of wagon, the family station wagon he has been driving.

At the dinner table, the son who once used to sit in a high chair and throw carrots now lingers at the table and tosses out opinions, some as irritating to his father as the airborne carrots of old.

In the kitchen, the kid who once was a babe in his mother's arms now, from time to time, wraps his mother in his thick arms and lifts her off the floor.

I am not sure if there is any big message in these chocolate-mousse recollections. It might be that time flies, or that memories live, or that bad water pipes will always be with us. But on Christmas Eve, I savor the chocolate mousse.

Chocolate Mousse

Serves 6

8 ounces semisweet, bittersweet or extra-bittersweet chocolate
1 tablespoon instant dry coffee
⅓ cup boiling water
5 eggs (graded large or extra large), separated
pinch of salt

Coarsely chop chocolate and place in small, heavy saucepan. Dissolve the coffee in the boiling water and pour over chocolate. Place over low heat and stir occasionally with small wire whisk until smooth. Remove from heat and set aside to cool for about 5 minutes.

Meanwhile, in the small bowl of an electric mixer, beat the egg yolks at high speed for 3 or 4 minutes, until they are a pale lemon color. Reduce the speed to low, gradually add the slightly warm chocolate and beat, scraping the bowl with a rubber spatula. Beat only until smooth. Remove from mixer.

Add the salt to the egg whites and beat with clean beaters until they hold a definite shape but are not stiff and dry.

Gently fold about one-quarter of the beaten whites into the chocolate mixture, then fold in the second quarter, and finally fold the chocolate into the remaining whites, folding only until no whites show.

Gently transfer the mousse to a wide pitcher and pour into six wine glasses, about 9-ounce capacity. Leave generous headroom for topping. (Instead of glasses, mousse may be poured into one large serving bowl, again leaving headroom.)

Cover tightly with aluminum foil and refrigerate for 3 to 6 hours.

Mocha Cream Topping

1 cup heavy cream
¼ cup confectioners sugar
1 tablespoon instant coffee

In a chilled bowl with chilled beaters, beat the above ingredients until the cream thickens to consistency of heavy custard, not stiff.

Pour or spoon the cream onto the mousse, completely covering the top. Refrigerate until serving.

From "Maida Heatter's Book of Great Chocolate Desserts"
(Knopf, 1980)

A Super Bowl snack

IT IS DIFFICULT AND ALMOST UN-AMERICAN NOT TO EAT TOO MUCH ON SUPER Bowl Sunday.

A few years ago, for instance, I tried to treat the Super Bowl as just another televised football game. I planned to sit in our family room with my kids and a few of their friends and simply watch the game. We wouldn't eat anything until half time. Then our family would go to the kitchen, sit down and dine.

Immediately, the kids objected. It didn't feel right, they said, to watch a Super Bowl without snacks.

So I rushed out to a 7-Eleven and bought an armful of chips, dip and soda. Upon my return I joined a roomful of guys who sipped and dipped and chewed as we watched football. By half time we had stuffed our bellies with junk food. There seemed to be little reason to eat any more or watch any more football.

Yet we did both. After the friends of the kids left, our family gathered around the kitchen table and ate supper as the television, with the sound turned down, flickered in the distance. By the end of the day, I felt bloated and lifeless. But I also felt like I was in the American mainstream because I had given a Super Bowl snack party.

It turns out that Super Bowl Sunday is, according to the American Snack Food Association, the biggest snack-eating day of the year. In 1997 on the big day, 10.8 million pounds of potato chips, 8.1 million pounds of tortilla chips, 4.2 million pounds of pretzels, 3.8 million pounds of popcorn and 2.5 million pounds of snack nuts were scarfed down. When I saw these statistics in a press release issued by the makers of Herr's potato chips, I realized the kids had been right. It is abnormal to watch a Super Bowl without wolfing down a salty snack.

These days I try to avoid chips on Super Bowl Sunday and instead eat chicken wings made with a recipe I call "Buffalo meets Baltimore." The Buffalo refers to the New York state community noted for the fiery chicken wings served in its eateries.

Several years ago, my wife found a recipe for Buffalo-style wings in "The Complete Book of Chicken Wings" by Joie Warner (Hearst Books, 1985). The book said the secret ingredient in the dipping sauce was Durkee Red Hot

Cayenne Pepper Sauce, an ingredient we had trouble finding in Baltimore. Over the years we have used a variety of hot sauces with good success.

We also added a new ingredient, seafood seasoning sold by Obrycki's restaurant in East Baltimore. Like most residents of Baltimore, we started sprinkling seafood seasoning on steamed crabs, but soon couldn't resist sprinkling it on anything edible, including chicken wings.

This is a great dish for Super Bowl Sunday, a day of excess, because it seems like a snack and because you always end up eating too much of it.

Buffalo Meets Baltimore

Serves 4 as main dish

2½ pounds wings trimmed Buffalo style (see below)
¼ cup butter
3-5 tablespoons hot sauce
1 tablespoon red wine vinegar
3 tablespoons, crab seasoning (Obrycki's)
olive oil

To make dipping sauce, slowly melt butter in a large saucepan. Add the hot sauce, (3 tablespoons for mild, 4 for medium, more for hot.) Add the vinegar. Remove from heat.

To make wings, first cut off the tip of the wing, and slice the remaining wing into two pieces; this is Buffalo-style trim. Brush both sides of wings with olive oil, or put wings in a large bowl and mix them with oil with your hands. Place oiled wings on a large rimmed, baking sheet and sprinkle top side of wings with about half of crab seasoning.

Put wings in oven, about 3 inches from broiler. Broil at 400 degrees for about 10-15 minutes, until the top of wings are browned. Remove from oven, drain off liquids from baking sheet. Flip wings, sprinkling their new top sides with remaining crab seasoning. Broil until brown, another 10-15 minutes. Serve with hot, dipping sauce.

Required side dish is celery sticks and carrots that have been soaked in ice water and are dipped in a blue cheese dressing.

Blue Cheese Dressing

Serves 4

2 ounces blue cheese, crumbled
½ cup mayonnaise
½ cup sour cream

Place ingredients in a food processor and mix until smooth. Chill.

From "The Complete Book of Chicken Wings"
by Jodi Warner (Hearst Books, 1985)

Making a great meat sauce

THE RECIPE CALLED FOR GROUND BEEF. I HAD A SLAB OF ROUND STEAK. Casting a glance at the food processor, I decided to give modern meat grinding a whirl. I put in the metal blade, tossed in a few thick slices of the round steak, snapped the lid on the food processor and let 'er rip. The machine sprang to life, bumping into the nearby television set, almost knocking a basketball game off the air.

After about three minutes of commotion, I stopped the food processor and looked at its work. In the bowl was some extremely ground beef. If the machine had kept going much longer, I would have ended up with meat toothpaste.

For the next go-round with round steak I eased up on the power. This time, instead of going gung-ho, I let the blade whirl for only a minute or two. This time the meat had a texture closer to that of the ground beef found in grocery stores.

I was getting the hang of high-power meat grinding, and it was a hoot. After a few more bump and grind go-rounds with the food processor, I had transformed a boring hunk of meat into a textured montage of meat. This was not mere ground beef. This beef had been "personally ground."

I wanted to admire my work, but I was on a tight cooking schedule. Rather than being an object of admiration, this beef had to be promptly plopped into the bottom of a deep metal pot. I used all of the meat, even the batch that was almost toothpaste. In the pot it joined an aromatic trio of sizzling onions, carrots and celery.

The meat was the central component of a ragu, or Bolognese-style meat sauce. And according to the instructions set out by Marcella Hazan in "The Classic Italian Cook Book," a key to a successful meat sauce is to cook it, at the merest simmer, for a long time. Marcella simmers her sauce for at least 3½ hours before she serves it over homemade pasta.

I have made this sauce many times and have never been able to wait that long before serving it. My personal best in simmering time is about 2½ hours, which, by no small coincidence, is about the length of most televised basketball games.

I have noticed that the longer a meat sauce is allowed to simmer, the better it tastes. The other day I was trying to get as much simmering time as possible, so I quickly moved through the early stages of the recipe. I put the meat in the pot. I added wine, then milk, then chopped tomatoes. It was only after the tomatoes went in, and the sauce began to cook in an uncovered pot, that I relaxed.

The bubbling meat sauce filled the house with an enticing aroma, and it quickly attracted kitchen visitors, the kids. "When are we going to eat?" the visitors asked. I replied that supper was still several hours away. I would serve no meat sauce before its time. The visitors grabbed some pretzels, watched some basketball and left.

I recalled that years ago, when I was a kid making forays into my mother's aroma-filled kitchen, I would occasionally get to grind meat. Our cast-iron grinder was a hand-operated device that, to a kid's eyes, represented a wondrous merger of the industrial and domestic worlds. Meat was dropped into an opening at the top of the device. The hand-turned auger moved it through the innards of the grinder. Strings of beef, looking like snakes, slithered out of its side, dropping into a waiting bowl. Sometimes, to appease the grinder after an especially strenuous session, it was fed pieces of stale bread.

I loved turning the meat-grinder handle. So did my three brothers. Mostly we tried to dodge all forms of kitchen labor, but when it came to operating the meat grinder, we fought over who turned the handle. Usually, we ended up taking turns.

On a winter afternoon, as I sat in my kitchen with the meat sauce bubbling on the stove and the basketball game dancing on the television set, I realized why grinding the meat in the food processor had given me such a charge. This time I had done it all by myself. This time I didn't have to share.

Meat Sauce

Serves 6

2 tablespoons chopped yellow onions
3 tablespoons olive oil
3 tablespoons butter
2 tablespoons chopped celery
2 tablespoons chopped carrot
¾ pound lean ground beef
1 teaspoon salt
1 cup dry white wine
½ cup milk
⅛ teaspoon nutmeg (optional)
2 cups canned Italian tomatoes, roughly chopped, with their juice

Use the deepest pot you own. Put in the chopped onion, with all the oil and butter, and saute briefly over medium heat until just translucent. Add the celery and carrot and cook gently for 2 minutes.

Add the ground beef, crumbling it in the pot with a fork. Add 1 teaspoon salt. Stir and cook only until the meat has lost its raw, red color. Add the wine, turn the heat up to medium high and cook, stirring occasionally, until all the wine has evaporated.

Turn the heat down to medium, add the milk and optional nutmeg and cook until the milk has evaporated. Stir frequently.

When the milk has evaporated, add the tomatoes and stir thoroughly. When the tomatoes have started to bubble, turn the heat down until the sauce cooks at the laziest simmer, just an occasional bubble. Cook, uncovered, for 3 to 4 hours, stirring occasionally. Taste and correct for salt.

Serve over pasta.

From "The Classic Italian Cook Book"
by Marcella Hazan (Knopf, 1978)

Big flakes? Time to bake

WHEN SNOW FALLS, BREAD EATERS SEEM TO HAVE TWO REACTIONS. ONE IS to buy every loaf in sight. Another is to hole up at home and bake.

I have experienced both responses. On a recent afternoon when the entire state of Maryland was digging out from a heavy snow, I drove to the grocery store. Cars were parked everywhere, including places that, in sunnier times, were considered exits. Inside the store, the aisles were jammed, the bread shelves empty.

I'm not sure why we buy more bread when it snows. Maybe the snow brings out our long-suppressed craving for sandwiches. But bread-lust probably has more to do with the fact that being in the grocery store after a snow is such an unpleasant experience that we are likely to do bizarre things, such as grabbing six loaves of taste-free white bread, if we can avoid returning to the store.

After I got shut out at the bread aisle, I bought flour and yeast and went home to bake my own bread. I wasn't alone. I called a neighbor and he quickly said he couldn't talk because he was busy baking bread. A woman who lives up the street told me that her bread machine had been going nonstop.

Later, a friend called from Oregon. She had heard reports of a big snow hitting Maryland. She said that folks in Oregon, like Marylanders, get a craving for bread when it snows. She gave me a recipe for sesame seed bread made in a food processor.

I include the recipe here along with my adaptation of Charles van Over's recipe for bread made in a food processor. In a previous column I told readers who wanted van Over's recipe to write me. The requests have been so numerous that I decided to print the recipe. Next time the snow falls, you can turn on the oven instead of slogging to the store.

Homemade Sesame Seed Bread

Yield: One 9-inch round loaf

1 package active dry yeast
1 cup plus 2 tablespoons warm water
¼ cup nonfat dry milk
1 tablespoon sugar
1 teaspoon salt
2 tablespoons olive oil
3½ cups flour
1 egg beaten
1 tablespoon sesame seeds toasted (black seeds if available)
1 teaspoon kosher salt

Grease a 10-inch-by-15-inch baking sheet. Sprinkle the yeast over warm water until it dissolves. Put nonfat dry milk, sugar, salt, olive oil and flour in bowl of food processor and pulse two or three times to blend. With machine running, slowly add water and yeast mixture and process until dough forms a mass. Continue to process for 1 more minute. Transfer dough to lightly floured surface, knead until smooth, adding more flour if necessary. Shape into 9-inch round loaf and place on baking sheet.

Cover loaf with plastic wrap and let rise in refrigerator for at least 2 hours and up to 6 hours. Preheat oven to 400 degrees. Remove loaf from refrigerator, brush with beaten egg, sprinkle with sesame seeds and kosher salt. Bake until done, about 30 minutes. Cool on wire rack.

From "Dungeness Crabs and Blackberry Cobblers"
by Janie Hibler (Knopf, 1991)

Adaptation of Charles van Over's Baguette Recipe

Yield: 2 loaves

12 ounces (weighed) flour
1 teaspoon sea or kosher salt
1¼ cups water, 55-60 degrees
1 teaspoon dry yeast

Weigh flour, put in food processor with steel blade. Add salt, process for 5 seconds.

With machine running, pour steady stream of 1 cup of water through processor feed tube. Process for 30-35 seconds. Dough ball should result. If dough is too wet, add tablespoon or two of flour and process for another 10-15 seconds. If dough is too dry, add remaining water and process for another 10-15 seconds.

Add yeast, process for another 15 seconds. Cover hands with flour, lift dough ball out of processor and put in a large bowl. Cover bowl loosely with plastic wrap or a dish towel. Let dough rise at room temperature. This takes a minimum of 1½ hours.

When dough has risen, cover hands with flour and dust a counter top with flour. Put dough ball on counter top and cut into two equal balls. Let dough rest for 15-20 minutes.

Dust tablecloth lightly with flour. Working on the tablecloth, press each dough ball flat, fold it over on itself, twice. You can then roll dough into long, snakelike baguettes, sealing seam, or you can simply form dough into round loaves. Place loaves in fold of cloth, cover and let rise until the loaves are about 1½ times original size. This takes 1-2 hours at room temperature.

Preheat oven to 400 degrees. Transfer loaves to lightly floured baking sheets. Make steam by spraying oven with water from spray bottle. Put loaves in oven. Spray again after five minutes. Bake at 400 degrees until crust is golden brown or internal temperature of bread is 210. This takes 25-40 minutes. Remove loaves, spray with water for shinier crust, cool on wire rack.

No waffling on waffle appeal

ONE OF THE MORE COMFORTING PHRASES IN THE LANGUAGE IS "WAFFLES FOR breakfast." It is a phrase that evokes thoughts of warm pajamas, soft slippers and leisurely mornings.

Waffles rush for no man. Until the light on the waffle iron signals that the great golden treasure cooking inside is ready to emerge, no amount of agitating can hurry the waffle along. To borrow a phrase from television's basketball analysts, waffles "dictate tempo."

Waffles, the good ones anyway, are still made one at a time. When I was a boy I kept a sharp eye on the family waffle iron. Usually one or more of my three brothers had beaten me to the breakfast table and had been rewarded with a waffle that emerged from the ancient yet trusty electric waffle iron. As the early-risers dug into their waffles, I would alternately gaze with longing looks at the light on the waffle iron and at my brothers' bountiful plates. I was the one who waited for waffles.

The wait was worth it. Eventually the waffle iron light signaled its approval and the batter cake emerged, crisp and exclusively mine. It was hot enough to turn a pat of butter into a yellow stream. That stream would meander through the peaks and valleys of the waffle's honeycomb pattern and would join the powerful syrup stream. Slowly the confluence of syrup and butter would become one mighty river, like the union of the Missouri and Mississippi, and would roll across my plate.

Usually this reverie would be interrupted by a voice from across the table: "You gonna eat that or just look at it?" The voice belonged to a hungry brother, who in the cycle of waffle distribution had moved from being a smug "have" enjoying his first waffle, to an impatient "have not" waiting for his second.

Despite the skirmishes with my siblings, waffle mornings were pleasant times. They had a much more relaxed pace than the cereal mornings in which we wolfed down bowls of boxed cereal before we shot out the door to school. They were much less foreboding than oatmeal mornings, which signaled that the weather was cold and miserable and your mom felt she had to put something warm and lumpy inside you.

Waffle mornings meant you did not have to get dressed for duty. They were days you kept your pajamas and slippers on all morning — a style of dress I still enjoy as a grown-up.

Until I was a grown-up I never paid much attention to the fine points of waffle-making. I did not think much about whether it was OK to use pancake batter to make waffles. I did not know how to keep waffles warm. I never thought that anything other than butter and syrup or maybe powdered sugar would ever appear in the company of a waffle.

I consulted a variety of waffle-making veterans on these points. Overall I found that there is not much agreement on waffles, other than that they are good to eat.

On the issue of batter, for instance, Elisabeth Alston, food editor of *Woman's Day* magazine and author of "Pancakes and Waffles" (HarperCollins), says that the "best ever" pancakes and waffles are made using the same batter recipe.

However, "The Joy of Cooking," the venerable cookbook by Irma S. Rombauer and Marion Rombauer Becker (Bobbs-Merrill, 1993), gives a slightly different batter for its buttermilk pancake recipe than for its buttermilk waffles. The waffle batter has less buttermilk and baking soda than the pancake batter. Moreover, while the pancake recipe calls for adding the whole egg, all at once, the waffle recipe calls for beating the egg whites separately.

In this debate, I tend to side with my favorite waffle-maker, my mom. Mom uses pancake batter for waffles, but adds an extra beaten egg all at once, and a little extra oil.

As for how to keep waffles warm, Alston says waffles can be placed, uncovered, directly on the racks of a 200-degree oven for no more than 15 minutes.

The answer on what is an appropriate waffle companion is varied. In her book, Alston goes so far as to suggest putting chopped walnuts in waffle batter, covering the cooked waffle with whipped cream laced with sugar and espresso, and serving the dish as dessert.

"The Joy of Cooking" advocates putting pieces of cooked bacon on the waffle iron and pouring a cornmeal batter over them, making a one-piece, bacon-laced waffle.

Jeannette Wiedmann, a Baltimore waffle-maker of some renown, sometimes serves kidney stew on waffles for big Sunday breakfasts. "I know a whole contingent of people who would never turn down kidney stew," said Wiedmann, adding that her stew relies on kidneys, not onions or potatoes, to carry the flavor.

The kidney stew and waffle breakfast is one she grew up eating at her family's Carroll County farm. To try to keep up with the demand of feeding a family of nine, her mother would have two waffle irons going, Wiedmann recalls. But sometimes, she didn't wait for the waffles.

"Any carrier for the kidney stew — cold biscuits, new biscuits, toast — would do," she says. "You don't really need the waffles."

Perhaps. But as one who rarely faces kidney stew, let alone at breakfast, I think I will stick to waffles with syrup and butter.

At the table of presidents

AS PRESIDENTS DAY APPROACHED, I FOUND MYSELF WONDERING: WHAT DID George and Abe like to eat?

George and Abe were George Washington and Abraham Lincoln, our first and 16th presidents, who, in addition to being responsible for this three-day weekend, also get credit for founding and preserving the United States of America.

Historians have dealt with the minds and motives of these men. I was interested in their palates. I wanted to know what they ate for breakfast, lunch and state occasions. I called researchers familiar with the lives and dietary habits of these men.

I learned that Washington was a fan of hoecakes, hominy and home-brewed beer.

I learned that Lincoln was a great man, but a light eater. When his wife, Mary Todd, chided him about his diet, she wanted him to eat more, not less.

I started with our first president. A typical breakfast for Washington was hoecakes — pancakes made of cornmeal — cooked on a griddle and served swimming in butter and honey. After polishing off a plate of hoecakes and a cup of unsweetened tea, Washington would usually hop on his horse and survey his Virginia plantation, an undertaking that meant he ended up logging about 14 miles a day on horseback.

I found this out by talking with Mary Thompson, a researcher at Mount Vernon, Washington's plantation, which sits on the Potomac River. Thompson told me she developed a sense of Washington's favorite foods by reading correspondence, by looking at Mount Vernon menus and by examining bookkeeping records of the estate.

In addition to his yen for hoecakes, Washington had a soft spot for hominy, she said. In Washington's time, the dish of dried, hulled corn kernels was often served to servants and slaves. But at Mount Vernon, hominy also showed up on the menu for the main meal, served at 3 o'clock in the afternoon to family and guests.

Washington also liked to eat a variety of fish caught in the Potomac, Thompson said. The river serves as the border between Maryland and Virginia, but the official Maryland state line is the opposing shoreline.

Maryland owns the water and so the Potomac River fish Washington found so tasty came from Maryland.

Like many men of his time, Washington brewed his own beer. The actual brewing was probably done by the servants and slaves who worked at Mount Vernon, Thompson said.

A house recipe for a so-called "small beer" has survived. It calls for hops, molasses and yeast, and a week's worth of patience — waiting as the beer "works," or ferments.

If it were sold today, the brew probably would be called Big George's Small Beer.

While Washington seemed to enjoy good food and drink, Lincoln did not seem to care.

"He was a real Spartan when it came to food," said Michael Maione, site historian at Ford's Theater in Washington.

The few times in his writings that Lincoln mentions meals, the fare was a boiled egg, tea and fruit, Maione said.

Menus from Lincoln's years in the White House describe elaborate meals, however. A menu for a White House feast in February 1862, for example, promised "stewed and scalloped oysters, stuffed turkey, aspic of tongue, canvas back duck, beef, ham, venison, pheasant, terrapin, jellies and ices."

But according to historians, Lincoln paid little notice to such spreads. "Food could be falling off the table, but he was not interested," Maione said.

Accounts from friends and relatives reported Lincoln would often forget to eat, said Linda Norbert Suits, curator of the Lincoln Home National Historic Site in Springfield, Ill.

Burdened by the responsibilities of his office and troubled by digestive problems, Lincoln lost weight during his years in the White House. He was about 6 feet 4 inches tall and weighed about 180 pounds when he took office in 1861, and was down to about 160 pounds when he was assassinated in 1865.

My glance into the eating habits of the two presidents did not yield profound insights into their character. But learning about Washington's weakness for hominy and Lincoln's inability to enjoy food reminded me that these towering visages of history had small, human moments.

Washington was not only the founder of our country, he was also a man who appreciated a good corn cake. Lincoln, on the other hand, was so devoted to the duties of office that he ended up missing the simple pleasures of eating good food.

My inquiry ended up reinforcing what major historians have been saying for years. These were two good men. We were lucky to have them.

Cooking polenta: a stirring experience

IT SEEMED LIKE AN ORDINARY MARYLAND TUESDAY, WHEN ROUTINE RULED and supper would be nothing special.

But onto the scene came a bag of polenta and a visitor named Luigi. The polenta, golden cornmeal, arrived via an Italian food store, Trinacria on North Paca Street, near Baltimore's Lexington Market. The visitor, Luigi Ferrucci, came to Baltimore from Florence, Italy, via Bethesda.

Luigi is a physician and was in Bethesda for one of his periodic research stints at the National Institute on Aging. He came to Baltimore to consult with my wife on a research paper. He ended up in our kitchen, with the polenta. The result was a magnificent meal.

It took a while. Instead of buying the "pronto," or instant, type of polenta, my wife and I had purchased the slow-cooking kind, the kind you stir for 45 minutes after it begins to boil.

I had eaten polenta before, in restaurants serving Northern Italian fare. But I had never cooked it, and that meant I had never appreciated the golden starch. Cooking it turned out to be a culinary marathon that required strong arms, a chunk of time and good conversational companions.

It started with a big pot filled with 12 cups of cold water. The water was brought to a boil and 4 cups of dry, grainy polenta were added to the pot. The heat was reduced, and then began the stirring marathon, an activity that required the constant movement of a long-handled wooden spoon through the mixture.

In the early going, the spoon moved through the mixture easily, like a knife cutting through butter. But as time wore on, the polenta thickened and stirring became difficult, like moving a trowel through a tub of concrete.

In Italy, Luigi said, making polenta isn't always such an ordeal. Italians use pots with tapered sides. There are no bottom edges for the polenta to stick to, and that makes stirring the polenta much less laborious, he said. He added that when he makes polenta for his wife and two boys, he uses a mechanical stirrer. The device sounded similar to the mechanized stirrer we have in our ice cream maker. And after attempts at pushing the spoon through the thickening polenta, I was ready to pour the mixture in the ice cream maker, turn on the motor and see what happened.

Instead, we took turns stirring the polenta. Luigi would stir for a few minutes. Then I would stir, trying to imitate the artful way Luigi had used the spoon to pull the cornmeal away from the sides of the pot. Then my wife would take a few turns. We even got our older teen-age son into the rotation by assuring him that stirring the polenta would put more muscles on his thickening arms.

With the stirring came conversation. Some of the talk was about cooking techniques. For instance, we watched Luigi make his tomato sauce by slicing three onions, drizzling them with olive oil, and tossing them and a large can of Italian plum tomatoes into a saucepan. He kept the sauce on high heat, boiling it for at least 20 minutes. Reducing the liquid this way, he said, is the secret to good sauce.

Some of the talk was lyrical. The bubbling polenta stirred the imaginations of the spoon pushers. To my eye, the hole formed after a bubble of polenta popped looked like the mouth of a hungry beast lurking in a thick, yellow sea. Luigi said that in the Italian version of "Sleeping Beauty," the sound that awakens the castle residents from their 100-year slumber is the sound of polenta bubbling.

After 45 minutes of such talk and much stirring, we noted that the polenta had changed. It had been transformed from grainy pellets to creamy mounds. It moved easily away from the sides of the pan. It took on a vibrant golden color. It was, Luigi ruled, ready to be put on the dinner plates.

He spooned five mounds of the polenta around the edge of each plate. Next to these golden mounds, he placed a lake of red sauce. The polenta and sauce rested for about 10 minutes, as we summoned the family to the table. Following Luigi's lead, we ate by mixing forkfuls of polenta with dollops of sauce. Some of us added pieces of cooked Italian sausage into the mixture as well. The mix produced wonderful, clean flavors. The polenta was light, not gooey. The tomato sauce was sweet, but not sugary.

In Northern Italy, polenta is often served in lieu of bread, Luigi said. Sometimes it is even served as dessert. He explained that the dessert is made by placing three equal portions of polenta, ricotta cheese and honey on a plate.

Later that night, I took Luigi to Penn Station to catch a late train to Washington. There he would connect to a subway that would carry him back to Bethesda, where he would be staying a few more weeks before returning to Italy.

Sated, we sat on the station's wooden benches, waiting along with other nighttime travelers for the train. Tuesday was drawing to a close. It had started as an ordinary workday, but thanks to a bag of polenta and a visitor from Italy, it had a golden finish.

An adventure in terrapin

NOT EVERYONE CAN EAT TERRAPIN. FEWER FOLKS STILL CAN EAT IT AFTER they have seen it made. Recently I did both.

When I told natives of Maryland that I had eaten some terrapin, they licked their lips and wanted to know where I got it. The dish is prized here and referred to by zealots simply as "terrapin."

When I told folks who hail from the rest of the world that I had recently eaten a soupy stew made from selected innards of the Chesapeake Bay turtles, they wrinkled their noses and asked, "Why?"

I was invited to join the ranks of the terrapin eaters for what in Baltimore is regarded as the best of all possible reasons: a neighbor asked me. One of the most appealing aspects of living in Baltimore is that neighborhoods matter to people here. When you meet at social gatherings in other cities, the first thing they want to know is what you do for a living. In Baltimore, people want to know where you live. And if your answer is "in the neighborhood," a bond is formed and all kinds of opportunities open up for you. Opportunities like the chance to watch turtles being cooked and cleaned.

And so when I was invited to watch terrapin being made by Nancy Rouse, who lives down the street from me, neighborhood honor required that I say yes. Rouse is a woman accustomed to having turtles in her kitchen. So commonplace were turtles in the Rouse family kitchen that, when her now-grown children were teen-agers, they financed weekend ski trips by making batches of terrapin and selling it to grateful customers for $30 a quart.

When I arrived at the Rouse kitchen one rainy winter morning, I met her friend, Shelby Strudwick, a woman who matched Rouse's enthusiasm for terrapin, shell for shell, claw for claw.

When I got in the kitchen I quickly realized that I was overdressed and out of my league. I was dressed in a tweed coat, shirt, tie and wool slacks, and was carrying a notebook and pen. The women were wearing cotton slacks and shirts, the sleeves of which they had pushed up over their elbows.

By 10:30 or so in the morning the two women had already taken apart the four live terrapins that had been driven up to Baltimore from Maryland's Eastern Shore. The terrapins cost about $3.50 each, Strudwick said, but in keeping with tradition she was close-mouthed about the exact source of her supply. Once a terrapin maker finds a good terrapin catcher, it is kept a secret. I did surmise that the terrapins were legally caught. The season runs through the winter.

Working as a terrapin twosome, Rouse and Strudwick had immersed the critters in boiling water, then removed the outer skin from their shells. They put the four terrapins back in a pot of boiling water and were cooking the turtles when I arrived.

The terrapins cook for about an hour or until they are done, Strudwick told me. The way you tell if a terrapin is done, she said, was to pinch one of the turtle's feet or claws. When it feels tender to the touch, she said, inviting me to pinch the cooked terrapin, it is done. I pinched the terrapin's toe and agreed it felt tender.

Pinching a toe was about all the work I did in helping the women prepare the terrapin. That was partly because I wasn't dressed for serious kitchen work but mainly because I didn't know my terrapin parts. For one thing, Strudwick said that unlike some terrapin cooks, she does not serve it with the bones in the bowl. She uses the bones to make the broth.

Rouse and Strudwick tried to teach me about terrapin parts. When they pulled the shell off a cooked terrapin and picked the innards apart by hand, they would stop in mid-turtle to point out to me the treasured eggs, the treasured liver, the dreaded gall sacks.

I nodded my knowing nod. But it was the same kind of nodding I do when my wife and I go to see a guy about our income taxes. Then my wife and the income tax guy sit there and talk about the fine points of straight-line vs. zigzag depreciation and every once in a while I nod at them. I'm not that interested in the details but in how things are going to end up.

And in terrapin-making, what I was most interested in was when I was going to eat the dish.

I learned that while terrapin can be made in one day, it should be served to an adoring audience. And since such an audience was not available the day Rouse and Strudwick picked apart the turtles, the women froze the meat and waited a few days to assemble some appreciative eaters.

The feast was in Strudwick's home in a neighborhood called Poplar Hill. And when Rouse, and my wife and I, arrived at the Strudwick home, we began the evening – as good Baltimoreans do – by talking about neighborhoods with Strudwick, her husband Lewis, and their son Nash. The Strudwicks said hills in their neighborhood were steeper, the trees taller and the fox sightings more numerous than in our neighborhood, Bolton Hill. I said I wasn't sure about that last point, that many nights in our neighborhood I heard guys on the street yell, "Yo! Fox!"

Soon other eaters arrived, Rick and Bobbie Hansen, and the terrapin, a mixture of dark meat and seasoned broth, was served in bowls. A bottle of Rainwater Madeira was passed around with the explanation that spoonfuls of the fortified wine could either be applied to the terrapin or drunk by the terrapin eater.

I poured my Madeira in my bowl of terrapin, then took a spoonful of supper. The terrapin was definitely strong and had a lot of what the wine guys call "mouth feel." I liked it. I liked it better when I didn't think about what I was eating. I liked it best when I ate it and thought about England.

During dinner several people told stories about the guest of honor, the terrapin.

Lewis Strudwick said he used to have live terrapins shipped to Baltimore from the Eastern Shore by bus in gunnysacks. The terrapins wouldn't sit still but would wander around in the sack, causing it to move across the bus station floor, he said. By the time Strudwick arrived at the bus station to claim his cargo, the leery baggage handlers were on one side of the room and the turtles on the other.

Discovering winter cress

IT'S SOMETIMES CALLED "CRESS," RHYMING WITH "YES." OR "CREASES," rhyming with "pieces." Or winter cress, its real name.

It's either eaten raw as a peppery salad green or cooked as an excellent companion to muskrat.

I had it both ways recently. I slogged into a snowy field at Windmill Farm outside Salisbury and sampled a green clump of cress popping out under the snow. It was crunchy and peppery stuff.

As the name winter cress implies, it does well in the winter.

"It doesn't like a lot of sun," said J. R. McGrath, proprietor of Windmill Farm. As he spoke, a strong wind swept over the snow-dotted fields in front of him. This was winter cress weather. The snow, folks say, makes the cress sweet.

They're right. The first bites of the cress leaves I sampled in the field were sweet and crisp. Then there was a pleasing, fiery aftertaste, like a good green pepper.

There had been plenty of snow, and later that night I ate some more snow-sweetened cress.

This time I ate cooked cress – steamed, actually. It tasted much less peppery but still faintly sweet, a flavor close to steamed spinach.

The only way to harvest the green is to wade out in a muddy field and cut the cress off the ground with a knife. This muddy work had already been done a few days earlier by Herb and Imogene Horton, devoted fans of cress. They had some cress growing in the back yard of their Mardela Springs home, but it was crowded. Successful cress likes room to stretch out. The cress the Hortons had for supper came from the roomy field on Windmill Farm.

The muskrat was also local, as were the oysters and the sweet potatoes in the sweet potato biscuits.

Although winter cress is a relative of the popular watercress, a green found at the trendiest of tables, winter cress is not so well known.

McGrath sells some of his winter cress to a wholesale produce operator in Jessup. But a fellow at the produce operation, W. D. Class and Son, said the demand for cress in the cities was mild.

Reference books say that winter cress can be found throughout the Northeast, but the center of "cress" or "crease" caters seems to be the Eastern Shore. This finger of Maryland and Delaware, separated from the rest of the world by the Chesapeake Bay and the Atlantic Ocean, is not over-whelmed by trends. The folks there seem to know what they like – crabs, oysters, fish, muskrat, cress, even an occasional raccoon – and don't much care if *Gourmet* magazine agrees.

"I've had winter cress all my life," said W. E. Dobson, 79, a native of the Eastern Shore and resident of Federalsburg.

"As a kid I remember having it with fried fish. When the herring were running in the spring," Dobson said, the dish often served was "greens and fried fish."

Another popular way to prepare winter cress, according to Dobson, was "to cook it like kale. Cook it with a ham hock ... or a hog back, something greasy.

"You ought to eat it with some muskrat," Dobson told me. When I replied that was exactly how I had eaten winter cress, Dobson was pleased.

As a matter of fact, said Dobson, shortly after he finished talking to me he was going to dine on muskrat at Johnny and Sammy's restaurant in Salisbury. The restaurant serves muskrat on Mondays, he said.

But Dobson doubted that he would get any winter cress to go with the muskrat. Winter cress has been hard to find, Dobson said, even on the Eastern Shore.

Jerome Framptom Jr., another longtime resident of the area, agreed. In Federalsburg, Frampton recalled, winter cress used to be sold door-to-door by the late Sewell Ricketts. Ricketts would forage nearby fields for the green, then sell it to townsfolk, including Framptom.

After Ricketts died about 20 years ago, winter cress was harder to come by, Framptom said.

According to Ron Wade, agricultural extension agent for Dorchester County, there are two reasons why the winter cress crop is decreasing. First, farmers are growing more wheat and barley than in previous years. These crops shade the ground and don't let winter cress start growing. Second, her-bicides used by farmers attack weeds, and winter cress, Wade said, is a type of weed.

Winter cress shows up periodically in at least one Salisbury supermarket, the Salisbury Warehouse Food Market. It's sold in the fall, said Jerome Williams, a worker in the store's produce section. The store stops carrying the green in the winter, Williams said, because the frost "burns" the winter cress, turning it reddish-brown.

But Joan Malone, who helps her husband, Danny, harvest the winter cress at Windmill Farm, said winter cress can take the frost. Frost may change the color of the leaves from green to a reddish-brown, she said, but it doesn't change the taste.

As for the taste of cress, Malone had a fresh opinion. Although she, too, had grown up on the Eastern Shore and had harvested winter cress, it was-n't until this year that she got around to eating it.

"Some people say it's stringy," said Malone. "But I don't think so. To me it tastes just as good as kale and collards."

In addition to its taste, there are other benefits of eating cress. Like many greens, it's high in vitamins. Another nickname for winter cress is scurvy cress. Eating it is said to have kept sailors from getting scurvy.

Besides preventing scurvy and bringing out the flavor of muskrat, winter cress, I believe, has other powers. Such as making you beautiful.

Wendi Bell, 17, lives on Windmill Farm, where the large patch of winter cress grows. She grew up eating the stuff.

Recently she was named Wicomico County Farm Queen. Before that, her mother, Becky, another cress eater, was named queen.

The conclusion?

Whether you call it cress, crease or winter cress, it is the stuff queens are made of.

Lake trout, a catchy name

THE ICE SNAPPED UNDER MY FEET AND A FIERCE WIND BIT MY SKIN AS I walked from my car to the Roost carryout restaurant at Reisterstown Road and Hayward Avenue in Northwest Baltimore. It was a bone-cold day.

A few minutes later, however, I was aglow. I was feasting on hot "lake trout." The fish had been rolled in batter and fried in oil. Steam rolled off the pieces of fried fish. The aroma filled my car as I headed down Reisterstown Road eating and remembering. The smell and taste of fried fish triggered memories of church suppers, of fish sandwiches for lunch, of fish on Friday.

Lake trout is probably Maryland's most popular alias. The fish draws long lines at the Roost and a handful of other Maryland eateries that sell it. But this lake trout never swam in a lake. Nor is it a trout. It is a whiting, a fish that swims in the Atlantic Ocean. It is caught by boats fishing off the coast of New England, and is shipped down to Maryland wholesale fish markets that sell the fish to retail markets and restaurants.

How a fish called whiting, or Menticirrhus to the scientists, became known as lake trout to the fish-eating public is an interesting tale. I pieced it together from stories, old and new, I heard from the folks who sell the fish.

The basic answer is that the name lake trout sells well. It is the same reason that Roy Scherer Jr. called himself Rock Hudson and Madonna Louise Veronica Ciccone became Madonna. The new name has more crowd appeal than the old one. Whiting, alias lake trout, is not the first fish to adopt trout as part of its moniker. To most, the word trout conjures up images of babbling brooks and gourmet meals. These are images that guys selling fish might try to capitalize on. And so one day, for example, a fish with a going-nowhere name such as ling becomes known as oyster trout, because it has "such pearly white flesh." The name catches on, the fish sells, and it is ling no more. It is oyster trout. It happens in the fish business.

Whiting, I was told, also got the "trout treatment." For years whiting was a fodder fish. It was ground up and used in fish sticks and other generic fish products. Sometimes it even ended up in plant food fertilizers.

But then someone, no one is quite sure who, got the idea of moving whiting up a notch on the ladder of seafood status and making whiting a "head fish." A head fish is a fish with status. It is sold with its head on, its body intact. Such a fish brings a higher price per pound than the headless, anonymous, fodder variety. Once whiting entered the head-fish ranks, it picked up the impressive-sounding title "trout."

The story of how the fish got the name lake is not clear. The most likely explanation is that lake is a corruption of late. It seems the fish was once called late trout because it arrived in the fish markets later in the day than other types of "trout."

I heard this story a few years ago from Bill Devine whose family runs Faidley's Seafood operation in Baltimore's Lexington Market. He said he first heard the story from another veteran of the seafood business, his mother-in-law, Albina Faidley.

Whiting were once caught by fishermen who journeyed out on the ocean for only a day of work, he said. Traditionally, these day boats unloaded their catch later than the boats that had been at sea for several days. So it was common that the whiting, or late trout, would arrive in markets later than other fish.

In the hurly-burly world of Maryland fish markets, where the king's English and the Lord's truth were sometimes subjected to manipulation, late was pronounced lake. Eventually almost everyone, from customer to fishmonger, ended up calling the fish lake trout.

The other day Devine told me that one new development on the lake-trout front is that some of his customers are once again calling the fish whiting.

Cliff Rose, who runs Shore Seafood in Baltimore's Northeast Market, told me he did a brisk business in lake trout. A few of his customers call it whiting, but not many, Rose said.

Lake trout probably outsells every other kind of fish sold in Baltimore, Rose said, adding that the biggest day for sales of lake trout, and all fish, was Friday.

"Friday is a big fish day," he said. "Part of it is the Catholic tradition of eating fish on Friday," he said. But Rose said customers from many different cultures and religious affiliations frequent his stand, which is located in a neighborhood east of Johns Hopkins Hospital and medical school. "Many people around here," he said, "gotta have their fish on Friday." Rose offered a quick assessment of the appeal of lake trout.

"It has a very mild flavor; not strong, not oily. It is very economical, averaging about $2.19 a pound retail. And it doesn't have many bones. When you pull out the backbone, most of the bones are gone."

I thought of Rose's critique as I polished off the last bites of my lake trout lunch from the Roost.

He was right on all counts. It had that familiar, crunchy fish-on-Friday flavor. It was cheap. For $4.26 I got enough fried fish for two meals. And the bones of that lake trout slipped out faster than you could say, "I thought I ate a whiting."

Soup makers' secrets

I HAVE ALWAYS THOUGHT OF SOUP AS A DE-ICER. A FLAVORFUL WAY TO TAKE the bite out of the winter wind, to loosen up the joints, to thaw the brain.

One recent bitter day when water pipes were bursting, knees were cracking and brains were numbing, I called a sprinkling of chefs and quizzed them on the secrets of soup-making.

Over on the Eastern Shore, Raymond Copper, executive chef of the Tidewater Inn in Easton, said pace was crucial. Soup cannot be hurried, he said. When Copper makes his snapper soup, a dish that takes its name from the snapping turtles that constitute its main ingredient, "it takes anywhere from six to eight hours to do it right," he said.

Much of that time is devoted to making the stock, a process that, when Copper does it, involves devoting long stretches of the day to watching liquids slowly bubble down.

"Some people use those canned stocks," said Copper. "But to get a good soup, I've always thought you gotta work from scratch . . . start with bones and vegetables, and reduce the sauce."

Most of his soups require two to three hours of chopping and watching, Copper said. He added that one notable exception to the idea that more time in the pot translates into more flavor in the bowl, is oyster stew. "People tend to overcook oysters. You don't need to cook them long, just cook them until they curl."

Chef Mark Henry agreed that time is the ally of the soup maker. Soups should not be rushed and most should be encouraged to spend the night, said Henry. He pointed out that many soups taste better on the second day. "Soups with tomatoes and beans and meats do improve overnight," he said. "Their flavors blend."

But soups with green vegetables in them are, he said, potages of a different color. "Soups with chlorophyll in them . . . broccoli or asparagus . . . taste better when they are fresher." This proves, I guess, that unlike wine, and most of us, green soups do not improve with age.

Henry, who has worked at several Maryland restaurants including the Milton Inn in Sparks, the Chester River Inn on Kent Island, and now the Oregon Grille in Hunt Valley, said that one trick he picked up in his soup-making career was putting a double dose of vegetables in vegetable soup. The first batch goes in the soup early, he said. As it cooks, this batch softens, virtually dissolves and releases terrific flavors, he said. The second batch goes in late in soup-making, then the soup is brought to a boil and simmers a few minutes until the newly arrived vegetables get tender. The second helping of vegetables gives the soup a nice texture, he said.

Henry also passed on his thoughts about the ideal shape of a soup pot. Big bottoms are good, he said, but pots with thick bottoms and thick sides are even better. When you turn up the flame under a pot with a thick bottom and sides, the soup isn't likely to burn as the flame licks the edges of the pot.

While Henry makes his own soup stock, he suggests that if home cooks want to buy canned stock, they should buy the low-salt varieties. "If you buy some canned chicken broth, get the kind that has the least salt in it. That way when you reduce it, it won't get too salty.

"If you cook your broth down and you think it needs salt, you can always add it."

Henry praised the practical, one-dish-feeds-all appeal of soup. "If I have a bowl of bean soup or Hungarian goulash, that takes care of lunch," he said.

But the chef also struck a philosophical note as he spoke about how the freewheeling nature of soup-making has always appealed to him.

"If you look at the two extremes of cooking," he said, "on one end there is baking, which is very structured, with a precise order of ingredients and all kinds of chemical reactions. And at the other extreme there is soup-making, which has almost no structure. You put some ingredients in a pot, and their flavors go together and it tastes good.

"For me, a good soup is the essence of what cooking is about. A soup has got to stand on its flavor. If a soup doesn't have the flavor, presentation doesn't matter."

Down in South Baltimore, the soups made by Bill Aydlett when he was chef at Sisson's restaurant sounded complicated: smoked duck and corn cream soup; gumbo with andouille, which is smoked Cajun sausage; gumbo with tasso, which is seasoned, smoked Cajun ham.

But Aydlett's approach to soup-making is remarkably straightforward. The secret to making a good gumbo, he said, is to make a good roux (a mixture of flour and fat used as a thickener).

And the way you know if you have succeeded in making a good soup, he said, is how you feel after you set down your spoon. Whatever the season, a good soup, he said, "makes you feel warm all over."

Memories are the icing on the sheet cake

ONE WINTER WEEKEND MY WIFE AND I THREW WHAT WE HOPE IS OUR LAST big birthday bash. Our youngest son turned 12, an occasion he and a gang of his buddies marked by shooting each other with lasers and eating chocolate sheet cake.

We figure that this noisy event might signal the end of the "mob of kids" style of birthday celebration. We are hoping that from now on, the kid will want to celebrate birthdays the way adults do: Either ignoring them or going out for a quiet evening with a few friends. We'll see.

The shooting-each-other-with-lasers part of the birthday experience was new to me, but not to the guys at the party. Most of them were veteran marksmen, having already plugged each other at previous birthday celebrations held at the same laser tag emporium, Ultrazone in the East Point Mall, where our party was held.

The chocolate sheet cake, however, was an old friend. As the birthday parties of our kids have moved from site to site, the cake has been a fixture.

The other day, during a pause in laser hostilities, I recalled some of the various birthday party venues where the cake had appeared. I remembered that when our older son, now a teen-ager, was small, he had a theme for each of his birthday parties. One year his theme was law and order, and little boys sat around our kitchen table wearing plastic police hats, looking like English bobbies as they ate chocolate cake. Another year the theme was the king and his court, and again all the "knights" in attendance wore the appropriate headgear and dined on chocolate cake.

As our sons grew older, their birthday celebrations moved out of our house. There were rides at the Baltimore Streetcar Museum, duckpin bowling outings at Taylor's lanes in Stoneleigh, indoor miniature golf games and swings in the batting cages at Sports in Cockeysville, trips through mazes at the now defunct Family Fun Jungle. Regardless of the backdrop, the birthday cake remained the same.

It is a simple, farm-country sheet cake, with eggs, buttermilk, butter, cocoa and a generous amount of sugar. It comes from "The Christian Home Cookbook," (1967, Gospel Publishers). The book is a collection of recipes sent in by Mennonite women, many of them living in western Kansas.

The recipe, sent in by Delma Friesen of Conway, Kan., and Bernice Giesbrecht of Glenn, Calif., makes a chocolate cake that is probably too sweet for most occasions, but just right for a birthday. It is also easy to make and serve. Using powdered sugar, you can write the age of the celebrant on the top of the cake.

The other day, for instance, my son blew out the candles on his cake and the "12" made of powdered sugar took flight. The collection of boys at the celebration loved the chaos.

There might be some cultural message in the fact that a sheet cake from the plains of Kansas has moved through the city of Baltimore leaving a series of sated celebrants in its wake. I'll let the anthropologists figure out exactly what the message is.

All I know is that as my kids get older I look forward to their birthday celebrations getting smaller and quieter, at least the ones I am invited to. And I am counting on getting a piece or two of that chocolate birthday cake.

Chocolate Sheet Cake

Serves 12

2 cups sugar
2 cups flour
½ cup butter
½ cup shortening
4 tablespoons cocoa
1 cup water
½ cup buttermilk
2 eggs
1 teaspoon baking soda
1 teaspoon cinnamon
1 teaspoon vanilla

Preheat oven to 400 degrees. Sift sugar and flour into large mixing bowl. Combine butter, shortening, cocoa and water in saucepan, bring to rapid boil, pour this mixture over sugar and flour and mix well. Add buttermilk, eggs, baking soda, cinnamon and vanilla; beat thoroughly.
Pour into greased rectangular pan, 10-by-15-inches. Bake for 20 minutes.

Icing

½ cup butter
4 tablespoons cocoa
6 tablespoons milk
¾ to 1 pound (1 box) powdered sugar (to taste)
1 teaspoon vanilla

Melt butter in saucepan, add cocoa and milk and bring to a boil. Remove from heat, add sugar and vanilla. Beat well. Pour on cake while still warm.

From "The Christian Home Cookbook"
(Gospel Publishers, 1967)

Second chances

LEFTOVERS ARE LIKE OLD FRIENDS. THEY AREN'T NEW AND EXCITING, AND that is why you like to have them around. They are the stuff comfortable evenings are made of.

When I heard about a report on the state of the nation's leftovers, I was encouraged. According to the 1998 Old Farmer's Almanac, the practice of cooking extra food, thereby guaranteeing that there will be leftovers, has increased 30 percent in America during the last 10 years.

I am not sure what survey method was used to come up with this finding. But I believe the report because it comes from a publication popular with farmers, a group of folks who, in my experience, know how to eat. If there aren't leftovers at the end of a farm meal, the farmer's wife is likely to think she didn't cook enough food.

I am a longtime admirer of leftovers. During my teens, I often could be found in front of the family fridge, studying its contents. Instead of saying hello, my father would routinely greet me by saying, "Close the refrigerator door." I still like leftovers, but usually by the time I get home the contents of our refrigerator have already been scavenged by my two sons. Sometimes I stare at the empty fridge shelves and feel like an old lion who has been beaten to his prey by younger, quicker members of his pack.

Not all foods are good as leftovers. Some dishes, like some marriages, work better the second time around. Fried chicken, for instance, is delightful when eaten warm, shortly after it has emerged from the skillet. But it tastes even better, I think, when it has had time to cool off. If, like me, you are a drumstick gnawer, feasting on a lunch of cold fried chicken is about as good as life gets.

Soups and big pots of chili also improve over time. This happens because the ingredients in soup behave like folks at a cocktail party. At first, most are standoffish, keeping to themselves. But after a while they start mingling, interacting with strangers, and the whole shebang develops an harmonious buzz.

On the other hand, some dishes do not make good leftovers. Carrots get mushy the second time around. Salads get soggy. And tacos, well, don't ask.

Some leftovers resemble old actors making a comeback. If they present themselves in a new package, they can be successful. Plain old mashed potatoes, for instance, are a pretty ordinary leftover. But if they are reworked — shaped into potato pancakes and reheated in a skillet coated with melted butter — they are a smash.

The allure of some leftovers, like take-out Chinese food, is overpowering. Any time I look in the refrigerator and find some leftover moo shu pork, I immediately eat it. Several factors are at work here. Among them are the pleasing flavor of moo shu pork, and the thrill of the hunt. At our house, you only get so many shots at bagging leftover Chinese food. If you pass on your chance at having the moo shu for lunch, other predators won't.

One of my favorite desserts is bread pudding, made with five cups of stale bread. There are a variety of explanations for my bread-pudding ardor. One is that the recipe for this bread pudding comes from Paul Prudhomme, who, like many Cajun cooks, can make anything except a tree stump taste like dessert. Another reason is that while this dish is made with leftover bread, it tastes surprisingly fresh and sweet. This bread pudding may be related to leftovers, but it rarely sees the dawn of more than one day.

New Orleans Bread Pudding with Lemon Sauce and Chantilly Cream

Serves 8

3 large eggs
1¼ cups sugar
1½ teaspoons vanilla extract
1¼ teaspoons ground nutmeg
1¼ teaspoons ground cinnamon
¼ cup unsalted butter, melted
2 cups milk
½ cup raisins
½ cup coarsely chopped pecans, dry roasted
5 cups very stale French or Italian bread, with crusts on

Preheat oven to 350 degrees.

In a large bowl, beat the eggs on high speed with an electric mixer until extremely frothy and bubbles are the size of pinheads, about 3 minutes (or with a metal whisk for about 6 minutes). Add sugar, vanilla, nutmeg, cinnamon and butter and beat on high until well-blended. Beat in the milk, then stir in raisins and pecans.

Place bread cubes in a greased loaf pan. Pour egg mixture over them and toss until bread is soaked. Let sit until you see only a narrow bead of liquid around the pan's edges, about 45 minutes, occasionally patting the bread down into the liquid. Place in a preheated 350-degree oven. Lower the heat to 300 and bake 40 minutes. Increase oven temperature to 425 and bake until pudding is well-browned and puffy, about 15 to 20 minutes more.

To serve, put 1½ tablespoons warm lemon sauce in each dessert dish, then spoon in ½ cup hot bread pudding and top with ¼ cup Chantilly Cream.

Lemon Sauce

Makes about 3/4 cup

1 lemon, halved
½ cup water
¼ cup sugar
2 teaspoons cornstarch, dissolved in ¼ cup water
1 teaspoon vanilla extract

Squeeze two tablespoons juice from lemon halves and place juice in a 1-quart saucepan; add lemon halves, water and sugar, and bring to a boil. Stir in dissolved cornstarch and vanilla. Cook 1 minute over high heat, stirring constantly. Strain, squeezing sauce from lemon rinds. Serve warm.

Chantilly Cream

Makes about 2 cups

⅔ cup heavy cream
1 teaspoon vanilla extract
1 teaspoon brandy
1 teaspoon Grand Marnier (or Triple Sec)
¼ cup sugar
2 tablespoons sour cream

Refrigerate a medium-size bowl and beaters until very cold. Combine cream, vanilla, brandy and Grand Marnier in the bowl and beat with electric mixer on medium speed 1 minute. Add the sugar and sour cream and beat on medium until soft peaks form, about 3 minutes. Do not overbeat.

From "Chef Paul Prudhomme's Louisiana Kitchen"
(William Morrow, 1984)

Lighting the way

I HAVE BEEN LIGHTING A LOT OF CANDLES. IT USED TO BE THAT CANDLES were reserved for weekend meals or semi-special occasions, which were also marked by the removal of the stack of newspapers from the end of the kitchen table.

But lately I have been lighting candles every time the tribe gathers for an evening meal. Sometimes I take the newspaper stack off the table, sometimes not.

There are probably a variety of reasons, some conscious, some not, for my increased fondness for candles on the dinner table.

It might be a reaction to the long, dark winter. The flickering flames of dinner-table candles seem warm and consoling, while outside, the winter night seems cold and forbidding.

It might be a reaction to the whopping utility bill we got in the mail. It seems to me that if the United States can bestow most-favored-nation status on its big trading partners, utilities should give most-favored-customer status on families like mine, whose members are reluctant to turn off the lights or shut the back door. It may not save much electricity, but somehow, turning off the kitchen lights for half an hour and using candles during dinner makes me feel frugal.

There is also the fact that in the dim light of candles, the world gets smaller. When the lights are on you can see the dishes stacked in the sink, the pots waiting to be washed, the briefcase sitting in the corner. The sight of them reminds you of work that needs to be done, of responsibilities that beckon. But in the candlelight, you see only the evening meal, and the faces of the evening eaters. For half an hour, the rest of the world fades into the background and the dinner table is the center of flickering light and attention.

Food looks better to me in the candlelight. A pink piece of beef looks pleasingly primal. A broiled silver rockfish seems to be slipping me a come-hither look. Even spaghetti seems sensual in the dim light. For tacos, however, I think you should turn on the lights. Even the magic of candlelight has its limits.

Not every member of the family shares my fondness for dim lighting.

Years ago when our kids were small, I tried to indoctrinate them. As soon as the kids were out of the highchair and eating something other than mashed bananas, I put candles on the family dinner table.

For a while, candles calmed the kids down. The kids looked at the candles like rabbits caught in the headlights of an approaching car. They were transfixed. Better yet, they were temporarily immobile.

As the kids got older, however, the candle became less of an object of adoration and more of a source of amusement. Attempts were made, in the guise of homework, to find the hottest point of the flame.

Later, one of the kids learned how, armed with bravado and a glass of water, he could snuff out a flame with his bare but water-soaked fingertips. All experiments with the flame, whether conducted in the name of science or self-confidence, were soon banned from the dinner table.

For a time candles became an object of sibling rivalry. One son did not like them on the dinner table. His younger brother claimed to be fond of them. The older kid regarded candles as too fancy for family meals. He considered candlelight dining another symptom of the family's larger problem of putting too much emphasis on meals. In his view, candlelight dining was like eating supper with his family. These were obligations he should be required to fulfill only a few times a week.

So I negotiated a pact with the candle-hating kid. Certain family meals would be candle-free. When word of the agreement reached the younger son, he promptly claimed that he could not enjoy a meal without the company of candlelight. He warned that if the family initiated a policy of candle-free suppers, he would take the candlesticks and dine in another room of the house.

So in the shank of a dark winter, I considered splitting the family supper table into two zones, one with candles, one without. But mostly I was hoping for an early, very warm, and very bright spring.

Chapter 3

Spring

You know it's spring when...

MY KID ASKED ME ONE DAY HOW TO TELL WHEN IT'S SPRING.

For a time I was stumped. All I could think of were adult answers.

Answers like you know it's spring when you don't have to twist arms to get people to walk across town for lunch.

Or you know it's spring when a source hasn't returned your phone call by 4 o'clock on a sunny Friday, and you get an uncontrollable urge to hightail it home and barbecue. As you fire up the coals, you get the feeling that in another part of town the guy who didn't call you back is doing exactly the same thing.

You know it's spring when women get the courage to wear sandals even though it might turn cold, and men get the courage to wear pastel ties even though they might get ribbed.

Or you know it's spring when folks start talking to each other on the street about the weather. In the spring strangers say things like, "Great day, isn't it?" as they stand on a street corner waiting for the light to change. When people stand on the street corner in the frigid winter or the scorching summer, what they say about the weather usually isn't printable.

I tried to tell him it was spring when the flowers and trees bloom, as they were doing that very morning during our walk to nursery school.

The kid,then 5 years old, had heard it before.

He pointed out that I had also told him that in the springtime he wasn't supposed to wear his heavy coat, the very coat he was wearing during our walk to nursery school.

How could I explain to him about cold fronts, erratic atmospheric pressure and the relationship between the falling barometer and the receding hairline of the TV weatherman?

I couldn't.

So I tried to explain that he could tell it was spring by the food we ate.

Like asparagus. You know it's spring when food publications and the chefs kick into asparagus overkill.

After months of trying to make soup sound and look exciting, food folk happily embrace asparagus. We wrap our figures, and different colored ribbons, around asparagus. We photograph it in more positions than a high-fashion model.

And we think up about 6,000 ways to get it on the menu, including putting a stalk in a Bloody Mary (my contribution).

But asparagus is a vegetable. And this kid, like most normal 5-year-olds, doesn't eat vegetables. So the asparagus-spring analogy was lost on him.

Next I said that he could tell it was spring when his dad started watching baseball games on television.

"You always watch baseball on television," he said.

I told him he was confused. I watch basketball in the winter. And baseball in the spring and summer.

"Is it spring now?' the kid asked. "Yes, sort of," I said.

"Then no more basketball?" he asked, a note of hope in his voice.

"Well, not exactly," I said, "there are the NBA playoffs. They last until June, which is summer."

Somehow the spring and televised sports explanation wasn't working. I dropped the kid off at nursery school and went hunting for some strawberries.

After several stops I found what I was after. Dark red ones. They weren't local; they were from California.

But they were juicy and fragrant, just like a good spring afternoon.

I picked up the kid, and took the strawberries home in a sack. Then I called the 5-year-old over for counseling. He came when I called, mainly because he thought I might have a toy in the sack.

I handed him a dark red strawberry, the best of the bunch.

"You know it's spring," I told him, "when the strawberries taste good."

A corned beef tradition

"WHAT IS THIS?" THE KIDS ASKED WHEN A PLATTER OF CORNED BEEF WAS placed on our supper table.

I rolled my eyes with disbelief. My offspring had failed to recognize corned beef, a traditional Irish dish. I was thankful that their grandmother or relatives on the Irish side of our family were not able to hear this remark.

When I was a kid I was familiar with corned beef. It was the bright red meat that showed up on your plate with boiled potatoes and hunks of cabbage. Hours before you ate it, you smelled it cooking. It was one of the regulars, the meat and potato meals that appeared in our Midwestern home on Sundays and special occasions.

St. Patrick's Day, March 17th, was one of those special occasions. It was a day that my Irish uncles treated as a holiday, taking off from work. It was a day when a constant stream of visitors arrived at our house. Monsignors with bone-crushing handshakes; musicians who played "When Irish Eyes Are Smiling" on the front porch at midnight; and a stream of men and women with creamy skin and curly hair who would stare at you and announce, "This one looks like his grandfather."

It was a day that my father, a German, always went to work. It was also a day that my brothers and I had to go to school, even though we could claim to be Irish. It seemed so unfair that on St. Patrick's Day some adults got to play hooky from the burdens of employment, yet we had to submit to the rigors of elementary school life.

One bright note of spending St. Patrick's Day in school occurred at lunch when I ate a sandwich made with green bread. The green bread, a gift from someone from my grandmother's old neighborhood, showed up at our house bright and early every St. Patrick's Day. My mother would make me a sandwich with it. At lunchtime, much to the horror of my companions in the school cafeteria, I would chomp down on bright green fare.

In between the slices of bright green bread was usually a slice of bologna. Corned beef was for supper and mostly for adults. As a kid, I didn't like the texture of it. It was too mushy.

So the other night when a plate of corned beef showed up on our

Baltimore supper table, I didn't expect my teen-age kids to like it. But I was disappointed that they failed to recognize it. I broke into a sales pitch for corned beef and found myself stressing the dish's connection to Jewish fare.

"This is brisket," I told the kids, "the same cut of meat that is used to make pastrami." At the mention of pastrami, the older one brightened. He is a big fan of the pastrami sandwiches found at Jewish delicatessens such as Attman's in Baltimore and Second Avenue in New York. He took a few bites of the corned beef but wasn't convinced. He said pastrami had a different, more spicy flavor. He was right.

His younger brother wouldn't eat corned beef because "it had too much fat." He got up from the table and cooked himself a burrito in the microwave.

At first, my kids' rejection of corned beef left me feeling downhearted. I was worried that a piece of my past was being tossed aside. But the next night, I felt much better. I opened the refrigerator and saw a hunk of the corned beef. I realized that if one generation rejects corned beef, it only means that another generation has enough leftover meat to make a thick sandwich.

Glazed Corned Beef

Serves 8 to 10

5-6 pounds beef brisket
3 onions, sliced
2-3 garlic cloves, minced
6 cloves, whole
3 bay leaves
1 tablespoon German (Dusseldorf) mustard
⅓ cup light brown sugar

Place beef in deep, metal pot or Dutch oven. Barely cover beef with boiling water.

Add the onions, garlic, cloves and bay leaves. Bring the mixture to a boil. Cover the pot tightly with foil and also put on pot lid. Reduce heat, simmering gently but not allowing it to regain boil. Cook 50 minutes per pound of meat or until the meat is tender when pricked with a fork.

Preheat oven to 350 degrees.

Remove meat from pot and drain. Place meat in shallow pan, fat side up. Trim excess fat with a sharp knife. Spread the mustard, then sugar on the top of meat. Bake until well glazed for about 15 to 20 minutes.

Serve hot or cold.

From "The New York Times Cook Book, Revised Edition"
(Harper & Row, 1990)

Celebrating Easter and Passover

THE BUDS ARE POPPING, THE BIRDS ARE SINGING AND THE KIDS ARE MORE fractious than normal. It is the time of year when the daylight grows stronger, when the breeze turns sweet and when the air seems to hum with the promise that good times, and good meals, are on the horizon.

It is time, in other words, to celebrate Easter and Passover.

At our house, about the only Easter menu item we seem to agree on is chocolate. We do have a long-standing disagreement over whether the chocolate bunnies that appear in the living room on Easter morning should be dark chocolate or milk chocolate. I favor dark chocolate. The rest of the family prefers the milk. I am the one who buys the bunnies.

However, I have discovered that even if you buy yourself a bunny made with the "wrong" kind of chocolate, it is still vulnerable to attack from rapacious family members. A few Easters ago, I left my chocolate bunny unprotected for a few hours and returned to find its ears had disappeared.

Often we end up cooking green beans and carrying them to the combination potluck meal and Easter egg hunt held in our neighborhood. The bean dish is flavorful and its bright green color seems appropriate for spring. I am pretty sure that one of our kids — who refuses to eat Easter lamb or Easter ham — also doesn't eat the Easter green beans. I don't care. As long as the kid eats something, other than my chocolate bunny.

I talked about Passover with cookbook author Marlene Sorosky. A resident of Danville, Calif., Sorosky lived in the Baltimore area from 1987 to 1994 and was back here in 1998 putting on cooking demonstrations for area Safeway stores. She used recipes from her book, "Fast & Festive Meals for the Jewish Holiday" (William Morrow, 1997).

She told me that at one demonstration, in Hunt Valley, she cooked a meal that could be served on the Seder, the feast at the beginning of Passover that celebrates the ancient Hebrews' escape from slavery in Egypt. Her menu included haroset, gefilte fish mousse, Cornish hens with apricots and prunes, baked spring vegetables and a carrot cake with orange caramel glaze.

The dish that intrigued me was the haroset, a mixture of chopped apples, fruits, nuts and wine and spices that represents the mortar that Hebrew slaves used for making bricks. I had my first haroset a few years ago during an

119

ecumenical Seder. I have been a fan of the fruity spread ever since. Sorosky said she makes two kinds of haroset, a classic version using raisins and walnuts, and a modern version, using cranberries and pistachios.

Haroset has a sweet taste and contrasts with the bitter herb, usually horseradish, that is also served as part of the Seder. Sorosky said that writing a book about the Jewish holidays had brought some sweetness back to a part of her life. She explained that when she was a child, Jewish holidays were not happy times for her. She grew up in Beverly Hills with "a tyrannical, Orthodox father and a mother who bent to his every religious desire." In this house, holidays "were about control, dominance and penitence."

But while writing the book, she collaborated with two women whose enthusiasm for Jewish holidays was infectious. Thanks to the time she spent with Joanne Neuman and Debbie Shahvar, Sorosky said she has discovered the warmth that comes from honoring her heritage.

And so after years of observing Passover, Sorosky said she now "celebrates" it. During Passover, Sorosky will gather with some of her children and grandchildren to remember the past and to hope for the future. A holiday meal, she said, can be the mortar that holds families together.

Green Beans and Goat Cheese

Makes 12-16 servings

4½ pounds fresh green beans, ends trimmed
1 cup plus 2 tablespoons olive oil
¾ cup white wine vinegar
3 cloves garlic, crushed
ground pepper to taste
2 cups chopped, toasted pecans
1½ cups coarsely grated hard goat cheese or Parmesan

Steam green beans about 7 to 9 minutes, until crisp-tender. Drain.

While beans are cooking, combine oil and vinegar and beat. Add garlic and pepper. Mix the drained, warm beans with dressing. Set aside about 10 minutes, longer if desired. If beans will not be served within an hour or two, refrigerate, but return to room temperature before serving.

Before serving, sprinkle beans with toasted pecans and grated cheese. (To transport this dish, cover marinated beans tightly with plastic wrap and carry grated cheese and pecans in separate containers. Add cheese and pecans just before serving.)

From "You've Got it Made"
by Marian Burros (William Morrow, 1984)

Modern Haroset

Makes about 10 servings

1 cup dried cranberries
½ cup shelled pistachios
1 large apple, peeled, halved, cored and cut into chunks
¾ teaspoon ground cinnamon
¼ cup sweet red Passover wine

In a food processor with a metal blade, pulse dried cranberries and pistachios until chopped. Add apple, cinnamon and wine and pulse until finely chopped or ground, as you prefer. Remove to a bowl, cover and refrigerate at least 1 hour. (May be refrigerated overnight.)

From "Fast & Festive Meals for the Jewish Holidays"
by Marlene Sorosky (William Morrow, 1997)

Break out the muddler — julep time is here

IT IS TIME TO SNIFF THE MINT, UNLEASH THE MUDDLER AND START MAKING juleps. That's right, honeylamb, the Kentucky Derby, the first leg of horse racing's Triple Crown, is run on the first Saturday in May. Two weeks later, the racing crowd comes to Baltimore for the Preakness Stakes, and then, in June, on to New York for the Belmont Stakes.

According to tradition, you are supposed to sip juleps on Derby Day, enjoy Black-Eyed-Susans on Preakness Saturday and toss back White Carnations on Belmont Saturday.

It is a tradition I have tried to honor, but have failed. I don't care for the Black-Eyed-Susan, a forced marriage of pineapple and orange juices and "sweetie-pie" liquors — vodka, rum and Triple Sec. Yet I recognize that during Preakness Week, some folks want to drink them. So I feel obligated to print here two recipes, an old one from the Junior League of Baltimore's "Hunt to Harbor" cookbook published in 1985 by Waverly Press, Inc., and a newer version the mixologists at Baltimore's Pimlico race track reworked in the late 1980s. As for the Belmont's White Carnation — made with 1 ounce vodka, 1 ounce peach schnapps, about 5 ounces of orange juice, a splash of club soda and garnished with a strawberry — it is too fruity to be viewed as a serious cocktail.

But the mint julep — a joyful union of whiskey and mint — has a long, noble history. And, Lordie, does it taste good! Every year on the first Saturday of May, I make mint juleps. And every year I argue with somebody over the julep recipe.

For instance, Robert E. Talbott, former proprietor of Morton's fine food and spirits shop in downtown Baltimore and now a country squire living in White Hall has criticized my julep in the past as an "error filled" concoction made by a "misguided Yankee."

One week, as the mint leaves poked out of my garden, I rang up Talbott and renewed our feud.

We debated the different kinds of sugar we use in our juleps. Talbott is a believer in using granulated sugar. "It is the grist of your mill," he contends, saying that the grains of the sugar, and the action of the muddler — a hallowed hunk of wood about 6 inches long — are all that is needed to grind the mint leaves into a sweet paste that is the base of his julep.

I advocate using powdered sugar and club soda, which along with a few artful moves with the muddler, transform the mint leaves into a willing partner of the whiskey.

We argued over the whiskey. Talbott puts rye whiskey, made from rye grain, in his juleps. Rye is the whiskey of choice for anyone who calls himself a true Marylander, claims Talbott, who was born in Baltimore and grew up in Glen Arm. I put bourbon, whiskey made from corn, in my julep because of a promise I made years ago. I got this recipe from a native Kentuckian, John Fetterman, who like most natives of the Bluegrass State, believed that bourbon was the one, true whiskey. When he gave me his recipe, he made me promise that I would never use any whiskey other than bourbon when making his julep. I honor that pledge.

Talbott and I agree on a few, crucial julep-making techniques, including the importance of good muddler maintenance. "Never wash your muddler," Talbott said, warning that a soapy film can cling to the wood, imparting harsh flavors as the muddler works on the mint leaves. "People who have a taste of Cascade on their muddlers," Talbott said, "are people to be avoided."

We also agreed that a successful julep maker also bashes his own ice. The ice that fills up the julep cup has to be the right consistency — pulverized. Ice in this state enables the julep to reach the proper, frosty temperature, and melts at the correct pace, allowing the flavor of the whiskey to come to "full bloom." Talbott told me that zippered canvas bags that banks use to transport money make terrific ice-bashing bags. You put the ice cubes in the bag, zipper it closed, and whale away at the captive ice cubes with a hammer, he said.

It sounded like a better way to bash ice cubes than clobbering them while they are wrapped in a towel, which is what I usually do. So now I have to sashay down to my neighborhood bank and ask the teller to "gimme a bag of quarters, without the quarters." If this ploy works, I'll be bashing my ice a new way this Saturday, as I make my julep and sing "My Old Kentucky Home."

Bob Talbott's Grind-It-Out Julep

Serves 1

1 shell (1 lean tablespoon) granulated sugar
4-5 mint leaves
pulverized ice
Maryland rye whiskey (bourbon as backup)

Put granulated sugar and mint leaves in bottom of medium-size metal cup — a "Jefferson cup" is best. Using family muddler, a 6- to 8-inch-long wooden rod that is never washed, work mixture together until it is uniformly green and clings to bottom of muddler. Add small amount of whiskey and work into mixture, until the muddler comes clean.

Pack cup with pulverized ice. Fill to rim with whiskey. Swirl several times with glass mixing rod or glass straw. Garnish with sprig of mint.

Rob Kasper's No-Sweat Julep

Serves 1

6-8 leaves of mint
2 tablespoons powdered sugar
2 tablespoons club soda
pulverized ice
bourbon

Place mint leaves, sugar and club soda in bottom of julep cup or tall glass. Muddle mint (press leaves with blunt, wooden instrument). Fill cup with pulverized ice (not cubes). Fill with bourbon. Insert straw all the way to bottom of cup, snipping off excess. Place decorative sprig of mint in julep cup within sniffing range of straw.

Old Black-Eyed Susan

Serves 1

1 ounce vodka
1 ounce rum
¾ ounce Triple Sec
lime wedge
pineapple juice
orange juice
shaved ice

Fill a 12-ounce glass with shaved ice. Add vodka, rum, and Triple Sec. Squeeze lime wedge and drop in glass. Fill glass with equal parts pineapple and orange juices.

New Black-Eyed Susan

Serves 1

6 ounces orange juice
1 ounce pink grapefruit juice
1 ounce pineapple juice
½ ounce vodka
½ ounce rum
½ ounce peach schnapps

Mix fruit juices and alcohol. Serve in tall glass filled with ice.

The perch weren't running

IT WAS A TEMPTING DAY. THE KIND THAT BECKONS OFFICE DWELLERS TO RUSH outside and revel in the warm excitement of spring.

And by 2 p.m. the escape had been made. The fishing rod was rattling in the trunk. The car was speeding away from a traffic jam on Lombard street and toward a golden afternoon of fishing at Wye Mills.

The perch were supposed to be running there, just an hour and a half away from Baltimore. The perch run is a rite of spring. The fish, responding to a combination of warm water and primal urges, swim from the Chesapeake Bay into freshwater streams to spawn.

As they spawn, they gorge. And if you are lucky enough to have a line in the water while the perch are running, it is, veteran anglers have said, a fisherman's dream. As soon as the hook hits the water, a strong-willed perch snips at it and gives you a tense, two-minute struggle. Land one, and start again.

Jay O'Dell, a biologist with Maryland's Department of Natural Resources, had mentioned the stream below the lake at Wye Mills as a good perch spot.

It was close to Baltimore – 50 miles. It was easy to get to. It looked like a good spot, the waterfall from the lake providing a good location for migrating perch and a feeding ground for big fish.

And best of all, no fishing license was needed. Below the dam the stream is considered tidal waters, O'Dell said, an area where men and fish can do battle as they have for generations, without government intervention.

While he was straightforward about where to fish, O'Dell was slippery about the other crucial fact – when to fish.

"The yellow perch should be running in a couple of weeks," he said two weeks ago. "But it is hard to tell."

A few long-distance calls to Wye Mills didn't produce anything more specific than "the perch should be running soon." So the decision of when to go fishing boiled down to choosing a promising afternoon.

Thursday afternoon was it.

The next day was a holiday, the beginning of a big Easter weekend, and bank tellers were talking about riding in convertibles. There was a rush, a delightful urgency, about the day. Surely the perch would feel it too.

Arriving in Wye Mills, two things became apparent. First, the perch were not running. Second, it didn't matter. A few hours spent on these grass-lined banks would be time well spent.

At the boat dock Chuck Schnaitman, who shook his head at the mention of perch, said, "Saw a few white perch in gill nets few weeks ago. But then it got to blowin'. You remember we had that big wind, and I think the perch didn't have enough water to get in the streams."

But recognizing a case of fishing fever when he saw one – "Something about this time of year, people start to want to get some perch" – he reached into the minnow box and sold the visitor a pint of minnows for $2.

"If they are biting, that is what they'll be hitting on," he promised.

Back at the stream, the water glistened and it was hard to 'alm down. The same charge of excitement that shot through a 12-year-old's back on his first day of fishing now tingled on an older spinal cord.

The ritual of getting the pole ready came back. A deep breath quieted jiggling hands. Then the light nylon fishing line was carefully fed through the pole eyes. A small weight, a split shot, was clamped on the line, about 6 inches above the small hook.

The fishing line, coiled from months of storage, fouled easily and city nerves were on edge. But soon the gently flowing water and the warm air made the line and its keeper relax.

Upstream, Glenn C. McCann, a distinguished looking fishermen with a wool cap and spinning rod, danced a light lure atop the water.

This quick, hopping action would attract restless perch. One white perch about 8 inches long went for the lure. After a quick fight, it was landed by McCann.

Downstream, another fishing line jerked in the sudden motion that meant something under the water was interested.

Interested, but not committed.

The tease began. The line moved, then stopped. Moved, then stopped.

The line, like a spring itself, was full of possibilities. What is down there? A fish? A branch? A turtle?

When should the hook be set? On the first strike? Too soon. Now, as the line quiets? Too late. After retrieving a few empty hooks, the reflexes returned.

Then it came. The long strike. It was a heart-pumping moment.

The pole bent to the water, and the fisherman could feel, just feel, that he had hooked one. But one what? It fought well. It ran for the safety of a sunken timber. It tried to toss the hook.

As it came out of the water, the whiskers solved the mystery. It was a catfish, a channel cat.

"Good eatin'," said McCann, as he strolled down the bank and eyed the fish.

The correct way of cooking catfish was discussed – skinned, rolled in milk and cornmeal, fried in hot oil – and the line quickly went back in the water.

In the next hour, ducks flew by, the red sun sank behind a stand of oaks, and three more catfish and two eels came slapping up out of the water. The eels were tossed back.

But the catfish, along with the perch, donated by McCann, were soon frying in a Baltimore kitchen.

Cold chablis, fresh fish and a vivid encounter with spring. Even though the perch weren't running, giving in to temptation had been worth it.

The perch, of course, will be running "any day now."

Ballpark is judged on hot food, cold beer

WHEN MY YOUNGEST BROTHER VISITED BALTIMORE, WE MET — WHERE else? — at the ballpark to eat ribs and sip beer. The swallows may fly to Capistrano, but our clan congregates at ball fields.

We inherited this trait from our dad. When he visited a town, he had a habit of locating the local stadium before any suitcase was unpacked.

I recall one family car trip when my dad gave us a driving tour of the campus of the University of Kansas in Lawrence. Dad wheeled the family's '57 Ford through a maze of buildings and roadways until he came to a promising vista and stopped the car. "There, boys," he announced with obvious pleasure, "is the stadium." My brothers and I were impressed. Our mother wasn't. My mom wanted to know why the highlight of a tour of university colleges was not a library or a fine-arts museum, but some ball field. We couldn't give mom an answer. To us, it seemed only natural that when you pass by a ball field, you stop and pay homage.

With this kind of upbringing it wasn't surprising that when my brother flew into Baltimore from Kansas City, we met at Oriole Park at Camden Yards. There I gave him a quick ballpark tour, eats included.

Technically we were both working the game. He is a news photographer for a Kansas City television station, KMBZ, and was here, along with a reporter, to file stories on how the Royals fared in the season's first game.

I was at the ballpark to do my annual report on how cold is the beer, how hot is the hot dog and how fast the concession-stand lines are moving.

My brother ended up working harder than I did. While he was busy shooting interviews with ballplayers, I went in search of a hot dog that I could stick my instant-read thermometer into.

I got a moderately hot dog, plucked from a pile of cooked dogs stacked on a slotted grill at the Grille Works Express on the Eutaw Street promenade in the right-field corner. In my six years of sticking thermometers into hot dogs, this spot has had some of the the hottest dogs in the ballpark. This year's dog, however, was merely warm, 126 degrees, some 30 degrees cooler than the sizzling dog I bought at the same stand on last year's opening day. Nonetheless this $4 dog still had good flavor, and the wait in line was four minutes, not bad for opening day.

As I walked around the ballpark, checking out the concession stands, several things caught my eye. First, the lines at the beer stands were moving quickly. My longest wait in line was three minutes, nothing like the 14-minute wait I experienced last year in a beer line. Second, there were more beer stands, at least those selling the expensive, $4.75, locally made craft beers. Old Line Microbrews, which sells the craft beers, has added two new spots, one behind home plate on the first level, and one on the top deck near the left-field corner. Thirdly, the selection of local beers has changed. Old Heurich, a beer with offices in Washington, was being poured at Camden Yards as were beers from Old Dominion Brewing Co. of Ashburn, Va. I saw beers made by some Maryland breweries — Clipper City, Frederick Brewing and Oxford Brewing. But I didn't see some of my old favorites from Baltimore breweries — DeGroen's and Olivers'. Later, folks at these two breweries told me that the way this year's deal was structured, they couldn't make money selling their beers in the ballpark.

After inspecting the concession stands at the ballpark, I meandered back to the press box and found my brother recharging his batteries. I persuaded him to walk with me out to the right-field pavilion for a brief stadium tour.

My first stop was at the Eutaw Street promenade for a locally made beer. We sampled a Clipper City Amber, full-bodied and satisfying, even if it was 50 degrees, some 10 degrees warmer than the beer I sampled last year on opening day.

The next stop on the tour was Bambino's Ribs, where I bought a $9 plate of barbecued ribs. We stood in the pavilion, eating ribs, sipping beer and reveling in the sights, sounds and smells of a baseball game. The Royals, ungrateful visitors, beat their hosts, the Orioles, 4-1.

My brother was a better-behaved guest. He praised the ribs. Coming from someone who lives in Kansas City — a town with a rib restaurant on virtually every corner, including the fabled LC's Bar B.Q., the temple of ribs — this was a considerable compliment.

He also liked the looks of the ballpark. And coming from our family, he has seen a quite a few.

Sweet on rhubarb pie

RAIN, ACCORDING TO FOLK WISDOM, IS "GOOD FOR THE RHUBARB." BUT ON the other hand, sunshine is also said to be "good for the rhubarb." There is probably a "cloudy-days-are-good-for-the-rhubarb" contingent as well.

That is the way it is with fans of the weird red stalks. As long as the plant is pushing up out of the ground, they are happy.

Rhubarb has many admirers. Both fruit and vegetable lovers claim it as one of their own. The ancient Greeks called it "the vegetable of the barbarians." They were referring to those rough foreigners who lived beyond the Volga (or Rha) River.

Moreover, in his new book "Chesapeake Bay Cooking With John Shields" (Broadway Books, 1998) John Shields describes rhubarb as a "misunderstood vegetable," a relative of the buckwheat family.

Yet in her new book, "Great Pies and Tarts," Carole Walter (Clarkson Potter, 1998) claims the courts have declared that rhubarb is a fruit.

"In a 1947 legal case at U.S. Customs Court in Buffalo, New York," Walter writes, "it was ruled that since rhubarb was normally prepared as a fruit, it should henceforth be classed as a fruit."

I guess this means that you are defined by the company you keep, at least in Buffalo.

Despite the disagreement about what food group it belongs to, there is little dispute that rhubarb makes a great pie filling. A pie made with rhubarb and strawberries usually draws fork carriers not only from the fruit and vegetable camps, but also from the ranks of dessert lovers.

One of our kids is a rhubarb zealot. The other night when our family was sitting around the kitchen table discussing our favorite dessert –a topic frequently discussed at our house – this kid nominated strawberry-rhubarb pie as his choice.

On one level, this nomination surprised me. Rhubarb is tart, even when paired with strawberries. And this teen-ager, like most kids, is normally a fan of sweet desserts. Then I remembered that this kid's grandfather, my dad, also loves rhubarb. The kid had inherited the rhubarb-eating gene from his grandfather.

In science this might be called "rhubarb recessive" behavior. In the kitchen, it means that when my wife makes strawberry-rhubarb pie, as she did recently, the kid can be counted on to polish off two pieces.

Strawberry-Rhubarb Pie

Makes one 9-inch pie

1½ pints strawberries, stemmed
2 cups diced rhubarb
1 cup sugar
3 tablespoons cornstarch
½ cup water
1 tablespoon lemon juice
¼ teaspoon salt
sweetened whipped cream

Preheat the oven to 425 degrees. Prepare the pastry dough (see opposite page) and roll it out to line a 9-inch pie pan. Flute the edge of the shell. Prick the bottom of the shell with a fork. Press aluminum foil into the bottom and sides of the shell and cover foil with dried beans to prevent crust from swelling during baking.

Bake for 8 minutes. Remove the foil and beans and continue to bake until the crust is lightly brown, 10-20 minutes. Cool before filling.

Place half the strawberries in a pot. Mash with a fork or potato masher. Add the rhubarb and 1 cup sugar. Combine the cornstarch, ½ cup water, lemon juice and salt in a small bowl and stir to dissolve the cornstarch. Add to the strawberry-rhubarb mixture. Cook over medium heat until the mixture is thick and rhubarb is tender, stirring often.

Halve the remaining strawberries and arrange them in the baked pie shell. Pour the strawberry-rhubarb mixture over the berries on bottom of pie shell, then top with remaining berries. Cover and chill.

Serve topped with whipped cream sweetened with 2 tablespoons sugar and 1 teaspoon vanilla for 1 cup of cream.

Adapted from "Chesapeake Bay Cooking With John Shields"
(Broadway Books, 1998)

Pie Dough

1½ cups all purpose flour
¾ teaspoon salt
½ cup vegetable shortening
3 – 4 tablespoons cold water

Sift together the flour and salt into a mixing bowl. Work the shortening into the flour with your fingertips or a pastry blender, until the mixture is the consistency of coarse meal. Add the water, 1 tablespoon at a time, and mix with a fork after each addition. Dough should not be wet, but just moist enough to hold together. Form the dough into a ball, wrap and refrigerate for at least 15 minutes before rolling.

Nobody cooks like Mom

EVERY MAY, IN THE NAME OF MOTHERHOOD, WOMEN ARE TREATED TO MEALS that would have tasted better if the moms had cooked the food themselves.

Not that the moms complain. Most are delighted at the attention they are getting from family members whose usual contribution to a meal consists of asking, "What are we havin'?"

So the moms do not roll their eyes when their French toast is blackened, or the meat is tough, or the service is slow at the restaurant with the lovely view and the brunch that every mother within a 50-mile radius has been escorted to.

On Mother's Day, moms are determined to enjoy the meals in their honor, regardless of what the food tastes like.

Not all the home-cooked meals whipped up in honor of Mom today will be awful. This is, after all, almost the dawn of a new century and lots of husbands and sons can cook.

While there are some guys who can cook everything from souffles to spanakopita, most guys have what we call our "specialties."

That means we have a few dishes that we cook for a big gathering, any big gathering. We fix them for wakes and weddings, and all the finest balls. And we cook them for Mother's Day. But the big difference is that on Mother's Day we also do the dishes.

A few specialties that guys will probably be cooking today are pancakes, steak and many varieties of lasagna.

Chili is a very popular cooking specialty of guys. But chili is not usually a good Mother's Day menu item. It presents too much of a threat to Mom's Mother's Day outfit.

My specialty is cooking food on the barbecue grill. As of this writing I do not know what my sons and I are going to serve at the Mother's Day dinner at our house. But I do know that whether it is pizza or pork loin, it will be grilled.

Moms, of course, have different levels of interest in food. Some are content with a Mother's Day meal that has been beeped in the microwave oven. Others prefer the food fixed by restaurant chefs or attempts at cuisine by family members.

Not all mothers cook. I think it is fair to say that women now feel comfortable with "fixing" dinner the way many men have been fixing it for years. Namely, picking up a phone and ordering takeout.

Nonetheless, I think the standard of excellence that most kitchen-cooked meals are measured against is still: Is it as good as Mom's?

And I think that is not going to change until the phrase "Dad's apple pie" causes the same warm glow of anticipation among eaters as the phrase "Mom's apple pie."

In our household, some of the most valued recipes — ones for corn bread, banana bread and baked beans — have "Mother's" scrawled atop their 3-by-5 recipe cards. These recipes came from my wife's mother. When my wife makes these dishes, she follows the instructions to the letter. And when the dishes emerge from the oven, they quickly draw a tableful of appreciative eaters. Other corn breads, banana breads and baked beans are sniffed at. Only "Mother's" will do.

On my side of the family, it is brisket. One of my goals in life is to be able to cook a beef brisket as well as my mother does.

Her technique is not complicated. She sprinkles a 4-pound brisket, trimmed of fat, with a packet of dry onion soup. She puts a cup and a half of water on the bottom of the pan, being careful not to pour the water over the beef. She cooks the beef uncovered at 300 degrees for about 45 minutes, then covers it and lets it cook until it passes the fork test — the brisket is done when a fork easily pierces it but the meat still holds its shape. It usually cooks for about three hours. About 40 minutes before the meat is finished, she tosses in peeled potatoes cut in half. The potatoes cook in the liquid in the bottom of the pan, next to the brisket. Everything comes out brown.

I have tried this recipe several times. The meat never quite tastes the same as when my mom fixes it. The meat is either dry or chewy. The crust of the meat is not quite right. And the potatoes are spotty brown, not the uniform Coppertone color that Mom's potatoes have.

In short, my brisket, while flavorful, is lacking that special something that takes a dish from the level of ordinary old food and moves it into the realm of an extraordinary dining pleasure.

That special something is "Momness."

The truth about pastrami

PROBING THE MYSTERIES OF PASTRAMI TURNED OUT TO BE A LONG-TERM enterprise. It began one spring day when I looked into the background of Romanian pastrami. After making several phone calls to delis in Baltimore and New York, and after polishing off a couple of sandwiches, I came to tentative conclusions about the name and the meat.

I figured pastrami was called Romanian because the Romanians were the countrymen who perfected the art of curing and smoking the meat. The meat, I decided, came from the belly of a steer and was fatter than brisket.

Faster than you could say "extra mustard," I was slathered with opinions on the origin of pastrami. I heard from Romanians, a deli owner and from just plain pastrami eaters.

First to speak for the Romanians was Adrian Barbul, a Baltimore physician, and native of Romania. The pastrami he recalled eating years ago as a lad in Bucharest was smoked goat meat, not beef, he said. He promised to telephone a few friends on this side of the Atlantic, or, as he said, "to beat the Romanian tom-toms" and come up with more details.

Soon Barbul was put in touch with another Romanian, Zalman Sandon, vice president of Homestead Gourmet Foods Company Inc. in Linden, N.J.

For Romanians, pastrami is a process, not a product, Sandon said. "To pastrami" is a verb, he said, adding that his New Jersey company " 'pastramis' beef, turkey . . . every imaginable kind of food."

There are three essential elements to the pastrami process, he said. The food has to be cured, injected with spices and garlic. Secondly, it has be salted. And thirdly, it must be smoked, he said.

In America the term Romanian-style pastrami is used loosely, Sandon said. Usually it refers to cuts of brisket beef that have gone through some version of the pastrami process.

In Romania, pastrami makers do not confine themselves to one cut of beef, or just to cattle, he said. There is goose pastrami, which Sandon described as "a real delicacy." There is pork pastrami. And there is goat pastrami, which is served in the fall with the partially fermented juice of recently harvested wine grapes. Goat pastrami, Sandon said, was "truly horrible, a salt brick."

The pastrami found in American delis, he said, mildly resembles the beef that has gone through the pastrami process in Romania. Americans use spices rather than smoke to color the beef, he said. Compared with Romanian pastrami makers, Americans go easy on the garlic, he said. Sliced beef that has been given the true Romanian pastrami treatment would knock the socks off most Americans, he said.

Also weighing in on the mysteries of pastrami was Seymour Attman, proprietor of Attman's Delicatessen, which sits on a stretch of East Lombard Street known as Corned Beef Row. In a two-page letter, Attman made several points about the type of beef pastrami sold in American delis.

Here, quality pastrami comes from steer, not from cows, he said. Steer are male cattle raised primarily for beef, cows are female cattle used primarily for milk and calf production. "Cow beef is not good enough quality to use. It is tougher and has yellow fat in the meat," Attman wrote.

He disagreed with the notion that pastrami comes from the belly of the animal. "It is the plate of beef that comes off the bottom of the brisket," he wrote. When I looked at an illustration showing the primal cuts of beef, I saw that the brisket was underneath the steer, closer to its chest than its belly. On some folks, the chest and the belly tend to slide together. But on cattle, I guess they remain separate.

This cut of beef is corned or pickled, Attman wrote, then rubbed with cracked pepper and various spices including garlic. The curing process takes several days. Finally the meat is placed on racks and smoked in large ovens, he said. "Essentially, pastrami is corned beef with a pedigree," Attman wrote.

After digesting all this information, I have rethought the way I will place my order of a pastrami sandwich. If I ever journey to Romania, I will not only specify that I want my sandwich with rye and mustard, I will also say what kind of meat — goat, goose, beef, or pork — that I want my pastrami made of.

In Baltimore, when I order a hot pastrami sandwich at Attman's or another deli, I'll say "Gimme a pastrami, and make sure the meat comes from a steer, one of those guy-cattle with a big chest."

The Larry Short breakfast

For an ordinary, at-home breakfast, I don't eat much. But when entertaining at a restaurant, I believe in strapping on the morning feed bag. One spring morning I ate breakfast with a guy I work with, Larry Short, at his then-favorite feeding spot, Cherylee's Big Bear's Den in Dundalk. The restaurant has since fallen from his favor. But at the time, back in 1994, Short regarded it as a good place to get his favorite breakfast offering, creamed chipped beef on toast with home fries.

It was good. And it was a bargain. Two plates of creamed chipped beef on toast with coffee came to $9 and change. I paid, but as I listened to my companion talk about the essential qualities of a big, restaurant breakfast, I was entertained.

Short has worked at *The Sun* and *The Evening Sun* for over 40 years dispensing newspapers, mail and earthy wisdom. He is a student of the big breakfast. One day at work he promised to introduce me to the fare at his neighborhood restaurant, which he calls The Bear's Den. After a few false starts, we got in his car and headed to the 7600 block of German Hill Road.

"Not many places you can take your lady for a real breakfast and get out the door for less than $15," Short told me as he drove through East Baltimore. This place, he said, was one of them.

Along the way we discussed what makes a good restaurant breakfast. Price was one component, he said. You don't want to blow a lot of money on breakfast, he said. You want to find a place, like the Bear's Den, where chipped beef and home fries go for about $4 a plate. And, he added, you want to get there early, before 11 o'clock in the morning. After 11, when the kitchen has to switch over to lunch food, the price of breakfast selections goes up 15 cents.

Some customers complain about the 15-cent surcharge, Short said, but not him. He looks at the big picture, two people getting out the door with a lot of food in their stomachs, and only $10-$15 gone from their wallets.

The size of the breakfast portions was also important, Short said. He scorned joints that served puny portions. Like a Fells Point eatery we drove past. "I'll never go back there," he said as he turned onto Broadway.

"Why?" I asked.

"Pigeon eggs," he answered.

"Pigeon eggs? I asked.

"The eggs were so small they looked like they came from pigeons," he explained.

A convenient location also matters in picking a good breakfast spot, Short said. One reason he was fond of the Bear's Den is that it was close to his home in the Charlesmont neighborhood of Baltimore County. And so on Saturday or Sunday mornings he could be sitting at the restaurant table a few minutes after walking out his door.

He said he once used to eat a 5 a.m. breakfast — two eggs, home fries, toast and coffee — at the Bridge, a small restaurant a few doors down Calvert street from the newspaper. A few years ago, when the newspaper moved its presses and the pre-dawn eaters who run them down to a new plant at Port Covington, the restaurant pushed the starting time of breakfast back to 6 a.m.

Years ago, he said, it was not uncommon to see a fellow drink a beer with his big breakfast. But those days, he added quickly, are long gone.

We slide into our seats at the Bear's Den, a place that apparently got its name from the large number of stuffed bears, big and small, that decorate its walls.

Following Short's advice, I ordered a plate of chipped beef with toast — not the biscuits. The chipped beef soon arrived. It was all the dish should be. Creamy, hot, strangely soothing. I had the $3.99 portion, which was almost enough food to feed the population of Ohio. Short had the large, $4.75 size, which could feed Texas.

We both cleaned our plates, paid the bill and headed back to work. As we rode along Merritt Boulevard, we discussed the distinguishing characteristics of a good plate of chipped beef.

I said the secret was in the sauce.

He said the freshness of ingredients mattered.

"Some people can't taste the difference between fresh and sittin'," Short said, referring to food that has been sitting on a steam table.

"I can."

Reeling in the rockfish

IT HAD BEEN A PERFECT SPRING DAY ON THE CHESAPEAKE BAY. THE SUN HAD been warm, the wind benign and the fishing-boat ice chests had filled up trophy-size rockfish, the best-tasting fish in the bay, if not the world.

As the boats docked at Harrison's Chesapeake House in Tilghman, the prized rockfish — 24 in all caught by some 40 fishermen — were held up for much admiration and for many photographs. Among those inspecting the fish was Bill Burton, outdoorsman extraordinaire and the organizer of the bay outing — a yearly event.

Those of us aboard Capt. Mike Lipski's boat, Tradition, had been so boastful that Gibby Dean, skipper of another fishing boat, threatened to spray us into silence with a dockside hose.

Once the hooting and swaggering had died down, it was time to proceed to the next part of the rockfish ritual, cleaning the fish and cooking them. Some fish were filleted at a fish-cleaning operation tucked under the drawbridge leading into Tilghman. One rockfish, a 45-pound beauty, was so massive that its fillets were passed around — like the Bible's loaves and fishes — to feed the multitudes. Other fish, of less miraculous proportions, were iced and carried to other kitchens around the state.

I kept my fish whole. When I got it home, there was more showing off to do, this time to family members and neighbors. Then I sharpened a knife, fired up the barbecue grill and carried the fish out to the parking pad behind our rowhouse. There I scaled the fish and filleted it. It was a messy process. Fish scales went everywhere — on me, on the parking pad and on the table I was using. When I finished cleaning the fish, I hosed down everything, including my shoes.

By then, the coals in the barbecue grill were just about ready. They were ashy, white and so hot that I could hold my hand over them only long enough to count "one Mississippi, two Mississippi" before the heat forced me to pull my hand away.

I stashed half of the fish in the fridge. I would cook it later. I brushed the other half with olive oil and grilled it until a fork could easily pass through the fillet. This took about 10 minutes per side, which was longer than it takes to grill most fish fillets. But this, of course, was exceptional fish. It was so fresh, so thick, so moist that it required a little more cooking time. It also had remarkable flavor, which I helped along for this meal only with a little salt and black pepper.

I got curious about what my fellow fishermen had done with their catch, so I called a few of them.

In Queen Anne's County, Mike Rossbach said he used "the mistake method" to come up with a new style of cooking rockfish. He said he rubbed the fillet with olive oil and red wine vinegar, sprinkled on some black pepper crab seasoning, topped the fish with basil and parsley and baked it in the oven at 350 degrees for 20 minutes.

He pulled the fish out of the oven and rested its pan on a burner atop the stove. He did not notice it, but the burner was turned on. "I heard this sizzling," Rossbach said. When he checked on the fish, all the pan juices had been seared by the burner.

This "pan-seared" rockfish turned out to be magnificent, he said. So a few nights later, when he cooked the rest of the fish for his wife, Lori, and their three boys, he used the same mistake-inspired method of baking and searing.

In Pasadena, Eileen Hyson was surprised when her husband, Bob, came home with something to cook. He had been going to such outings for years, she said, and "had never come home with a fish."

When the rockfish fillet showed up in her house, she knew she wanted to put some dill on it. "I like fish with dill on it," she said. So she made a basting sauce by sauteing some sliced shallots in butter, and sprinkling in some ground-up dill. She brushed the sauce on the fillet, and broiled it for about 10 minutes. "It was delicious," she said. "It was so fresh, so moist. It did not taste or smell fishy."

In North Linthicum, Alan Doelp gave his rockfish fillet the simple treatment. He brushed it with olive oil, coated it with bread crumbs, topped it with butter, then cooked it in a 475-degree, "not quite broiling" oven for 10 minutes, until he thought it was done.

When he tasted the fish, its moist texture made him think he had undercooked it. His wife, Carol Benner, had him put the fish back in the oven for a few more minutes. When the fish emerged the second time it had the same texture, Doelp said. "Until I cooked my own, I had never thought of rockfish as a moist fish. Every one I had eaten in restaurants had been dry. I had never had a more delicate, moist or tender piece of fish."

Doelp spoke for many of us when he summed up the experience of paying to go on a charter boat to catch our own supper.

"It was the best rockfish I have ever eaten. I figure it cost me about $70 a fillet." It is one of those experiences — like eating in fine restaurants — "that every so often, you owe yourself."

A puffer's paradise

ANOTHER SOLD-OUT CIGAR DINNER, THE THIRD IN THREE YEARS, WAS HISTORY. The man who organized the dinners, Ira B. "Bill" Fader Jr., sat in the office above his Baltimore Street tobacco shop and savored the highlights of the previous evening. He also savored a cigar, a Por Larranaga Delicados.

He told of how a collection of well-turned-out gentlemen and a sprinkling of well-dressed ladies had gathered in the turn-of-the-century splendor of the Engineering Society in downtown Baltimore to feast on seared beef tenderloin, sip cognac and port, and puff on hand-rolled cigars.

Most of the cigar devotees were from the Baltimore area, but the prospect of smoky enjoyment had drawn a few from out of state. A threesome had journeyed in from Seaford, Del. Another fellow, Fader said, was visiting from Evansville, Ind.

The crowd had numbered 160, up from 130 the year before, and 90 the year before that. The crowd was not supposed to exceed 150, Fader said. But then the general manager of the Engineering Society discovered that all the tickets ($100 each) were gone, and that he couldn't get a seat to a dinner in his own establishment. So he made an executive decision and added a "house" table for himself and nine of his friends.

As an occasional puffer, I think the appeal of cigar dinners is that they offer you an opportunity to behave like a connoisseur, a gentleman who appreciates his Fonseca port and Upmann cigars. At the same time you get a chance to indulge in the boyish delight of doing what some folks say you shouldn't.

On the matter of sophisticated tastes, Fader said that when you combine fine cigars with vintage wine and artfully seared beef and follow them with vintage port, what you end up with is "a whole evening dedicated to the pleasures of good living."

On the boyish-delight front, Fader, a graying grandfather, said, "There are so many places you can't smoke a cigar, that when you have a dinner where you not only can smoke cigars but can smoke them all evening, then it is just fun."

The irony around cigar dinners is almost as thick as the smoke. As more regulations have been passed restricting smoking, cigar smoking and cigar dinners have become increasingly popular.

Sales of imported hand-rolled cigars, the kind that cost from $1.25 up to

$20 each, increased some 16 percent in 1994, according to cigar industry figures. The number of big-ticket cigar dinners, events often underwritten by cigar and liquor companies, climbed to an estimated 400 nationwide in 1993. In smoking circles, the first such celebration of the stogie is generally said to have been a 1985 dinner put on at the Boston Ritz-Carlton hotel by then-hotel manager Henry Schielein. Since then the cigar dinners have spread to other cities. One night in 1995, for example, 31 Ritz-Carlton hotels around the world, including several in the Washington area, held International Cigar Celebrations. These $250-a-plate dinners, which were a joint venture with *Cigar Aficionado* magazine, featured vintage wine, fine food and rare cigars.

In Maryland, I know of a few other smoky tributes besides the Fader shindigs that have been paid to the cigar. In January, 1995 I read about the First National Women's Only Cigar Dinner held at the Ruth's Chris Steak House in Baltimore.

A colleague told me about a cigar- and beer-tasting he attended one winter at the Manor Tavern in Jacksonville. It was a terrific event, he said, even though his wife made him take his aromatic clothes off before she would let him back in the house. I went through a similar strip routine in February 1994 when I returned home from a cigar bash held at the Cafe Tattoo in Northeast Baltimore.

The Engineering Society dinner had a cigar menu. It listed the Credo Magnificat, the Macanudo Vintage #1 and the Pleiades Perseus as the reception cigars, the equivalent, I guess, of appetizers. The Credo Athanor was the dinner selection, and the Fonseca 5-50 and Fonseca Triangular were the "finale," or after-dinner, offerings.

Fader told me he did not follow the menu. "I don't smoke any cigar during dinner," he said. "When is there time during a meal? Are you going to puff and eat? I smoke before or after the dinner."

The second floor of Fader's Baltimore Street tobacco shop has become a smokers' lounge. Fader created the lounge as a place where folks who are prohibited by recent Maryland regulations from smoking in their offices, can "relax with a smoke, have a cup of coffee, read the newspaper or even conduct a business conference."

Already many of the customers of the Baltimore Street shop know each other, said Julie Fader Gilbert, one of Fader's three daughters. "It's like a club; they call each other by name," she added.

Gilbert, a public relations consultant, attends the cigar dinners, where she tries what she describes as her "annual cigar."

This year she started, but did not finish, a Pleiades Perseus.

While she does not love cigars, she is, she said, tolerant of smokers.

She lets her father smoke cigars in her house. But not her husband.

Getting creative with shad

NOT LONG AGO I HAD A PIECE OF HEAVEN AND WASN'T SURE HOW TO HANDLE it. I had a hunk of fresh shad and some shad roe.

The shad had been deboned. That is a big deal when you are talking about shad, because the fish has an extraordinary amount of bones. The bony nature of shad is one reason it is not as popular with eaters as, say, bone-free fillets of orange roughly.

Another reason is that shad is seasonal. Shad is sold in Maryland fish markets from about December to May. These shad have to be imported from other East Coast states whose river systems support a healthy shad run. When shad arrive in Maryland waters, usually in early spring, they are protected. In the hope of reviving the once-plentiful supply of shad, Maryland law prohibits fishermen from catching shad for commercial purposes. A Maryland commercial fisherman can keep two shad for his own personal use, but he can't sell them.

The shad I ate was a "loophole legal" local shad. The fish had died while tangled in a commercial fishermen's net in the Chesapeake Bay, and the fisherman had sent me the fresh fish, which a friend deboned. Maybe I should have felt guilty, but mostly I felt grateful — and nervous.

This was a gift from nature, and I didn't want to blow it. I immediately began worrying about the best way to cook it.

I recalled eating shad in two Baltimore-area restaurants, Rudys' 2900 in suburban Finksburg, and Tio Pepe in downtown Baltimore. At Rudys', hickory-smoked shad roe, or fish eggs, were served with leeks, morel mushrooms, garlic mashed potatoes and fiddle-head ferns. At Tio's, the shad was covered with a sauce made with red and green peppers, tomatoes, mushrooms and a touch of wine. Both dishes were delicious but required considerably more skill and ingredients than my household kitchen could muster.

So I considered simpler treatments. I learned that a traditional, Eastern Shore style of cooking shad was to cut it in chunks, batter it and fry it in a cast-iron skillet filled with oil. That is what J. C. Tolley of Toddville, Md., told me. Tolley assured me that the flavor of skillet-fried shad was terrific. But he admitted that eaters who cooked the shad this way had to be willing to pick a lot of bones out of the fish.

Sous-chef Tom Winter of the Crab Shanty restaurant in Ellicott City warned me that if I overcooked the shad roe, the egg sacks could explode. On the other hand, he said, if I under-cooked them, the roe would get gummy. Winter suggested cooking the fish the way he does at the restaurant, sprinkling it with butter and paprika and cooking it for three to five minutes in a 500-degree oven. It sounded appealing, but I was not sure my oven could get that hot.

Then I came across a recipe for "charcoal-broiled shad" in the old "Maryland's Way" cookbook. Like many recipes in old cookbooks, this one was somewhat hard to follow. It told me to cover the fish with slabs of bacon and cook it over a charcoal fire for 14 minutes, flipping the fish about every 10 seconds. I did not follow this intensive-flipping routine. Instead, I rubbed the fish with bacon, and cooked the fish over a charcoal fire until its pink flesh turned white.

The fish fell apart on the grill. While my charcoal-grilled shad arrived at the table looking somewhat like scrambled eggs, it had a wonderful, slightly smoky flavor. The roe, which my wife had sauteed in butter, was bliss. To accompany the shad we had a tart white wine, a 1992 Christian Salmon Sancerre.

It was a wonderful meal, especially for an ordinary Tuesday night.

I was pleased with myself, until the next day, when I heard how some friends had cooked a portion of the shad I had given them. They had placed the roe and the fish on a metal cooking sheet. They basted the fish with a solution of lemon juice, white wine and butter, and sandwiched the roe between slabs of bacon. Next, they pushed the fish-laden sheet under the oven broiler and watched the bacon. When the bacon was almost done, the fish was almost done. At that point they pulled the bacon off the roe, basted the roe with the lemon-butter mixture and broiled everything for another minute.

My friends made their bacon-basted shad sound even better than my charcoal-scrambled version. Which proved, I guess, that whether you are telling stories about cooking exceptional fish, or catching them, somebody's always out to top you.

The best of beef

WHEN I SAW THE COWS, I RELAXED. FOR ME THE SIGHTING WAS PROOF THAT I had cleared the city and was traveling in the land where the cattle, not the Miatas, roam.

Somewhere between Frederick and Hagerstown, on the north side of Interstate 70, I saw the cows, a barn, grass and dirt. The sight of cows feeding gave me a liberating feeling that comes from being in the country.

I felt even better a short while later when, as one of three judges for the 1995 Maryland Beef Cook-Off, I sat in the Hagerstown Sheraton Inn and feasted on the beef dishes competing for the title of best in the state.

After much chewing and some second helpings, we judges declared the winners. Margaret McConnell of Annapolis won the top prize of $250. For her winning dish she cut some top round into cubes and soaked them in a marinade made of soy, ginger, molasses, garlic and apple butter. She put the marinated meat and some pearl onions on skewers, and cooked the skewers over a charcoal fire.

Second place went to Marjorie Farr of Rockville, who fried a tenderloin, then covered it with a topping of Roma tomatoes and herbs. Frank Mullin of Washington got third place for his steaks crowned with onions and bell peppers. Dorrie Mednick of Baltimore, who covered steaks with a ginger and apricot sauce, and Karen Stephens of Middletown, who made tortillas stuffed with sausage and beans, received honorable mentions.

As the nation's appetite for meat has been trimmed, so have the trappings around beef-cooking contests. (The state contest is sponsored by the Maryland Beef Council; the national by the American National Cattle Women Inc. in cooperation with the Beef Industry Council and Cattlemen's Beef Board.) Once an annual event, the National Beef Cook-Off is now held every two years. And the practice of inviting a cook from each of the 50 states to the finals has been scaled back. Now only the cooks of the top 15 recipes, determined by a national board, are invited to compete for the top prize of $25,000.

Cooks are required to use no more than eight ingredients in their recipes, and must whip up their dishes in less than an hour. Speed and convenience reign.

When it comes to cattle, Maryland is not exactly the Ponderosa. There are 315,000 cattle, both beef and dairy, in the state. This puts Maryland 40th among the 50 states in number of resident cattle, according to Bruce West, who keeps the cattle count, and other statistics, for the state's Department of Agriculture. Texas leads the nation in cattle with 15.1 million, followed by Kansas with 6.8 million head.

While there are crossbreeds of cattle in the state, the two dominant breeds seem to be Angus and Hereford. I found this out when, after finishing my duties as a beef taster, I ventured into the section of the hotel where the Maryland cattlemen were holding a trade show. I picked up literature touting the breeds of cattle, including a glossy publication that looked like a magazine, complete with centerfold. It turned out to be the program for the April sale of bulls, cows and calves of the Wye Angus herd in Queenstown.

I leafed through the publication, looking at lineage charts, admiring the photographs and names of the prize bulls. I decided that if, in another life, I come back to this earth as an Angus bull, I want to come back as Bolton of Wye. What a body.

Later, to find out more about the Angus breed, I telephoned Bill Knill, an Angus cattleman from Carroll County. Knill talked about his cattle the way a car salesmen might describe an expensive car. Perfectly proportioned, classy, no wasted space.

"Angus are a little smaller [than most cattle] and that means you don't have as much body to feed," Knill said. These midsize cattle produce the medium-sized cuts of beef that buyers want nowadays, he said.

Eleanor Free spoke to me by phone on behalf of Hereford cattle. She and her husband, Joe, have about 200 head of the cattle on their Frederick County farm. "Herefords have a good temperament, they are very easy to work with, you don't have to chase them all around the field," she said. They "are good, muscular animals." Recently the breed has been refined so that less fat, or "white meat," as it is called in the trade, appears on the animal, she said.

Most beef shoppers, of course, don't ask about breeding lines when they buy meat. Most behave like McConnell, the Maryland Beef Cook-Off winner. Right before the contest began she went to the grocery store to buy the meat to use for her contest entry. She bought the top round, she said, not because of its lineage. She bought it because it was on sale.

A fruitful search for strawberries

AS SOON AS WE CROSSED THE BAY BRIDGE I BEGAN LOOKING FOR STRAW-berries. This was a springtime weekend trip to the Atlantic Ocean. The water would be too cold to swim in. But the mosquitoes would be on vacation. Moreover, the sun was warm, the air was sweet and travel has always made me hungry.

When I take a family trip, I plan some reward for me, the chief driver and trail boss of the outfit, to enjoy at the end of the trip.

Sometimes the only thing that keeps me calm during Route 50 traffic jams is the thought of the sybaritic feast that awaits when we reach our destination.

Usually when we make a journey, we pack enough food and drink to satisfy a family of four for a month. My reward is often included in these provisions. Sometimes it is a well-marbled steak that I toss on the grill even before the bags are unpacked. Other times it is fresh shrimp, bought at a roadside seafood stand, and steamed for a feast redolent of melted butter and Muscadet.

In the doldrums of family travel I think of joys potable, as well as edible. At journey's end I have been known to imitate a favorite in the 1994 Preakness horse race, and "Go For Gin," pouring myself a gin rickey — equal parts gin and lime juice, followed by ice cubes and club soda.

There was talk among the passengers about food, but it concerned which fast-food emporium we were going to pull into.

Picking a fast-food stop for the family is often a complicated procedure that requires skillful negotiation among hostile parties. There is the hamburger faction, the McDonald's chicken nugget contingent, the Subway cheese steak loyalists and the Popeye's chicken fans.

My only requirement was that the place we picked had to be located on the right side of the road. The only reason for stopping at a fast-food place was speed. I figured it was contradictory to waste time getting to a joint on the wrong side of the highway.

Eventually the fast-food factions came up with a compromise candidate, Burger King. I was told to pull over at the first sign of a Whopper. I missed the first one, somewhere around Grasonville. I was in the wrong lane. My failure to make the turnoff was roundly criticized by passengers who claimed to be suffering from parental cruelty, starvation and dehydration, at least until I pulled into the Burger King in Easton.

Once the tribe had been given its fast-food fix, I began my search for my reward, fresh strawberries. En route to Cambridge and Salisbury, I looked for signs put up by owners of roadside produce stands. I was looking for a particular type of sign. Nothing too fancy would be acceptable. I figured, any produce-stand operator who spent a lot of money on a sign wouldn't think twice about shipping strawberries in from California.

A hand-lettered sign would be best, perhaps with a misspelling. I didn't see one.

It was two weeks before Memorial Day and the pickings were pretty slim. I did spot one stand outside Salisbury that looked promising. But as I got closer I saw it was advertising "local" tomatoes and that scared me away. I know everything grows faster on the Eastern Shore than it does west of the Bay Bridge. But I found it hard to believe that even the fabled Eastern Shore farmers could be harvesting tomatoes in May.

I turned south on Route 13 and saw a promising stand outside Pocomoke City. It was just a guy selling something, maybe strawberries, from the back of his truck. But he was on the wrong side of the highway, with no turn-around in sight.

It looked like I might have to make a trip without a reward. But just south of the Maryland-Virginia line, when I slowed to make the turn onto Route 175 and head toward Chincoteague, Va., I spotted a homemade sign. It read simply: "Strawberries."

In a parking lot next to a gas station and video rental store was a battered truck. Next to the truck was a simple wooden table, and on the table were a couple of boxes of strawberries.

The berries looked like locals. They were imperfect and sandy. Some had spots of greens. Some were a little lumpy. But they had a wonderful aroma. We bought two boxes at $1.75 a quart.

My wife whipped up a shortcake using a recipe from an old Good Housekeeping cookbook. And that night I spooned down the first strawberry shortcake of the season. One small trip for the family, one sweet reward for the driver.

The long and short of homemade shortcake

A GOOD SHORTCAKE CAN MAKE UP FOR SHORTCOMINGS. IT CAN, FOR instance, transform a bunch of so-so strawberries into one of the world's most appealing desserts, strawberry shortcake.

Homemade shortcake has several clear advantages over the stuff you find in the stores. First of all, the homemade variety is not too sweet. In the proper strawberry shortcake scenario, the berries take the lead and the cake is complementary, providing supportive, background flavor notes. If the shortcake has too much sugar, it competes with the sweet berries, not to mention also tussling with the whipped cream, which is the required topping.

Then there is the texture. Shortcake should be crumbly, not springy. It should make you think of scones, not sponges. When it encounters any stray strawberry juice on the bottom of the bowl, a properly made shortcake embraces the juice, and the union is a happy one. Such a shortcake usually comes from a home oven, not a commercial one.

I live in a household of short-tempered shortcake eaters. When my wife makes shortcakes, our two kids immediately start arguing over who gets how many cakes.

One night, for instance, as soon as a sheet of shortcakes emerged from the oven, one kid appeared in the kitchen, ready to divide the goods. This kid likes to start off eating his shortcake straight, without berries. To get himself ready for the strawberry-covered shortcakes served for dessert, he eats an uncovered shortcake as an appetizer.

However, if this kid is allowed to eat too many of these appetizers, the portions of dessert served to the rest of the family get smaller. When desserts get smaller, tempers get shorter, at least in our house.

Thanks, no doubt, to the many hours spent in his seventh-grade math class, the kid was able to quickly make the shortcake calculations. There were seven shortcakes and four eaters. The kid figured he could eat one shortcake as an appetizer and there would still be enough to supply him and his brother with their required double serving at dessert time. Or, in shortcake math — one appetizer, plus two dessert cakes each for the two kids, plus one shortcake each for the two parents, wipes out all the sheet of shortcakes.

I didn't have to be a math whiz to figure out that when it came to divvying up dessert, I was getting the short end of the shortcake.

Basic Shortcake

Yields about 7 cakes, 3-4 inches wide

1¾ cup sifted all purpose flour
½ teaspoon salt
3 teaspoons baking powder
1 tablespoon sugar
5 tablespoons chilled butter
¾ cup milk

Preheat oven to 450 degrees. In a bowl, mix flour, salt, sugar and baking powder. Add the butter to the dry ingredients by cutting butter with two knives until mixture is consistency of coarse cornmeal.

Make a well in the center of this mixture and add milk all at once. Stir until the dough is fairly free from the sides of the bowl. Turn the dough onto a lightly floured board. Knead gently and quickly, folding it about 8 to 10 times. Roll with a lightly floured rolling pin, until the dough has the desired thickness. Cut with a biscuit cutter or coffee cup.

Place on ungreased baking sheet. Bake until lightly brown, about 10 minutes.

A driver's choice: good speed or good food

WHEN TRAVELING DOWN THE ROAD, DO YOU MAKE GOOD TIME, OR DO YOU pull off and sample the local delights? Until recently, I held the make-good-time view. I treated family car trips as if they were lower-speed versions of the Indianapolis 500. The idea was to keep those wheels rolling.

Consequently, any stop along the way, whether for gas or grub, was treated as the equivalent of an Indy pit stop. I never made good on my threat to time our roadside breaks with a stopwatch. But several miles before we reached a fast-food restaurant, I would start quizzing my passengers, making sure all knew exactly what they were going to order when they walked, at a purposeful pace, into the restaurant.

We stopped at fast-food joints because they were located right next to the highway, because our kids were familiar with the menus and because we could carry the food to the car. This meant lunch could be consumed as we were rolling down the road, eating up those miles.

Except for stealing a few french fries from the kids, I didn't eat while driving. I found that rather than filling up on fast food along the way, I tended to make very good time on the highway and then reward myself at journey's end with a big meal.

Recently, however, this keep-'em-rollin' philosophy of family travel was challenged. It happened on the New Jersey Turnpike a couple of hours out of Baltimore, heading toward Boston.

We had just pulled out of the turnpike rest stop carrying the name of American novelist James Fenimore Cooper and the fried food of American cowboy hero Roy Rogers. I was congratulating myself for only having lost 20 minutes of road time when I heard rumblings of discontent. It seemed that the stop at Roy's and James Fenimore Cooper's place had not delivered a satisfying culinary experience. To paraphrase our teen-age passengers, lunch was a disaster.

Like most dads at the wheel, I listened to the complaints of my kids with a deaf ear. My attitude was, so what if the chicken tasted funny — that's life on the road.

This time, however, amid the murmurings of discontent from the back seat, I heard a new, positive note. Instead of merely criticizing his parent's choice of lunch spots, the teen-ager offered an alternative proposal. Instead of skirting the big cities — New York and Philadelphia — along our route, he asked, why not drive into these burgs and pick up some real sandwiches?

The kid had me going. I was conflicted. As a wheel-man I knew that a side trip to the Second Avenue Deli in lower Manhattan, at midday, without a good street map to guide me, could add two or three hours to our Baltimore-to-Boston trek. But as a fan of the deli's juicy pastrami sandwich, I knew the detour would be delicious.

As parents say when we aren't sure what to say, I said, "No." I would not divert the family vehicle from its plotted course.

But the kid, as kids do, sensed I was wavering. He kept the detour idea alive, not just for the remainder of our drive to Boston, but on the return trip as well.

We will pass this way only so often, he kept telling me. Shouldn't we stop and sniff the pastrami in New York? Shouldn't we smell the cheese steak in Philadelphia?

On the drive back from Boston, I caved in and steered the car toward Philadelphia. I tried to tell myself I had switched routes for traffic reasons. I tried to convince myself that getting off the Jersey Turnpike early and driving to Baltimore on Interstate 95 would let us miss the congestion that comes at the end of the turnpike when cars line up at the toll booths. But deep in my gut, I knew it was the taste of a sizzling cheese steak more than the threat of traffic congestion that lured me off my plotted path.

We got off the turnpike at Cherry Hill, N.J., headed over the Ben Franklin Bridge, followed the signs for Independence Hall, and after a few quick turns, most of them correct, found ourselves at Jim's Steaks, at Fourth and South streets.

Jim's is an aromatic, hectic joint with a precise style for ordering sandwiches. You don't merely say you want a cheese steak, you describe in quick, clipped terms what you want on the sandwich. As in, "Gimme a steak, with American and onions, for here."

Instead of grabbing our sandwiches and hitting the road, we sat upstairs in Jim's in a room that overlooked Fourth Street. There were several other families in the room, and over in the corner, a table occupied by two young ladies. The ladies had caught the attention of the young men working at Jim's.

When one of these fellows came upstairs, ostensibly on an errand, he shouted "I love you" to the young ladies. After the second or third such proclamation, another customer, a guy sitting with his kids at a distant table, hollered back to the amorous cheese-steak maker, "I love you too, man." Nothing like that ever happened when we stopped at the James Fenimore Cooper rest stop.

We polished off the sandwiches and headed down the road to Baltimore. It was a weeknight, and traffic was light. The cheese-steak stop had added about an hour to our trip. I tried not to think about the extra time. Instead, I tried to get comfortable with my new philosophy. Namely, that no detour is too far if the sandwich is that good.

Making perfect pickles

I APPRECIATE A GOOD PICKLE. A PICKLE THAT IS CRISP AND FIRM, THAT HAS maybe a little salt, and maybe a little fire. A pickle that lets you know it is there.

While there are a handful of folks who pickle cucumbers in their basements, most of today's pickling work is done in factories. For instance, the 550 acres of cucumbers that Eastern Shoreman Harry Nagel grows in his Federalsburg fields are shipped to the Bloch & Guggenheimer Inc. pickle plant in Hurlock, Md., the Vlasic Foods Inc. plant in Millsboro, Del., and the Mount Olive Pickle Co. in Mount Olive, N.C.

There was a time when pickle-making in Maryland was personal, when eateries either made their own pickles or bought them from local pickle houses like Louis Borshay's operation in East Baltimore or Samuel Luchinsky's factory, which sat on land that is now the Camden Yards baseball stadium.

There was a time, said Seymour Attman, owner of Attman's Delicatessen in East Baltimore, "when people used to get excited when the first crop of cucumbers would arrive from the Eastern Shore." The first cucumbers of the season meant that in a few days there would be a fresh barrel of "half sours," the pickles made by soaking cucumbers in spicy saltwater brine for about seven days.

Attman said his East Lombard Street deli now gets its half sours, dills and full sours from a pickle house in New York. But Attman, who is in his early 70s, remembers participating in the pickle-making ritual his father supervised back in the 1940s.

"My father would buy the cucumbers in the old Mash Market," Attman said, using the local pronunciation of the Marsh produce market that once stood at Lombard Street and Market Place in downtown Baltimore. Cucumbers were purchased at the end of the day, Attman said, because that was when vendors who were stuck with a surplus of unsold cukes were willing to cut a deal.

Once the deal was struck, barrels were rolled out, and garlic was smashed. Attman remembers putting heads of garlic in a rolled-up apron and clobbering them with a device that looked like a sledgehammer. The smashed garlic, along with salt, water and a pickling mix formulated by the Baltimore Spice Co. just for Attman's, was tossed in the barrels with the cucumbers.

"Then you would get a cooper to seal up the barrel, like a whiskey barrel, so it wouldn't leak," Attman said. Next, a crew would help cart the barrels to the Baltimore Cold Storage company. There the pickles would sit, with the cold temperature slowing the pickling process, until the pickles were needed at the deli. When the time came, the barrels would be taken to the deli and opened. And then the cured cukes would go on sale.

"If you got bad pickles, soft ones, that meant something was wrong with your mix . . . too much salt, or too much water," Attman said.

He also told me a few terms used in the old pickling trade. A "bloater," he said, was a puffed-up cucumber, a pickle gone bad. A "dead green" was a young pickle on its way to becoming a "half-sour." A "full sour," or "New York sour," was a cucumber that had been sitting in brine for almost a month. It was often called a "well-done" in Baltimore.

Many of the pickles now sold in supermarkets are made using processes that either cook the cucumbers or douse them in vinegar. These processes preserve the products' shelf life. Most deli pickles are fermented in a salt-water mixture and are not cooked. The uncooked, saltwater pickles usually have a shorter shelf life, but more defined flavors.

One man who ships "gourmet" pickles around the country has taken the pickling process in a new direction. Zev Dorfman, head of D Z Pickling in Los Angeles, said his kosher pickles are cured in their jars. In a telephone conversation, Dorfman, a native of Romania, said he was relying on a 150-year-old recipe — saltwater, no vinegar, lots of garlic — and a modern toll-free number to satisfy America's craving for a good crunch.

He puts 4-inch cucumbers in plastic jars, douses them with the pickling mixture, seals the jars and ships them. The cukes pickle as they travel, Dorfman said. He advises his customers to eat a pickle as soon as the shipment arrives. If they like the flavor of the first pickle, they should put the other pickles in the refrigerator to stop the pickling process. But if they want their pickles a little stronger, they should keep the pickle jar at room temperature and allow the pickles to cure longer.

A five-jar package of his pickles costs about $30 when shipped to Maryland, Dorfman said.

Pickles, which are low in calories but high in salt, have long been the source of curious theories. Pickle eaters in California, Dorfman reports, claim that pickle brine has both livened up their salad dressings and their love lives.

Some folks in Baltimore, deli owner Attman said, like to drink the pickle brine because they believe it relieves the pain of arthritis. But Attman believes that too much of a good thing, even a good pickle, can give you problems.

"When I eat too many of those pickles," Attman said, "I get the gout."

The forgotten carrots

A COUPLE OF TOUGHS SURPRISED ME ONE SPRING DAY IN THE GARDEN.
They were carrots left over from last year's gardening efforts. My kid, then 9 years old, had sprinkled some seeds in a corner of the garden. The seeds had not done much last summer, and they were virtually forgotten until a few days ago when I was poking around in the dusts of April.

When I first stood over the swaying green tops of the carrots, I thought they were a variation of my biggest crop, weeds. Then I thought they might have been survivors of our long-lost dill crop.

But the green tops didn't smell like dill. They didn't taste like dill, either. That is one of the joys of fooling around in your garden. When you find something that looks promising, all it takes is a little washing from the hose, and you have an immediate, on-premise dining opportunity.

This particular tasting was not thrilling. The mysterious green tops didn't taste like weeds, but they did not taste much better. The mystery ended when I looked down at the ground and saw the bottoms that these tops had been attached to. I had almost stubbed my toe on the carrots.

It was a good thing I had not bumped up against these big, orange orbs. If I had, I might be limping. These were not svelte carrots, the tall, thin types that spend their formative months being fussed over in perfect carrot-growing environments. These were outlaw carrots. They looked like fireplugs. Short, squat. Thick.

They weren't pretty, but I was proud of them. I was also determined that these carrots were going to appear on my family's table. I took them home, where they received a mixed reception. "Awesome," said the kid who had planted the seeds. At my urging, the kid put the fattest carrot on a ruler, it measured 1 inch wide, and 3 inches long. It was a porker.

I knew the fact that the kid had planted the carrots was no guarantee that he would actually eat them. I am no longer one of those adults who believe that if you get the child involved in the preparation of a vegetable, the kid will end up eating the vegetable.

I used to believe that — before I had children. Now I believe that getting kids to eat anything, other than cookies, is pretty much a roll of the dice. You serve the dishes, you take your chances.

The kid who planted the carrots, for instance, also helps me grow tomatoes. He helps me plant them. He helps me water them. He helps me pick them. When we get the tomatoes home, however, he won't go near them. The kid doesn't like the taste of tomatoes. No amount of cajoling, or moaning with pleasure as I feast on the sweet tomatoes can deter the kid from his no-tomato lifestyle. (His big brother, who rarely sets foot in the garden, loves tomatoes.)

I console myself with the thought that maybe some day this will change. That maybe later in life, the younger boy will discover the pleasure of tomatoes, the happy way I discovered, on my 30th birthday, the pleasure of yeasty champagne. In the interim, however, it is clear to me that just because a kid grows something, or helps you slice it, does not mean he will put it in his mouth.

As for the tough carrots, I figured they had a 50-50 chance of getting eaten. I cut them into carrot sticks. When the kids were younger, I could sometimes humor them into eating carrots by pretending that we were gangsters and the carrot sticks were cigars. On nights that Mom was away, the guys and I would sit around the supper table with carrots stubs dangling from our lips. I guess you could call it gangster nutrition.

Those days are long gone. Usually when I am pushing raw vegetables, I rely on that friend of parents everywhere, ranch salad dressing, or as the kids call it, "dip." I believe that if you dip it, they will eat it — most of the time.

As I sliced these stubby carrots, I could see they needed help. They were so old that they had more growth rings than most trees. They were also very chewy.

The kid who had said they looked "awesome" reported that they "tasted weird," no matter how much dip they were dragged through.

I had to agree. The flavor of these carrots reminded me of a taste of my youth — the old No. 2 pencils I used to chew during school math tests.

The ugly carrots, our first garden crop of the season, were not a culinary success.

But that doesn't mean the kid and I won't plant more. In gardening and in kid-feeding, I believe in a brighter tomorrow.

A strong presence in the family

WHEN I WAS A BOY GROWING UP IN THE MIDWEST, BALTIMORE WAS WHERE my dad went to meet his boss. My dad was the manager of a Social Security office in St. Joseph, Mo., outside Kansas City and every so often he and other office managers from around the country would be summoned to Social Security headquarters in Baltimore for a week of meetings with the brass.

The end of "Baltimore week" meant a family trip to the Kansas City Municipal Airport to greet Dad on his return. This was the late 1950s, when airports were simple structures and airplane travel was a big deal.

Standing on the breezy observation deck of the airport, my mother, my three brothers and I waited for the plane from Baltimore. Suddenly the "Connie," or Constellation — a massive TWA plane — swept out of the night sky. It rumbled to a noisy stop near the terminal. Stairs were rolled up to the plane's door and men in suits walked down them, happily waving to all on the observation deck.

My brothers and I engaged in competitive dad-spotting. Each of us claimed to be the first one to see Dad coming out of the airplane. But we couldn't verify our identifications. From certain vantage points, all dads look alike.

Father's Day is the day that a lot of us size up our fathers, and our relationship with them. I now live in Baltimore and my dad lives outside Kansas City in a fog. Alzheimer's has him in its cruel, creeping grip.

Now communication with my dad is faint and garbled. Mostly my dad treats me as a friendly if mysterious visitor. "What do they call you?" he asked me when I spent a week with him. Not long ago my mother put my dad on the telephone to speak to me, and he simply whistled me a tune.

One odd effect of losing the ability to talk with my dad about family, sports, politics and the like, is that I find myself going over old ground. I dredge up the small stuff, the old habits of his everyday life, and compare them with my own.

My dad was a strong presence in our family, a man who lifted his hand to calm the nightly clamor at the supper table by calling for "Peace, peace." His conversational technique was to go around the supper table and ask each of us what we had done that day "for the good of the cause." Responses such as "cut some grass" or "trimmed the hedge" were smiled upon. "Nothing much" was an invitation for parental intervention.

One June morning when my older brother and I were teen-agers reveling in our fresh freedom from school, we got to the breakfast table to find the "help wanted" section of the newspaper waiting for us. Earlier that morning my dad had circled likely summer-job opportunities. By 10 o'clock, he had called us to make sure we had pursued the leads. One Baltimore morning I found myself writing a classified ad for a neighborhood newsletter, advertising my teen-age son's eagerness to do odd jobs.

The fine points of food and drink matter much to me, little to my dad. Food couldn't cook fast enough for him. He once fried hamburgers in two minutes. He created what became known in family lore as "the night of the bleeding burgers."

He drank the local beer, but not because it was fresher or had superior hops. He drank it out of loyalty to the nearby brewery, Goetz, and because it was cheap.

He liked bourbon, but didn't care about its pedigree. Once, when I lived in Kentucky, I presented Dad with a bottle of Makers Mark, a boutique bourbon I had just discovered. I watched him combine my prized whiskey with a bottle of standard-issue Old Crow. It was all brown water to him.

Dad plotted family car trips with precision and always knew which direction the car was headed. Last summer, when I drove him to the Atlantic Ocean for a family vacation, I found myself telling him we would head "east on Route 50, then south on 13," even though he couldn't grasp what I was saying.

Late in my dad's career there were more trips to Baltimore, and to Omaha, Neb., and Cedar Rapids, Iowa. Dad had become a supervisor of Social Security offices in several states. By then, the novelty of a flight from Baltimore on a Connie had given way to the deadening routine of rising before dawn to catch a 7 a.m. jet to Omaha that Braniff, an airline with quixotic ideas of scheduling, might or might not be operating that day.

One Friday night when I had been driving for a few years, I was tapped to pick Dad up at the Kansas City airport. This time there was no dramatic waving from the observation deck, just a gentle greeting at the gate. Dad was a tired traveler.

At home he was our editor, marking up drafts of school term papers that my brothers and I had written in what we thought was golden prose. Dad routinely chopped 10 lines of our typing into three comprehensible thoughts.

"Keep those sentences short, those verbs strong," he would tell us. A few weeks before Father's Day, while editing one of my son's school papers, I heard myself passing along exactly the same advice.

Chapter 4

Summer

A plug for watermelon

ON NIGHTS WHEN NOTHING IS STIRRING, WHEN THE TREES HANG HEAVY WITH humidity, I seek solace in ice-cold watermelon.

For some reason, when watermelon juices are running down my chin I forget about the sweat trickling down my back. The riper and colder the melon, the more pleasure it offers.

One summer night, a steamer, I found myself slicing a chunk of reasonably cold, relatively ripe melon for my then-12-year-old son and telling him watermelon stories. Both he and his younger brother are fond of the fruit, and watching either of them eat it is always a welcome sight. My kids and I may disagree on whether an order of french fries constitutes lunch, but we agree on the glories of watermelon eating, a practice that spans the generations.

My son and I examined the heart of the melon, a spot in the middle of the melon where the sugar content rises and the number of seeds diminishes. There are two theories, I told him, on when to eat this sweet spot. One is the immediate gratification theory: You eat it right away. The other is the delayed gratification approach: You eat around the heart, saving the sweetest bite until last.

We looked at the color of the flesh close to the rind. One mark of a great melon, I told him, is that its flesh is red and sweet right down to its "bone" — that is, the white pulp that sits next to its rind. The melon we were eating was good but not great; its sweetness started fading about half an inch before the pulp.

We talked about the common methods of determining whether a melon is ripe. There is the "thump" method of tapping the melon with your fist and listening to the sound move through the melon. Most folks have trouble distinguishing the deep thump sound given off by ripe melon from the dull thud of a run-of-the-mill melon. Hearing the deep thump is, I said, like having perfect pitch. It is an ability you are born with. Next, there is the bottom-ogling method of picking a ripe melon. You examine the pale underside of the melon. A mature melon has a creamy bottom, not bright white and not pale green.

When I told my son about testing a watermelon by having it "plugged," he didn't know what I was talking about. And so I told him about the night we plugged the 40-pound melon.

I told him it happened on a hot August night, when I was a bored teenager, anxious to get away from my family. The kid seemed interested, especially at the mention of getting away from family.

One of my friends, I continued, had his driver's license. And like most summer nights, this one began with my friend picking me up in his old Chevy. We picked up two other guys and drove around town. We cruised, checking out the miniature golf course and a couple of drive-in restaurants, until we found ourselves in a park, wanting to do something wild.

We considered the various forms of vice. Drinking beer was pondered but was voted down on several counts. We were under the legal drinking age by about five years. Besides, we didn't really like beer. It was bitter.

We considered girls. They were complicated. Only two of the four of us had girlfriends. And they had fathers who wouldn't let their daughters out of the house on such short notice.

So eventually we considered watermelon. We decided to go out and buy the biggest watermelon we could find. Right outside the park was a fruit stand. The store kept its melons floating in a big tank, along with big blocks of ice, making the water so cold that it hurt your hand if you stuck it in to fetch a melon. We told the fellow tending the melon tank we wanted a mammoth melon. He selected a 40-pounder and asked if we wanted it plugged.

We said we did. We watched as he cut a small cylindrical serving of the melon and presented it to us to taste. Supposedly, if a buyer didn't like the taste of the plug, he could refuse the melon. There was pressure associated with tasting the plug. Rather than putting all the melon-testing pressure on one guy, all four of us tasted the plug. We approved. Years later, when restaurant wine stewards present me with a cork from wine bottles, I am tempted to take a clue from my watermelon-plugging days and pass the cork around the table for all to sniff.

We took the prized melon back to the park. There, sitting on a picnic table in the dark, we devoured it. We ripped the melon apart with our hands. We let juice stream down our faces. We spit the seeds into the night. It was a melon to remember.

Somehow that melon made a long, dull summer a little shorter.

Into the frying pan

I CRAVE FRIED CHICKEN. IN THE SUMMER, THE BEST KIND OF FRIED CHICKEN is cold fried chicken, the kind pulled from a picnic basket. In hot months this kind of fried chicken is more appealing than the kind that you eat right after it is pulled from a sizzling skillet.

The skillet, of course, is a key to success. It should be big, dark and storied. The best fried-chicken skillet is one that has a tale that goes with it. Such a skillet might be described as "that old skillet, the one Grandma used to threaten us with."

I thought about this when I tried to teach my kids how to cook fried chicken. I looked around for the oldest skillet in the kitchen cupboard. Nothing new or coated with Teflon would do. It had to be old, and cast iron. I found one that I swore belonged to my mother, or maybe my wife's mother. When I held that skillet in my hand, I just knew it threatened somebody, sometime.

I put that no-nonsense skillet on the burner, poured in the oil and cranked up the heat. I used olive oil, which I realized later was a mistake. Olive oil has many wonderful properties, but when you cook fried chicken in it, your chicken doesn't taste like "home," unless you happened to have grown up eating fried chicken in Italy.

I soaked my raw chicken pieces in buttermilk, which I thought was a clever, geographically correct touch. Fried chicken is a celebrated dish of the South. While I am not a child of the South, I have lived there and have, by marriage, become acquainted with the foods and habits of the region.

In my mind, two signs that someone hails from the South are if she answers "Yes, ma'am" when her mother is mad at her, and if she drinks buttermilk.

I dropped the buttermilk-soaked chicken in a bowl of flour seasoned with salt and pepper. When the ½ inch of oil in the skillet was hot enough to make a bread crumb float and bubble, I set the floured pieces of chicken in and cooked them, uncovered, for about 25 minutes.

The result was OK. The skin was crisp, but the interior lacked flavor. This was not as it should be. A good piece of fried chicken, like a good book, is supposed to get more interesting as you go along.

After I fried my less-than-successful chicken, I consulted two expert sources to find out what went wrong. The first was "Southern Food" (Knopf,

1987), a lively and thoughtful book about the food of the region, written by John Egerton. Egerton has lived in Lexington, Ky., Tampa, Fla., and Nashville, Tenn.

In his book, Egerton says the crucial ingredients to good fried chicken are the skillet, the size of the bird, the method of applying the flour, and whether you put a lid on the skillet.

The skillet, he says, should be deep, heavy and black. The size of the bird should be small and lean. Egerton soaks his chicken, as I did, but not in buttermilk. He uses cold, salted water and soaks the pieces for about an hour. The purpose of soaking, he explains, is to get any blood out of the chicken.

He also has a different way of putting the flour on the chicken. Rather than dipping the chicken pieces in a bowl of flour, Egerton puts some seasoned flour in a paper bag, then shakes the chicken pieces in the bag until the pieces are coated. Something in the shaking process, I guess, makes the chicken more amenable to frying.

Egerton drops the coated chicken into a skillet filled with half an inch of sizzling oil. He uses melted shortening fortified with 4 tablespoons of bacon grease.

The oil, he writes, should be sizzling but not smoking. Moreover, the chicken pieces shouldn't be pushed together in the skillet. A crowded piece of chicken does not, he says, make for a happy fryer.

He cooks the chicken until it is golden brown on each side. How long this takes depends on the size of the chicken and the heat of the oil, but usually the chicken is cooked within 20 to 30 minutes, he says. There is no lid on his skillet. An uncovered skillet, he says, yields dry, crisp chicken. Cooking with a covered skillet yields chicken with moist inner meat.

After consulting with the author, I talked to a home cook, Kay Purvis of Baltimore. When my kids were younger she helped care for them. And on special occasions, she cooked fried chicken. Ever since then, Kay's fried chicken has been the standard that all fried chicken has been measured against. After tasting my attempt at fried chicken, for instance, one of my kids told me, "It is good, but it is not Kay's."

When I called her on the phone, Kay told me flat-out that the secret to good fried chicken "is good, hot grease."

"I use Crisco or Mazola . . . now real old cooks will use lard," she said. Not only must the oil be hot, there must be plenty of it, she said. "I don't have the oil covering the chicken, but I have it right up on it."

Kay, who was born in Brownwood, Texas, said her fried-chicken-cooking style was taught to her by her late mother, Ruby Stafford.

Kay said she realized that these days some people regard fried food as something to be avoided, not embraced. "Those people on diets, they don't want you to talk about grease," she said. But those folks, she said, are simply going to have to miss out on one of life's treats — real fried chicken.

So I am saving paper sacks and bacon drippings in preparation for my next attempt at greasy fried chicken.

Weiners with ... whatever

WHAT YOU PUT ON YOUR HOT DOG DEPENDS ON WHERE YOU LIVE. THAT IS what I learned recently when, in honor of July, National Hot Dog Month, I called hot-dog sellers around the United States. The hot dog has been charged, but never convicted, of crimes ranging from increasing the risk of cancer to causing bratty behavior in kids. Nevertheless, we continue to love the hot dog, eating an average of about 80 per person per year. And, in different regions of America, the hot dog gets special treatment.

In Baltimore, for example, the distinctive hot dog topping is a slice of beef bologna. The bologna is wrapped around a grilled, all-beef hot dog, said deli owner Seymour Attman.

Over the clatter of the lunchtime crowd, Attman told me of the typical topping of a Baltimore dog: "The mustard — it is deli style, not the salad style — the sweet relish and the fresh onions, and the bologna."

Attman said he thought the practice of putting bologna on hot dogs got started in the early 1940s at Nathan Ballow's delicatessen. Over the years the Ballow deli moved from North Avenue to Reisterstown Road, where it became Mandell and Ballow, and eventually went out of business, Attman recalled. But Ballow's practice of serving hot dogs with bologna stuck and spread through the city.

The practice apparently did not reach Western Maryland. In Hagerstown, I was told, folks like their hot dogs uncluttered.

"Up here people don't put much on a hot dog, maybe hot onions, because they want the flavor of the meat to come through," said Donald Hoffman. Last year Hoffman's family started making old-fashioned hot dogs, out of pork and beef. The dog is smoked over white hickory wood. It is the same smoking technique the family business has used for years to make its bacon, Hoffman said. The hot dog is sold by mail order and at the Roy L. Hoffman and Sons shop on Cearfoss Pike in Hagerstown.

In New York, the hot dog, like most everything else in Gotham, turns out to be complicated.

Manhattan hot-dog eaters, I was told, have to have onions. But out on Long Island the required hot-dog companion is dark mustard, with the seeds still in it, said Ron Dragoon. Dragoon is president of Ben's Kosher Deli

Restaurants, which sell hot dogs at nine locations on Long Island, one in Queens and one in Brooklyn.

"In suburbs, it is mustard with a little sauerkraut," said Dragoon. Occasionally, he said, a customer will "perform a sin" and ask for ketchup on his hot dog. "When that happens, we do a double take. But we give them the ketchup."

Dragoon, a native New Yorker, also noted differences in the various cooking styles used by hot-dog merchants throughout the city. Boiled and steamed hot dogs come from the propane-fired cooking devices found on the pushcarts operating on Manhattan street corners, he said. Grilled hot dogs are found in the more established delis, where the kitchens use electricity. Grilling, Dragoon said, is the best way to cook a hot dog.

On the plains of Nebraska, what folks put on their Wahoo Wieners depends on what ingredients have gone into the hot dogs. That is what Barb Coenen told me. She works for the O.K. Market, makers of Wahoo Wieners, smoked hot dogs that take their name from Wahoo, a town midway between Lincoln and Omaha. Wahoo Wieners are sold via mail order around the country.

On the fine-grind Wahoo Wiener, folks are likely to deposit a mixture of ketchup, mustard, onion and pickle relish, Ms. Coenen said.

When they are eating a Wahoo Wiener made with garlic, folks put on the sauerkraut, she said.

And when they are dealing with Wahoo Wieners made with jalapeno peppers, they add melted cheese.

I ended my survey of hot-dog toppings with a phone call to California. Los Angeles hot dogs, I was told, are being made out of vegetables and are being topped with anything from creamed spinach to guacamole. But at the Hollywood Hot Dog Co. in Beverly Hills, the biggest seller turns out to be the traditional, all-beef Hebrew National dog. The topping on the traditional dog, however, sounds like something that came off of a Wolfgang Puck pizza. "It is corn relish, black bean salsa, with chopped onion and a honey-mustard," Hollywood Hot Dog's Marty Halfon told me.

The corn relish topping, Halfon explained, was designed to "put fire through your nose."

I hung up and summarized my hot-dog findings. In Baltimore, the hot dog is covered with bologna. In Hagerstown, it is a smoked dog with next to nothing on it. In New York, the dog travels with onions in Manhattan, and with seedy mustard and a sprinkling of kraut in the outer boroughs. In Wahoo, ketchup and mustard go on the mild wieners, kraut on the warmer wieners, and melted cheese on the fiery dogs.

And in Beverly Hills, the dog itself is traditional but the topping is exotic. Or, as they like to say in the city of smog and sunshine, their hot-dog topping is "healthy."

Great to eat, difficult to pronounce

I AM NOT SURE HOW TO PRONOUNCE THEM, BUT I DO LOVE TO EAT THEM. I AM talking about apricots, the fruit that looks like orange golf balls and can taste like nectar.

Some folks stress the solo sound of the "a" in their pronunciation of apricots, so that the first syllable sounds like "ape." Others emphasize the marriage of the "a" and "p," so that the first syllable sounds something like "lap."

I tend to be more of a "lap" than an "ape" kind of guy, at least when it comes to apricots.

Whatever the fruits are called, they were in abundance Sunday morning at the Farmers' Market in downtown Baltimore. Boxes of them dotted the produce stands set up in the parking lots running underneath the Jones Falls Expressway north from Saratoga Street. They had even spilled north into an expanded section of the market, a parking lot north of Pleasant street.

After listening to a few farmers talk about what is involved in growing apricots around here, apricots sound to me like big stars playing gigs in small towns. They are only on the scene for a short time, a few weeks in July. They are very sensitive. They bruise easily. They demand to be handled by hand.

They may be the prima donna of tree fruit, but like many prima donnas they can deliver so much pleasure, they are worth the trouble.

When shopping I looked for apricots that had high color. That meant no green spots and plenty of bright orange and gold tones.

The juice of a truly ripe apricot can make you sigh with pleasure. I remember having some nectar experiences many years ago when I lived in western Kansas, and my family bought two bushel baskets of apricots trucked in from the nearby orchards of Colorado. Since then I have come to the reluctant conclusion that semi-arid climes, like eastern Colorado, have a leg up in the apricot nectar department over fruit grown in places like Maryland and Pennsylvania.

But I continue my quest for the nectar-filled apricot east of the Mississippi. The other day, after I brought my apricots home and washed them off, I popped a few in my mouth. One was very juicy. One was pretty pulpy. Nonetheless, I enjoyed eating them. Apricots offer more fun for your mouth than most fruits. The skin is soft, with no annoying fuzz. The juice can be a sweet surprise.

I am even fond of the seed, it is so smooth and symmetrical. As a kid I saved seeds of the apricots I had eaten and planted them in our back yard. None sprouted. The backyard bare spot where I planted them also ended up doing double duty as second base in summer baseball games. It was probably too tough at second base for apricots.

Sunday morning I popped a few more apricots into my mouth and began thumbing through cook books, looking for things I could make with the fruit. A chutney, made with apricots, onions and sugars, looked inviting. It was supposed to go on grilled fish.

I also saw a recipe for a compote made with fresh apricots and fresh raspberries. I had bought some raspberries at the market as well. The compote was something you could put on top of some pound cake, or simply serve topped with some cream, as a dessert.

Faced with using the apricots for a main course or for a dessert, I naturally chose dessert.

I may be unsure how to pronounce the first syllable of apricots, but I know what you are supposed to say when you have finished eating them. You are supposed to say "AHHH."

Everything is peachy

IT WAS TIME TO SNIFF THE PEACHES. THE PEACH HARVEST WAS GETTING SERIOUS, and three of the most popular varieties grown around here — Red Haven, Sun High and Loring — were coming off the trees and going into local kitchens.

This meant that kitchens would be filled with the enticing perfume of ripe peaches, an aroma that signals to eaters that juicy days were here again.

The summer has been a hot one. While the heat made most of us more irritable, it made many of the peaches sweeter. That's what Kay Ripley told me in a telephone conversation from Baugher's orchards in Westminster, a family-run operation presided over by her father, Allan Baugher.

Heat increases the sugar content of peaches, she explained. The summer heat, coupled with a lack of rainfall, produced peaches that will probably be skinnier but sweeter than the plump peaches of prior summers, she said.

Having digested the happy forecast, I began thinking of ways to enjoy this sweet harvest. I plotted a peach-eating regimen.

I began with breakfast. Eating fresh peaches at breakfast is a sure sign, I believe, that you are living the good life. On mornings when I feel nutritionally correct, I will mix peach slices with my cereal. On days I feel decadent, I will feast on peach slices swimming in a pool of cool, sweet cream. I think the decadent days will dominate.

In the hours leading up to lunch, I plan to feed on the pile of fresh peaches that will sit on the kitchen counter. If I get lucky at lunch, I might scrounge up some peach cobbler or pie, leftovers from a previous night's pleasure.

Peaches will also be coming to dinner. When there is grilled fish on the menu, I will accompany it with a salsa made of red onions, lime juice and fresh peaches.

As for dessert, there are the old favorites: peach pie, peach cobbler, peach cake. But I promised myself that I will try something new, a peach adventure. John Martin Taylor, author of several cookbooks, including "Hoppin' John's Low Country Cooking" (Bantam, 1992), told me I should try "peach leather."

In a telephone conversation from his Charleston, S.C., home, he described this treat as a homemade fruit roll-up, and told me how he makes it. He peels and purees five or six partially ripe peaches with one to two tablespoons of honey. He greases a cookie sheet, spreads the peach-honey puree out on the sheet, then puts it in an oven that has been turned to its lowest setting. He leaves it in overnight. By the next morning, the peach mixture has turned into a delicious "leather," he said.

Taylor and I also talked about my ultimate peach delight, homemade peach ice cream.

Taylor said there are two keys to making peach ice cream. First, you must crush the peeled peaches in your hands. There is no other way to get the right consistency, he said. Second, the hand-crushed peaches must be thoroughly chilled before they are added to the custard used to make ice cream. If they aren't chilled, the peach bits will get icy.

The reward, a bowl or two of fresh peach ice cream, is worth the work. Eating homemade peach ice cream is about as close to bliss as a middle-aged, middle-income person can get.

So this summer I have vowed to make the perfect peach ice cream.

Peach Ice Cream

Makes 1 quart

8 – 10 peaches
½ teaspoon almond extract
2 cups milk
6 egg yolks
¾ cup sugar
1 cup whipping cream

Peel the peaches, remove their pits and mash by hand. Chill in refrigerator. Add almond extract to milk and scald milk in a heavy saucepan. Remove from heat. Beat the yolks in a bowl by hand or with a mixer until light colored. Add the sugar and continue beating until mixture has doubled in volume. Gradually add some of the milk to the egg mixture. Pour egg mixture into the remaining milk in the saucepan and cook, over low-medium heat, stirring constantly until the custard coats the back of a spoon, about 8 to 10 minutes.

Add the whipping cream to the custard, let mixture cool, then chill in refrigerator. When both the custard and the peaches are thoroughly chilled, combine them. Freeze in an ice cream maker according to the manufacturer's instructions.

From "The New Southern Cook"
by John Martin Taylor (Bantam, 1997)

Corn lovers, lend me an ear

SAY HALLELUJAH AND PASS THE BUTTER! THE SWEET CORN HAS ARRIVED.

I had a couple ears of corn that were so sweet that eating them had me curling my toes with delight. There I was, barefoot in the kitchen, attacking two pieces of sweet corn. I was in such a frenzy, the corn cobs moved like the carriages of a typewriter — left, right, return.

All I knew about the corn was that the kernels were white and it was delicious. But after talking with Ronald Sewell, the Taneytown farmer who grew the corn, and with a couple other farmers — John Selby in Centreville and Pam Pahl in Woodstock — I got a quick education on the sweet corn scene.

The good news is that not only has the sweet corn landed, it has arrived by the truckload. For the next two weeks we could be up to our ears in ears. This is not the way the farmers planned it. They would prefer that the corn crop ripens in a more orderly fashion. But Mother Nature apparently had other ideas. The cool and quirky spring weather played havoc with farmers' planting schemes.

Back in the spring, some corn plants popped out of the ground, and just stood still. Other fields had to be replanted. So now, after weeks of sunshine and thundershowers, these crops are ripening at the same time. "For the next 10 days or so the supply will probably be abundant, then it will level off again," said Sewell who farms in Carroll and Frederick counties.

Over on Maryland's Eastern Shore, Selby agreed the early sweet corn crop looked good. But he reminded me that the cool weather of May was followed by blistering heat in June. The part of the corn crop that was scheduled to sprout during those "dust-bowl days of June," could have an uneven yield, he said. That part of the crop should come to market in August, he said.

Speaking to me on a car phone as he bounced along Route 50, Selby, 77, said this summer was "the hottest one I can remember. Other years it got hot in July. This year it started in June," he said.

The extended hot weather kept Pam Pahl and her husband, Les, busy irrigating the couple's farm in western Baltimore County. Their corn crop is in good shape but has attracted unwanted consumers. "The deer love it," said

Pam. "The corn is green, everything else is dry, so the deer come into those cornfields and do some damage."

The other thing I learned about the sweet corn scene is that all white corn is not the same. Fans of certain varieties of white sweet corn ask for them by name, the way some wine drinkers request vintages of their favorite Chardonnay.

As I understand it, the breakdown of white sweet corns goes something like this: First is the Silver Queen, a traditional variety. Fans say that it is sweet yet still tastes like corn. The drawback to Silver Queen is that it loses much of its flavor a day or two after it has been picked.

Next are the very sweet varieties, which feature weird spellings — one is SuperSweet — and higher sugar contents. Fans of these corns like their sugary flavor and their longer shelf life, saying they hold their flavor for 3 to 5 days after picking. But some eaters contend the flavor is not corny enough, and that the kernels are chewy.

Finally there are varieties called "sugar-enhanced" that try to strike a middle ground between Silver Queen and the super-sweet corns. Fans say the sugar-enhanced varieties are sweet but still taste like corn. The drawback of the sugar-enhanced varieties is that they have a shorter shelf life than the sweetened varieties.

The corn that curled my toes was a sugar-enhanced type. Sewell gave me other information about the corn's pedigree: it is an Abbott and Cobb, a 73W, of the Summer-flavor group. I also found out where I can buy more. In addition to the truck in Taneytown, at Route 140 and East Baltimore Street, Sewell sold the corn in Westminster, from a truck parked on Gorsuch Road behind Crouse Ford.

So I plan to conduct a summer-long taste test of white corn. I'll try some sugar-enhanced from Sewell, I'll get some Silver Queen and super-sweet types from the Pahl's stand at Baltimore's Sunday morning Farmer's Market. When I go the Eastern Shore, I'll swing by Farmer John's stand off Route 50 and try Selby's corn.

Who knows if I will come to a conclusion. But I am looking forward to the research.

Marvelous melon

LATELY I HAVE BEEN LOUPING ALONG.

When I get hungry I crack open a cantaloupe. I feast on it at the day's three main eating events: breakfast, supper and dessert.

For breakfast I cut a slice of the melon and eat it with a spoon. It is a fragrant start to a summer morning. At supper I mix chopped 'loupe with minced onion, green pepper strips, a little red wine vinegar and use the mixture to top grilled tuna steak.

For the main event of the day, dessert, I make cantaloupe ice cream.

One of the reasons I'm now so sweet on 'loupes is that earlier this summer I had a run-in with a sour one.

I was driving back to Baltimore from the Eastern Shore when I stopped at a roadside stand in Salisbury off Route 12. I bought some good corn and reasonable tomatoes there, but the cantaloupe turned out to be soft. I should have known better. It had been raining for the better part of a week, and melons soak up water.

Moreover, if I had paid attention I would have noticed that none of the other customers were interested in the 'loupes.

One woman, who apparently lived nearby and shopped regularly at the stand, saw me eyeing the 'loupes and tried to drop me a hint. "I haven't had a good melon this year," she said. "They have been mushy."

I wasn't listening. By then I had begun checking out the cantaloupes, trying to find a ripe one. I examined the skin, looking for even "netting." I eyed the color of the skin, looking for a slight yellow undertone. I pushed the end opposite the stem, and felt slight pressure and got a pleasing whiff of cantaloupe perfume.

I was convinced this was the 'loupe of my dreams. It turned out to be like a dream, one of those mushy ones. When I got home and opened the 'loupe up, the meat of the melon almost fell out. It was too ripe and watery even to use in homemade ice cream.

All I could do was carry the spoiled 'loupe to the trash. Only rotten crabs smell worse than a 'loupe past its prime.

So the next time I bought a melon — at a stand in the Sunday morning Farmer's Market in downtown Baltimore — I let the fella selling the melons pick it out.

"When do you want to eat it?" he asked.

"For breakfast tomorrow," I said.

He handed me a big melon, with perfect netting, and slight, yellow undertone to the skin. "Put it in the refrigerator when you get home," he said.

I intended to do as I was told. But when I got home the fridge was jammed.

And the 'loupe smelled so inviting. I couldn't wait. I opened it up, cut off the skin and cut the melon into bright orange slices.

After eating a few, I tossed the rest in a plastic dish and carried them to a spot where they might catch the attention of my marauding children — the neighborhood swimming pool.

When the the kids came out of the water, not only did they eat the fruit, they devoured it. Kids who have been swimming all day are like fish, they have feeding frenzies.

Cantaloupe Ice Cream

Makes 1 quart

1 large or 2 small, very ripe cantaloupes
juice of 1 lemon
sweet cream base (see below)

Cut the cantaloupe in half and clean out the seeds. Scoop fruit into a mixing bowl, add the lemon juice and mash until the fruit is pureed. Drain the juice into another bowl and reserve. Cover the melon puree and refrigerate. Prepare the sweet cream base and whisk in fruit juice.

Transfer the mixture to an ice cream maker and freeze following the manufacturer's instructions.

After the ice cream stiffens (about 2 minutes before it is done), add the cantaloupe. If more juice has accumulated, do not pour it in because it will water down the ice cream. Continue freezing until the ice cream is ready.

Sweet Cream Base

2 cups heavy or whipping cream
¾ cup sugar
⅔ cup half and half

Pour the cream into a mixing bowl. Whisk in sugar, a little at a time, then continue whisking until completely blended, about 1 minute more. Pour in half and half and whisk to blend.

From "Ben & Jerry's Homemade Ice Cream & Dessert Book"
(Workman Publishing, 1987)

Getting picky about crabs

THERE ARE TWO KINDS OF CRAB PICKERS IN MARYLAND: THOSE WHO USE wooden mallets to crack the shells of steamed blue crabs, and those who use knives.

I'm a mallet man, with aspirations to be a knife-wielder. I feel at home among the noisy, crustacean-clobbering crowds of Baltimore. But as soon as I cross the Bay Bridge, I feel inferior. On the Eastern Shore, the knife-wielders work so swiftly and silently that almost faster than you can say, "I'm not from around here," a crab has been separated from its shell.

One such knife-wielder is Betty Tall. She picks crab meat for a living, this year getting $2.25 a pound at the Meredith & Meredith Seafood packers in Toddville, Dorchester County. She is a claw cracker, which means she specializes in removing meat from the crab claws.

Using a crab knife, a knife that resembles a short steak knife, she cracks the claw at the point where it is connected to the crab's body. Then she cracks it again near its "elbow." She removes the meat as she goes along.

Sometimes she will go after the "crab fingers," the meat at the end of the claw. But, she said, only if the crab is a "big Jimmy."

She comes from a family of claw crackers, Tall told me during a telephone conversation. When she and her sister, Audrey Murphy, were growing up on the Eastern Shore, their mother, Pauline Abbott, assigned them the duty of picking meat from the claws served at family crab feasts.

One of the reasons the girls got claw duty, Tall recalled, was that her mother didn't think they were skilled enough to pick meat from other parts of the crab's body.

She and her sister took to this task. "Back then, nobody much picked claws, so if you did pick claw meat for somebody, my Lord, they loved you to death," she said.

Now some 50 years later, Tall, who is in her early 60s, still cracks claws at the seafood factory in Toddville from May until November. Her sister, a picker at a seafood house in Crapo, Dorchester County, also works on claws.

I asked Tall how she felt when she saw folks hammering away at a pile of steamed crabs.

"I just want to help them," she said.

Blondell Pritchett of Bishops Head, also in Dorchester County, told me she, too, disapproved of hammering hard-shell crabs. Pritchett has picked crabs with a knife for 48 years.

She learned from her father, Wilson Pritchett, who gave her a job at Crocheron Brothers, an old seafood factory in Crocheron, Dorchester County. Pritchett described her crab-picking technique. Holding the crab by its swimming fin, she sticks her knife under the back of the shell and, in one motion, pulls the top shell off by lifting and pushing the knife.

Next she cuts away the gills and the yellow mustard, and trims off the legs, or fins. Then, using the knife more as a pusher than a slicer, she removes the meat from the top of the crab's body. Again using the knife as a pusher, she removes the lump meat from the back of the crab, and finishes off by pushing out meat on the sides of the crab's body.

She often doesn't look at what she is doing. Instead she just "feels" what is going on, she said. She works standing up, and has picked as much as 100 pounds of crab meat a day, she said.

The knife is sharp, but she doesn't worry. "I get a little nicked up now and then," she said. "But I don't get cuts."

I told Pritchett about some of the techniques used in a picking contest I participated in at Baltimore's Harborplace during Preakness Week of 1994. I was clobbered, finishing fifth in a field of seven.

The 1994 winner was Lisa Willis, then a newscaster for television station WBFF-Channel 45 in Baltimore. Wayne Brokke from Wayne's Barbecue in Harborplace finished second and Guy Reinbold, chef of the Baltimore hotel then called Stouffer's, finished third. Both Brokke and Reinbold used knives to pick their crabs. Willis had an unusual technique. First, she pulled the top shell off. This, Willis later told me, was a tip she had picked up from Shirley Phillips, proprietor of the Phillips seafood restaurants.

Next Willis pulled off the crab legs, and split the crab in half. Then, using the heel of her hand she smashed the body of the crab and tossed the meat, and some shell into a pile.

Willis called this her "smash and grab" maneuver and admitted that she used it only in contests that emphasized speed and didn't distinguish how much shell was in the meat. When she is picking crabs at home, Willis said she uses a knife and employs a more methodical method of removing meat from shell. When I told Pritchett about Willis' smash-and-grab crab-picking style, she laughed. On the Eastern Shore that kind of crab meat, she said, would never pass inspection.

So this summer, as the crab season begins to warm up, I am trying to improve my crab-picking technique.

I am weaning myself from the hammer. And slowly, carefully, I am wielding a knife. But for the first few crab feasts, it will be a dull knife.

The crab cake contest

ONE CHARACTERISTIC OF MARYLANDERS, WHETHER THEY ARE BORN HERE OR have moved here, is that they have strong opinions about crab cakes.

Another characteristic is that they tend to believe the best crab cakes known to mankind happen to be made by them.

This was the case at a Saturday night dinner party held at the Ruxton home of Jim and Anita Gabler. There, a dozen Marylanders — some natives and some immigrants — held a crab-cake tasting.

The idea for the contest stemmed from boasts made at a previous gathering of the group, whose members meet in one another's homes about four times a year to eat good food, drink fine wine and engage in spirited conversations.

At one of these gatherings the topic turned to crab cakes, and according to Gabler, virtually everyone in the group claimed to possess the recipe for the world's greatest crab cake. And so, Gabler, a local attorney who has written several books on wine, organized a crab-cake tasting to coincide with the group's next dinner party. I was invited, along with my wife, as guest eaters.

The crab-cake portion of the evening was marked with displays of secrecy, precision and hooey. The crab-cake mixtures had been prepared by the contestants in the quiet of their own kitchens and then carried to the Gabler's house, where they were handed over to a caterer who was presiding over the kitchen for the evening.

Instead of carrying the name of their creator, each of the seven competing crab cakes was assigned a letter, A through G.

Each was formed by the same ice cream scoop, ensuring they were all the same size. Moreover, all the crab cakes were cooked the same way, broiled.

When the seven sizzling beauties appeared next to their appropriate letters on the diners' plates, the tasting began. Twelve hungry men and women — the Gablers, Nancy Sandbower, Jim and Ginny Ryan, Ed and Loretta Lakatta, Sue Powers, Hank and Kathy Sabatier, and my wife and I — tasted the crab cakes and recorded our top three choices. As we tasted, we sipped a magnificent white wine that Gabler had pulled from his cellar. In keeping with the custom of this group, the wine bottle was wrapped in foil, and imbibers were encouraged to guess where the wine came from. I guessed heaven. The correct answer was Burgundy, a 1995 Premier Cru from Puligny-Montrachet, La Truffiere.

As the scoring sheets were then read aloud by Jim Gabler, the count was tallied by Kathy Sabatier, Ed Lakatta and Sue Powers. When the crab-cake title was on the line, this was not an especially trusting group.

Even when the tally was completed, the results were questioned. The scoring system gave three points for every first-place vote, two points for every vote for second and one point for third. The crab cake made by Hank Sabatier finished with the most total points, 16. But the crab cake made by Sandbower finished with 15 points and ended up garnering the most first-place votes, five. The crab cake made by the Gablers finished third, with 14 points.

The results were subjected to more questioning when it turned out that both the first- and third-place winners had used the same recipe. Both had mixed a pound of fresh crab meat with half a cup of mayonnaise and the ingredients found in the 1.24-ounce package of Old Bay Crab Cake Classic mix. This mix has been around since 1985 and contains the same ingredients found in the familiar blue and yellow can of Old Bay Seasoning, plus bread crumbs and dried egg. Supporters of this Old Bay crab cake cited its ease of preparation — simply open a $1.80 package of ingredients — and they reminded all that it had garnered the most points.

Supporters of the Sandbower crab cake — made with capers, fresh red pepper and paprika — countered by saying that because the Old Bay crab cake had two entries in the event, it had an unfair advantage. They said this procedure reminded them of the technique Maryland political machines used to employ to win elections: Namely, if you load the ballot with your candidates, one of them is likely to win.

Later when I called McCormick and Co. and told Old Bay brand manager Art Zito about the results of the contest, he scoffed at the notion that two spots on a ballot was an advantage. "It could work the other way — it could split the vote," Zito said. Championing the crab-cake makers who had used Old Bay, Zito added, "We got a win, we'll take it."

Sandbower, a Catonsville potter who teaches at Towson University, said the tasting was fun, but the results did not change her opinion. She was sticking to her family's recipe. She said she was taught to make crab cakes this way — adding red pepper that has been sauteed in butter, adding capers, keeping the cakes in the refrigerator before cooking them — years ago by her grandmother, Katie McLean, who lived in Baltimore's Charles Village.

Sandbower said she has passed the recipe on to her children, Beth Harbinson, Katie Milleker and John Cary. She makes crab cakes this way because it keeps tradition and taste buds alive. And that, she believes, is why her family's crab-cake recipe is the best.

Nancy Sandbower's Maryland Crab Cakes

Serves 4

1 pound jumbo lump fresh crab meat
1 red pepper, chopped
2 teaspoons dry mustard (Coleman's)
1 egg yolk from large egg or 2 yolks from medium eggs
1 heaping tablespoon Worcestershire sauce
1 or 2 dashes of Tabasco sauce
1 tablespoon capers, finely chopped
3 heaping tablespoons mayonnaise
6 saltines, pulverized, lightly cooked in butter
4 dashes Hungarian paprika (Fuchs)
butter

In a small pan, first saute chopped pepper in butter, then put lid on pan and cook a minute or two more until tender. Remove pepper from pan and save.

In a bowl, mix the pepper, mustard, egg yolk, Worcestershire sauce, Tabasco, capers, mayonnaise and paprika.

Fold in crab meat, trying to keep the crab meat in lumps. Putting some of the saltines in your hands, form the seasoned crab mixture into four cakes. Pat remaining saltines on outside of cakes.

Put crab cakes on a plate, covering them with plastic and letting them cool in the bottom of refrigerator for at least an hour.

Cover bottom of frying pan with butter, saute crab cakes in pan, cooking until brown, about 4 minutes per side.

A delicious lesson in cooperation

I JOURNEYED TO THE MIDDLE OF THE CHESAPEAKE BAY TO FIND THE SWEETEST crab meat. At the Smith Island Ladies Crabmeat Co-op I hit gold.

Getting there was an effort. I drove to Crisfield, hopped on the Captain Jason ferry boat, and took a 12-mile ride out to Tylerton, one of three communities on Smith Island.

There I bought a pound of crab meat for $14 from Carol Ann Landon. Her husband, Everett, had caught the crabs a few hours earlier in the waters that surround the island.

The crabs had been hurried back to the newly opened co-op in Tylerton. There they were steamed and passed on to Landon, who picked the meat and put it in 1-pound containers bearing the co-op's label.

I paid, iced down my container of crab meat, hopped on a boat back to Crisfield and drove back to Baltimore. That night I enjoyed a supper of crab cakes that was so good I later dreamed about eating it again.

The crab meat of Smith Island has been sending eaters into ecstasy for years. Moreover, the women of the island have traditionally made extra money by picking crabs caught by their husbands, fathers or brothers. What is new in this arrangement is that rather than picking the crab meat in their own kitchens, the women of the island now pick and pack their crab meat under the roof and auspices of the Smith Island Ladies Crabmeat Co-op.

The co-op is situated in a sparkling structure in Tylerton, a community of about 75 folks. This summer's opening of the co-op represented the end of a tussle between the Smith Island women and the state Health Department.

Four years ago authorities clamped down on women picking crab meat in their homes. At first some of the women of the island bristled at the suggestion that crab meat picked in their homes could be anything less than perfect. But eventually they accepted the notion that to sell their crab meat to the wider world, they would have to abide by the regulations followed on the mainland.

The women formed the co-op, got a few grants, a few donations, and a lot of advice. Last month the co-op's picking house opened for business. It has a steaming room, stainless-steel tables, glistening white walls and a floor so clean you could almost eat off it.

I was given a tour of the facilities by Janice Marshall, who, along with her daughter, Robin Bradshaw, is among the 14 women who make up the co-op. Each woman has her own, self-selected seat in the picking house. They work all hours of the day and night, some rising before dawn with their husbands. The men ride their boats out to catch crab. The women ride bicycles or golf carts to the co-op to pick the crabs caught in an earlier harvest. There are no cars in Tylerton.

At the picking house, the women begin the day with a Bible reading. The evening I was there, a handful of women talked and kidded each other as they worked.

Rather than using the wooden mallets found in Baltimore crab houses, the women used small, sharp knives to separate the meat from the crab shell. "I doubt there is a mallet on Smith Island," said Christine Smith. "Even the men here know how to pick."

Connie Marshall disagreed. "Mine don't," she said. "They can crack a claw and that is about it."

Some of the women teased R. Wade Binion, a young, handsome rural-development specialist sent out from Washington by the U.S. Department of Agriculture to help the co-op set up its books.

Binion, who grew up on a family farm outside Indianapolis, told me the structure of the crab-picking cooperative was similar to grain co-ops set up in Midwestern farming communities. Participants share evenly in the proceeds and losses.

Despite their easy laughter, some of the women said they had anxieties about being in business. So far this year crabs have been scarce. "It is not a sure thing," Marshall said. "You're just depending on the bay. It is scary."

Marshall said the co-op had not done any marketing. While it has a few devoted customers, such as Jay Prettyman, owner of the Rusty Rudder restaurant in Dewey Beach, Del., the co-op is looking for more outlets for its crab meat.

Two trucking firms in Crisfield can transport packages of the crab meat to Baltimore and Wilmington, she said. A minimum 10-pound order is required. Rather than separating the lump and claw meat, the Smith Island women put both types of meat in their 1-pound packages.

In a telephone conversation from his restaurant, Prettyman sang to me the praises of the co-op's crab meat.

"In my 30 years in the restaurant business this is the best meat I have found anywhere," he said. He added that at $14 a pound wholesale, the co-op meat is priced higher than other crab meat on the market. But he said he is willing to pay more because "the quality is much better.

"You don't have to handle it, to tear the meat up and look for pieces of shell. The ladies start with such good crabs, caught by their husbands. And when they pack them, it is a matter of family pride," he said.

In their dreams, the women see boatloads of visitors buying freshly cooked crab cakes at the co-op. But for now the only crab meat sold on the premises comes in those pound containers. The only way to get to the island is by boat. The ferry arrives at Tylcrton at 1 p.m and leaves around 4 p.m.

If you go, be sure to take a cooler that holds more than 1 pound of crab meat. My family quickly polished off the 1 pound I carried back to Baltimore. Then we were hungry, and a long way from Smith Island.

The Crab Queen's royal gesture

I WON A CRAB PICKING CONTEST. ME, A GUY WHO WAS BORN IN KANSAS AND grew up believing seafood was fish sticks. Me, who once thought a crab hammer was something you put in your tool box. Me, who wouldn't know a crab knife from a putty knife, pulled 7 ounces of meat and some shell from about four crabs in three minutes to win the First Annual Preakness Crab Picking Contest in 1992 at Harborplace.

I have the placard for my wall, and the cuts on my hand to prove it.

I should remember that this was not a contest for crab-picking pros. The contestants were local celebrities, which meant the players were anybody who could convince a boss that picking crabs on a beautiful May afternoon was work.

Still, a Midwesterner who picks crabs the way a combine works wheat — threshing it — won a contest in crabtown.

This event carries great geographic significance. Winning a crab picking contest in Baltimore is the equivalent of a corn shucking contest in Indianapolis, a chili making contest in Houston or an herb sniffing contest in San Francisco. It proves I can eat like a native.

And it breaks a 13-year losing streak for me. That is how long I had been in this town, practicing at home, then showing up at contests wearing an aw-shucks expression and hoping to sneak up on the Marylanders. This tactic almost worked a few years ago at a contest at Harrison's Pier 5 restaurant. I surprised former Baltimore Oriole Brooks Robinson, former Baltimore Colt Jim Mutscheller and nine members of the Boumi Drum and Bugle Corps. Nonetheless, I lost that 1989 contest to Jack Edwards, who was then an announcer at WFBR radio. So when I got to the contest at Harborplace, the first thing I did was look around for Edwards. I didn't see him. But I did see people who had beaten me in other food-related contests, like Tony Pagnotti, then of Channel 2, and Gary Murphy, then of station WBSB-FM Variety 104.3, one of the sponsors of the contest. Both Pagnotti and Murphy had creamed me in an ice cream eating contest at Lexington Market last year.

As I waited for the contest to begin I sized up some of the competitors. Jockey Charles Fenwick and tailor Steve Haas are both in jobs that require quick hands. Caterer Charles Levine was in his element, food. And professional lacrosse players Jeff Jackson and Brian Kronenberger are masters at wielding lacrosse sticks and could, I figured, also do a sizable amount of damage with crab hammers.

But the real sleeper in the field was a sweet woman named Shirley. I didn't get her last name until shortly before I sat down with her in the preliminary, one-picker against one-picker stage of the contest. Her last name was Phillips. She, along with her husband Brice, operate Phillips restaurants, the biggest crab houses in Maryland and probably the world. To get to the finals of the contest, I had to beat the Queen of Crabs.

I was too nervous to look directly at royalty, but out of the corner of my eye I saw that the Queen was going to use a knife to remove the meat from the crab shells. That scared me even more. Real crab pickers, people who live on the Eastern Shore, use a knife. Amateurs, like me, use our fingers. Wielding that knife, she went through that crab like Grant went through Vicksburg. She sliced off legs, then off came the shell, and quicker than you could say, "God bless the backfin," she was lifting great lumps of white meat from the shell.

Mercifully, the one-on-one contest ended. The winner would be the contestant with the heaviest pile of crab meat. The Queen's pile of meat was higher than mine. But just before her plate was weighed, the Queen did a strange thing. She ate a large portion of her contest entry. That is why I won and advanced to the finals. Call it noblesse oblige. Call it good public relations (her restaurant, Phillips, was a sponsor of the contest). Call it a tainted victory. I called it a win. After 13 years of losing, I was willing to take any victory, spotted, stained or soiled.

In the finals I again used my shredder technique, and again I thought I would lose. But when the crab meat stopped flying and the trays were weighed, I had won, edging out the two lacrosse players, Jackson and Kronenberger, by half an ounce and three-quarters of an ounce, respectively.

Looking back, I owe my victory to two factors. First, the generosity of the Queen of Crab. She could have smoked me. And the other factor in my win was the fact that both crab meat and crab shell are the same color. My tray was not closely examined for illegal shell parts.

Nonetheless, I have my crab picking placard, and my tale to tell visiting Midwestern relatives.

Most importantly, I'm not from Kansas any more, at least not during crab season.

The physics of soup

FOLKLORE SAYS IF YOU MAKE CRAB SOUP DURING A THUNDERSTORM THE soup will spoil. Believers say it has happened to them. They blame anything from a drop in atmospheric pressure to the electrical charge in the storm air for turning their soup.

Skeptics say thunderstorms have nothing to do with spoiled soup. They contend the spoilage is usually caused by improper cooling of the cooked soup when it is stored in a refrigerator.

A few cooks say they don't know if there is any scientific basis to their behavior, but they don't make soup during a thunderstorm because their Mama and Papa told them not to.

That is what I found out when I called cooks and scientists around Maryland and attempted to find out if there was any fact behind this nugget of Maryland folk wisdom. The truth of the matter, like the soup itself, seems turgid.

Chef Mark Henry, a native of Maryland, said he is a believer in the dangers of thunderstorms to culinary efforts. Henry said several years ago he was working at a restaurant in Columbia called Crystal's when a thunderstorm hit and his crab soup spoiled. That taught him a lesson, he said. "There is a drop in pressure when a thunderstorm comes through. And your soup boils at a lower temperature. So you think you have cooked your soup all the way through and you haven't."

When the partially cooked soup ingredients are stored, the bacteria in them remains active and turns the soup, he added. So now when Henry sees dark clouds on the horizon, he cooks his crab soup longer.

Fred Davis, the National Weather Service's chief meteorologist at Baltimore-Washington International Airport, confirmed that atmospheric pressure drops when a thunderstorm rolls through the area. Once the storm leaves, the pressure goes back up, he said. And Dick Berg, a physicist at the University of Maryland, College Park, said it is fundamental physics that when the atmospheric pressure drops, so does the boiling point of liquids. But he was skeptical that a slight drop in the pressure during a passing thunderstorm would have a significant impact on the temperature of the crab soup.

Chef Mike Baskette, who teaches at Baltimore International Culinary

College, also doubts that a slight drop in the boiling point of the soup would cause the soup to spoil. Even though the soup might boil at a lower temperature, because of the drop in pressure, that temperature would still be high enough to wipe out bacteria, he said.

Baskette suspects two other culprits for spoiling the soup. One is the soup pot. Uncoated aluminum pots, for instance, can increase the chance of spoilage. During a thunderstorm the electrical charge in the air could facilitate a reaction between the pot's aluminum surface and the acid in tomatoes used for making crab soup, he said. The reaction could cause the soup to spoil.

Baskette recommends using either a stainless-steel pot or an aluminum pot lined with stainless steel. He added that the reaction between the pot and the acid could also occur on a sunny day, but that the chances for spoilage were probably higher during the charged air of a thunderstorm.

Another common soup spoiler is improper cooling, Baskette said. Sometimes containers of cooked soup stored in a fridge do not cool down below 40 degrees, he said. Usually the soup around the edge of the pot cools down, but the soup in the center of the pot stays hot, even in the fridge. This means that bacteria in the warm center of the soup go to town. He recommends storing the soup in small containers, checking the temperature of the soup as it cools, and stirring it.

Finally, I came across some cooks who don't believe that thunderstorms spoil crab soup, yet can't bring themselves to make it in stormy weather. One is Bill Cusick, a retired Baltimore Gas and Electric Co. worker, who whips up 8- to 10-gallon batches of crab soup at home for special occasions. Cusick said that when he is thinking of making soup in his Timonium home and "sees those dark clouds gathering up over Cockeysville," he hears his father's voice.

"My father was from the Eastern Shore down around Fishing Creek, and he always told me if you make crab soup in a thunderstorm, the soup would spoil," Cusick said.

And so, as a tribute to his father, Cusick postpones his soup-making plans. "No matter what my father told you, he was right," Cusick said. "Even if he wasn't."

Crabs on the other coast

DURING AN EATING VACATION IN PORTLAND, ORE., I SPENT A FAIR AMOUNT OF time comparing their local crab, the Pacific Dungeness, with ours, the Atlantic blue.

Rather than restricting my comparison to the culinary question of which crab dishes can make me shiver with delight, I also looked at crab culture. I looked at what kind of art the local crab inspires. I looked at what kind of bait and tactics crabbers use. I looked at which crab was nastier.

Shortly after I got off the plane from Baltimore, I went to a Portland seafood restaurant, McCormick & Schmick's. It has since set up shop in Baltimore. I ordered crab cakes made with Dungeness crab. The crab cakes were golden, warm, but somewhat shy of crab flavor. My dining companion, Janie Hibler, a Portland resident and author of "Dungeness Crab and Blackberry Cobblers," (Knopf, 1991), told me a better way to show off the flavor of Dungeness was to serve it as a crab cocktail, with a little horseradish and tomato sauce.

So the next day Hibler, her daughter, Kristin, and I sat on a sun-drenched balcony of their Portland home feasting on a crab cocktail made with fresh, boiled Dungeness. The crab meat was sweet. It was a decisive win for the West Coast crab.

On the question of how the local crab influences the local artists, I started with T-shirts. I had carried a T-shirt from Baltimore that I considered a good example of the way crabs and art can interact.

It came from Obrycki's restaurant, and showed a giant crab skewering bite-sized humans with its claw. "Revenge," read the caption on the shirt. I presented this shirt to Hibler as a gift. She was thrilled, even if she did not wear it.

Finding T-shirts decorated with images of crab is a challenge in Portland. McCormick & Schmick's restaurant did sell a T-shirt, but instead of a crab, the shirt featured a moose.

Moreover, during my four-day stay in Portland, I did not see one person wearing a baseball cap with a crab perched on the bill. In Baltimore I see such caps frequently, especially at the seafood stands in the Lexington Market.

While I wasn't able to go crabbing in Oregon, I did question several local folks on the matter of bait.

Bill White, who rents boats and crab-catching equipment at Bay Shore R.V. Center and Marina in Nehalem Bay, about 50 miles northwest of Portland, said most of his customers use frozen fish to catch Dungeness crabs. But he said he had seen some crabbers use watermelons or cans of cat food with holes punched in them for bait.

Later, Nick Furman of the Oregon Dungeness Crab Commission told me that a few years ago, a fellow tried to harvest crabs using a helicopter. The idea was that the helicopter would haul giant crab pots, 7 or 8 feet long, from the local waters.

The venture went bust shortly after a copter crashed into the water.

I had to admire the imagination, if not the common sense, of folks who try to catch crabs with cat food and helicopters.

There's a difference in the way the West Coast and the East Coast treat soft crabs, crabs that have shed their shells. Throughout Maryland and most of the East Coast, when blue crabs shed their shells, people pursue them. Chefs can't wait to saute them. Eaters line up to taste them.

In Oregon, when the Dungeness crab sheds its shell, folks lose interest in it. According to Furman, Dungeness meat loses a great deal of density when the crab molts. These lighter crabs are called "floaters," Furman said, and are usually considered unpalatable.

I tried but was unable to determine which crabs are meaner.

I know from finger-numbing experience that the blue crab is a feisty critter that can do real damage with its quick-moving claws.

The Dungeness, however, is a heavy fellow with a reputation as a big hitter. I was told by Dungeness supporters that when their crab is put in a tank with a lobster, the lobster often ends up dead.

I left Portland thinking that the blue crab has the advantage in crab-cake and soft-crab competition. And I would say the blue crab has inspired more artistic expression — some might call it tackiness — than the Dungeness.

But the gap is closing. Oregon now has several giant inflatable Dungeness crabs, which appear at various civic functions wearing sunglasses.

The fine points of skewering

SKEWERING — THREADING MORSELS OF FOOD ON A SHAFT AND COOKING them over a charcoal fire — is a lot of trouble and a fair amount of fun.

Cutting up the tidbits and positioning them on skewers can be tedious. It is one of those jobs that restaurant chefs tend to delegate to their assistants. On the home front, however, assistants are hard to find. Occasionally you might be able to entreat your kids to load a few morsels on a few sticks. But their enthusiasm for extended piercing — the kind of workload required by most serious skewerings — is slight.

More often than not, you have to do the skewering yourself. That is what I found myself doing recently — loading pieces of shrimp and asparagus on some wooden and metal skewers.

Like many seemingly dreadful undertakings, this one turned out to be surprisingly enjoyable, after I lowered my head and got to work.

Running things through with a sharp stick seemed to bring out the musketeer in my subconscious. "Take that, you spineless rascal," I said as I impaled a slippery shrimp. "Now I gotcha," I announced as I nailed an elusive chunk of asparagus. These were not uplifting thoughts, but they got the skewers loaded.

I grappled with the question that every skewerist must face — namely, does he want to use a tool made of wood or of metal? There are advantages to both. The main thing the metal skewer has going for it is that it does not burst into flames.

Wooden skewers that have not been soaked in water can do that. While fiery skewers can add a dramatic touch to any dinner gathering, a four-alarm outburst can also ruin the flavor of the food.

The effect that an artful skewerist is after is less what happened to Joan of Arc — burned at the stake — and more what happened in "The Magic Flute" to Tamino. He was tested by fire and emerged from the experience with improved character.

A drawback of metal skewers — at least of the long, skinny type I found in the kitchen junk drawer — is that they allow the food to spin.

The other night, after I put on a pair of insulated mittens, I tried to turn over the metal skewers that held the shrimp and asparagus. I wanted to do this so that the food would cook evenly. But the food on the metal gave me the slip.

It kept spinning. The shrimp and asparagus pivoted on the skinny metal shaft. This meant that the food on the hot side of the grill — close to the fire — got even hotter and cooked quickly. The food on the cold side — the side away from the coals — cooked slowly.

There were a couple of wooden skewers on the fire as well. These had thicker shafts, and they didn't allow the shrimp and asparagus to play games.

The food impaled on these wooden skewers turned over on command, and cooked evenly.

I probably could have hurried out to a kitchen-supply store and purchased some fancy metal skewers that have "food lock-down" features. But simply spearing my food and roasting it over an open fire seemed like a primal act. Making a run to a mall would have sullied the experience.

So instead of going shopping, I speared the food with what was at hand — a handful of metal and wooden skewers.

For a moment I considered grilling dangerously, putting the wooden skewers over the coals without first soaking the skewers in water. There was a pretty good chance that the unsoaked wood would not get hot enough to ignite.

But I quickly realized I wasn't willing to take the chance.

I knew that if even part of supper burst into flames, my goal of becoming an artful skewerist would suffer. So I soaked the wood in water and hummed a little tune that went something like: "I don't want to set the skewers on fire."

Grilled Shrimp and Asparagus

Serves 4

8 spears of asparagus, bottom ¼ trimmed
16 medium shrimp (about 1 pound) peeled and deveined
1 tablespoon vegetable oil
salt and pepper to taste

Dipping Sauce
⅓ cup soy sauce
1 tablespoon sugar
¼ cup fresh lime juice (about 2 limes)
1 teaspoon red pepper flakes
1 tablespoon freshly cracked white or black pepper

Fill a large bowl with ice and water. In a large saucepan, bring about 6 cups of salted water to a boil over high heat. When water comes to full boil, add asparagus and cook for 2 minutes. The asparagus should be tender but should still retain its bright color and crisp texture.

Drain the asparagus and plunge it into the ice water to stop the cooking process. When the asparagus is cool, drain it, and cut each spear into thirds.

Make dipping sauce by combining all ingredients in a small bowl and whisking together. Set aside.

Thread the asparagus and shrimp alternately onto skewers, rub lightly with the oil, and sprinkle with salt and pepper to taste. Grill over medium-hot fire for 4 to 6 minutes per side. To check for doneness, cut into one of the shrimp and be sure it is opaque all the way through. Remove skewers from grill and serve. Pass the sauce on the side for dipping.

From "License to Grill"
by Chris Schlesinger and John Willoughby (Morrow, 1997)

Ribs by the numbers

BARBECUING RIBS IS A SIMPLE, SINFUL PLEASURE. IT MIGHT SEEM contradictory to slap rules on such primal behavior, but life is full of contradictions, and good ribs are worth a few hours of unquestioning obedience.

Here, culled from talks with local and national barbecue barons, are the Ten Commandments of Cooking Ribs in the Back Yard.

The 1st Commandment: Cook low and slow. We are talking hours here, not minutes. Count on a slab of ribs cooking for at least three hours over a low heat, 250 degrees tops.

The 2nd Commandment: Good barbecue comes from good meat. Selecting a slab of pork ribs is like buying a car: You need to pick the right size. Spareribs are sized by numbers, which roughly refer to how many pounds the slab weighs. The full-size model, referred to by butchers as "3½ to 5's" (3½ to 5 pounds a slab), are the big-bone ribs. But these big guys also tote more waste than smaller models.

The four-door sedan, best-selling slab is called "the 3½ and down." Baby-back ribs are the sports car of ribs: smaller, leaner, pricey but considered by some to be too lightweight for anything other than an appetizer. The new rib in the model line is the loin-back: bigger than the baby-back, smaller than the 3½ and down. A slab usually weighs 1¾ pounds to 2¼ pounds. Your butcher can help you determine how much meat to buy.

The 3rd Commandment: Buy American pork. American pigs taste better than pork from across the ocean. Just ask J. R. Roach of De Witt, Ark., and Rodney Cheshire of Memphis, two of the big Bubbas of the national barbecue circuit. One June they taught a one-day barbecue school at Andy Nelson's Southern Pit Barbecue in Cockeysville. Their ribs, which had been rubbed with spices and smoked, were wolfed down by their 45 or so students. But the profs weren't pleased. The ribs, Roach said, had come from Denmark (they couldn't find locals) and had a foreign flavor. I thought they tasted too salty. "Fish-fed pigs," sniffed Cheshire. The lesson: Always ask your butcher where he gets his pigs.

The 4th Commandment: Skin your ribs. Using a knife, peel off the membrane that coats the bone side of the ribs. This trick, taught by Roach and Cheshire, helps smoke and spices penetrate the meat.

The 5th Commandment: Avoid flames. The ribs and the fire should be kept apart. Champion barbecuers take several steps to control the contact between heat and meat. They let their wood logs burn down to coals. They put water in their cookers. Backyard cooks can imitate the champs by using an indirect cooking method. Put the ribs on one side of the grill, put the coals nearby, but not directly under the ribs. Gas grills do the job, but are seriously lacking in soul.

The 6th Commandment: Know the temperature. Backyard cookers now come with thermometers in their lids. A less accurate but more colorful way to measure the heat of a fire is to hold your hand over the coals and count "one Mississippi, two Mississippi, three Mississippi," etc., until the heat forces you to pull your hand away. Ribs do best over a three-to-four Mississippi fire.

The 7th Commandment: Dunk or rub according to your beliefs. There are two schools of thought — the dunkers and the rubbers — on what to do with ribs before you put them over the fire. The dunkers immerse the pork in vinegar-based marinades, producing a "wet rib." The rubbers massage the rack with a dry mix of spices, yielding a "dry rib." Combining the two methods is regarded as heresy.

The 8th Commandment: Never boil ribs. "The only reason you put meat in water is to make soup," said Rick Catalano, then-proprietor of Cafe Tattoo in Northeast Baltimore. "It takes the juices and flavor out of the ribs," said Jerry Railey, then-proprietor of a barbecue stand in the Cross Street Market.

People boil ribs because they are in a hurry, a sin against the first commandment. But for the ribs cook who gets caught by a thunderstorm, a better, if not sanctioned, way to proceed is to bake the ribs in a 250-degree oven until the meat can be pulled from the bone.

The 9th Commandment: Use tricks to keep them warm. When the ribs easily pull apart, they are done. If the ribs are ready before the eaters are, keep the ribs warm by stacking racks of them on top of each other, and basting the top rack with a watered-down version of your favorite sauce. If the wait will be especially long, wrap ribs in aluminum foil. Put two ice cubes in the bottom of the foil packet, then seal it. Set packet on the grill. As ice melts, it will keep ribs moist.

The 10th Commandment: Don't forget the finish. The sauce that is served with the cooked ribs when they hit the table is called the finish sauce. Tomato-based sauces tend to burn if applied to ribs that are on the fire. But they make good finish sauces. Finish sauces can be hot or sweet. Hot means peppers. Sweet means brown sugar, molasses or honey. Applying a honey-based finish sauce also gives the ribs a beatific glow.

Confections of a fig lover

AFTER SITTING AROUND MOST OF THE SUMMER DOING NEXT TO NOTHING, MY backyard fig trees suddenly began producing a glut of fruit. This rush to ripeness resulted in a race between me and the critters — birds, bees and ants — to see who could eat the figs first.

Fresh figs are a prize worth pursuing. They have a unique texture, and a flavor that is sweet but not cloying. So I put on a pair of gloves — protection against surprised critters — and went out and pinched the figs. The pinching helps determine how ripe the figs are.

I had read that Italians, who seem to know a lot about figs, don't harvest them until they see juice dripping out of the blossom end of the fruit. They call the drip "a tear in the eye." I was not that patient. I thought that if I waited until the juice started dripping, the crowd of critters would ravage the figs. And that would put tears in my eyes. So I started pinching the figs. If they felt pliable, I picked them.

After I had a bowl full of fresh purple figs, the question was: What was I going to do with them? There was the usual solution, washing them quickly with water and eating them while they were still warm from the sun. This was satisfying. But soon I was sated on sun-warmed figs, and looking for other ways to reduce the pile of purple fruit.

I went the appetizer route, stuffing each fig with a toasted almond and some fennel seeds, then drizzling them with red wine and baking them in a hot oven (400 degrees) until the heat caramelized the wine. The process took about five minutes. The figs were wonderful, for a while.

After stuffing myself with some 60 stuffed figs, I tired of this taste. So I experimented with figs, honey and mascarpone cheese. This dish was easy. I split the figs, drizzled them with honey and ate them with the mascarpone. This cheesy fig treatment had its days of glory, then it, too, grew tiresome.

Next I fell back on a technique I had tried in previous years — wrapping the figs in basil leaves and a slice of prosciutto, brushing them lightly with olive oil and grilling them until the prosciutto is barely brown at the edges, about half a minute per side.

After a few servings it was the same old story. The first few times were thrilling, but by the fourth time around, I had lost interest in eating the figs.

Meanwhile, a recipe for a salad made with grilled figs and grilled plum tomatoes had caught my eye. I will probably try that one as well.

This love-them-then-leave-them routine will probably last a week or so.

Then one of two things will happen. Either the trees will stop producing figs, or I will run out of recipes.

Figs with Honey and Mascarpone

Serves 4

8 figs
about 1 cup mascarpone cheese at room temperature
about ¼ cup honey

Cut figs into halves. Place ¼ cup of mascarpone on each of 4 plates. Surround the mascarpone with figs. Drizzle with honey. Serve immediately.

From "A Fresh Taste of Italy"
by Michele Scicolone (Broadway Books, 1997)

The solution to summer squash

UNTIL RECENTLY, I HAD NOT BEEN ABLE TO WORK UP MUCH ARDOR FOR summer squash.

It was just another vegetable in the market. It was not as well known as its green cousin, zucchini. And with its crooked neck and bright yellow skin, it was not good-looking.

What changed my attitude toward summer squash was proximity. Many summer squash moved into our home. They filled up bowls that were supposed to hold fruit. They stretched out on kitchen counters. They sunned themselves in the back yard.

This invasion of the summer squash was similar to the zucchini influx that had visited the household a few weeks earlier. Both were caused by a garden gone bonkers. I had planted some summer squash in a community garden in Druid Hill Park. It grew. Man did it grow! It spread out faster than urban sprawl, crowding out the cabbage, overpowering the beans. Even the thistles — among the toughest of weeds — seemed to give the summer squash wide berth.

Unlike their zucchini cousins, the summer squash were hard to get rid of. People may laugh at a zucchini, but eventually they will take it off your hands. Its big, green form is friendly. It looks like an overgrown cucumber.

Summer crookneck squash, however, looks twisted. Its skin is a color I would describe as toxic yellow. When you rub your hand on its skin, it feels bumpy. Looking at its bent neck, you can't help but wonder: "Is that what will happen to me if I eat this stuff?"

So when I brought several yellow crookneck squash home from the garden, they piled up in the house. Nobody ate them and I began to consider other uses for them. I thought of calling them gourds, and putting them around the house as decorative accent pieces.

Eventually, what got the squash off the kitchen counters and into the oven was a potluck supper. Our neighborhood, like many in Baltimore, has a lot of potluck suppers in the summer. The idea behind these meals is that everybody cooks, but nobody cooks very much. You whip up one dish or so. The organizers of the potluck meal provide something substantial — from roast beef to hot dogs — as the main dish. The potluck dishes brought by the folks attending the meal serve as accompanying fare. One recent hot afternoon, my wife was trying to figure out what to take to a potluck supper that evening. I suggested the squash. I had mixed motives.

I wanted to share this source of carotene, the yellow pigment that our bodies convert to Vitamin A, with our friends. And I wanted to get rid of the squash. I figured people will eat most anything at potlucks. So let's dress the squash up, put it out there and see what happens.

These squash were the wrong size. Yellow summer squash, like fashion models, are supposed to be young, thin and supple. Few squash on earth seem to fit this description. Most are aged, wide, lumpy and getting stiffer by the minute. When my wife sliced our aged squash open, the seeds looked like they had seen a lot of life. So she discarded the seeds, sliced off the yellow skin, and cut the yellow, pulpy flesh into little pieces. You go through a lot of squash when you discard their mid-sections. But in our case, all this waste was a plus. The goal was to lower the number of squash.

Which we did. After the surgery, there was no longer a summer squash in every kitchen corner. There were a few left. But they were under control. We had, as the cattlemen say, managed the herd.

We put the pieces of sliced squash on a baking sheet, brushed them with olive oil and sprinkled them with sea salt and black pepper. Then we baked them in a very hot oven, 450 degrees, for about 45 minutes. When faced with this dramatic heat, the pieces of summer squash did what most of us do in the summer heat, they shrank. When the squash pieces had cooled, we put them in a bowl and carried them to the potluck supper.

At first, I didn't eat any. Instead, I concentrated on the selection of brownies, which were also offered as side dishes. But I heard other eaters remarking favorably on the flavor of the yellow squash. I was surprised. This was supposed to be a give-away dish, not a gourmet dish. I tried some. The squash had a sweet flavor.

The squash dish was so good that my wife and I made it again the next night, when we were feeding ourselves, not the neighborhood. Summer squash and I have now become intimate. In the garden, I seek it out. I fight off its prickly leaves and can't wait to get my hands on its bumpy, twisted neck.

On vacation with popcorn

MAYBE IT IS BREATHING THE SEA AIR. OR MAYBE IT IS SWALLOWING THE SALT water. Whatever the reason, popcorn tastes better when you are at the ocean.

Among the rituals I engage in when my family makes its summer pilgrimage to the Atlantic Ocean is the midday popping of the corn. After a few hours of floating on the waves on an air mattress, I crave popcorn. Retreating to the kitchen of the beach house, I put a pan on the stove, heat vegetable oil in it until two or three test kernels of popcorn burst. Then I cover the bottom of the pan with more kernels, put a lid on the pan, start popping, and finish off with salt and melted butter. There is something about being barefoot at 3 o'clock in the afternoon and eating a bowl of pleasure that makes you feel like you are on vacation.

With or without their shoes on, Marylanders have been eating popcorn at the beach for years. I found this out after talking with two barons of the Ocean City popcorn scene, Rudolph William Dolle Jr. and Donald R. Fisher, and with Joe Bernard, whose Queenstown firm, Wye River Inc. was hoping to capitalize on the region's popcorn-eating habits by calling its bags of cheese, butter and caramel corn "Downy Ocean Hon!"

After operating a merry-go-round in South Baltimore on the grounds of what is now the Harbor Hospital Center, the Dolle family moved themselves and their carrousel to Ocean City in 1910. Once there, they started making salt water taffy and a year later added fresh-popped popcorn to the menu. Ever since then, folks have been lining up at the Dolle Candyland stand at the Boardwalk and Wicomico Street for containers of buttered or caramel corn, which today range from 70-cent boxes to $17 tubs.

The popularity of popcorn is based on two factors, said Rudolph Dolle. The first is habit. "When people get to the beach, they just have to have popcorn, ice cream, french fries."

The other factor is taste. When people are treating themselves, he said, they don't want imitation flavors. "We use honest-to-God butter," Dolle said. "We say if you put good in, good comes out."

Donald R. Fisher, the 64-year-old proprietor of Fisher's Popcorn, learned the business from his father, Everett. At the age of 7, Donald folded popcorn boxes, and at the age of 14, he became chief popper when his dad was drafted to fight in World War II.

Back in 1944, his popcorn business was a summer-only operation. Now Fisher's, at Talbot Street and the Boardwalk, is a year-round enterprise, supervised by Fisher, his son Donald and daughter Cindy. In addition to having healthy summertime sales, the business also does a brisk trade around Christmas, shipping tubs of popcorn ranging from $4.50 a gallon to $28 for 6½ gallons to customers around the country.

Some customers give the tubs of popcorn to neighbors who took care of the dog, or watched the house, while the family was at the beach, Fisher said. A lot of doctors and dentists send gifts of popcorn to thank people who sent them referrals, Fisher said.

Such a friendly reception to popcorn from members of the medical community is interesting in light of the furor raised about the high fat content of movie-theater popcorn cooked in coconut oil. Until then, popcorn had enjoyed something of an undeserved reputation among snackers as a health food. Groups such as the National Cancer Institute, the American Dental Association and American Diabetes Association recommended air-popped popcorn as a good source of fiber and a sugar-free snack.

Gail A. Levey, a registered dietitian in New York and a spokeswoman for the American Dietetic Association, gave me some perspective on popcorn's nutritional value. Popcorn, she said, is like bread. If you don't put anything on it, it is good for you. But if you coat it, either by cooking it in oils high in saturated fat, or by topping it with butter, the nutritional benefits fade.

Air-popped popcorn with no toppings is probably the most nutritionally correct popcorn, high in fiber with virtually no calories or sodium, she said. But many people can't stand the taste. Popcorn cooked in coconut oil is high in saturated fat, but also has excellent flavor. Both Dolle and Fisher use coconut oil to pop the corn used to make their buttered popcorn. Their caramel corn, which gets much of its flavor from its sugary coating, is popped over an open flame without oil. Downy The Ocean Hon! popcorn, which is coated with cheese, butter or caramel, is popped in canola oil, a lower-fat oil.

One good strategy for a popcorn lover concerned about nutrition, Levey said, is to shop around for a popcorn cooked in low-fat oil that has enough flavor to satisfy a craving for popcorn. Bags of microwave popcorn, she said, now have the fat content on the label. At home you could experiment with air-popped corn or with popping corn in canola, olive or vegetable oils.

Another strategy, she said, is to go ahead and enjoy an occasional bag of good old high-fat, high-flavor beach popcorn, but not every day. To which I add, be sure and take your shoes and socks off. Popcorn always taste better when your toes are sandy.

Pursuing sandwich perfection

IT IS A SIMPLE SANDWICH. IT IS MADE OF BREAD, TOMATO SLICES, OLIVE OIL, salt and pepper. Yet its flavor can vary. Sometimes this sandwich can be an amazing blend of textures and juices. Other times, however, it can taste ordinary, like doughy bread and watery tomatoes.

Success with this sandwich seems to depend on two factors: the technique of the sandwich maker and the quality of the ingredients.

I say "seems" because I am not yet a master of this sandwich. Sometimes the versions of this sandwich I have made have been heavenly; sometimes they have just been OK. None has been as satisfying as the ones made by Luigi Ferrucci.

This is perhaps the 1,000th time I have cited Luigi as an expert on eats and the second time I have mentioned him in this book. He is a physician who lives outside Florence and stays with my family during business trips to the United States. During these stays Luigi has taken up kitchen utensils and shown us ways to make polenta, pasta, gnocchi and tomato sandwiches.

When I find someone who knows a subject well and has an effective way of communicating insights, I listen closely. For instance, when Mike Flanagan and Jim Palmer talk about pitching strategy during a TV broadcast of an Orioles game, I am delighted. They tell me things about a game that I have played, coached and watched for years.

The same thing happens when I listen to Luigi talk about food. I learn things. Take, for example, how he makes a tomato sandwich. One night early this summer, Luigi mentioned that in his student days, he had virtually survived on sandwiches made with bread and tomatoes. The next morning I left Luigi in the kitchen for a few minutes while I drove my wife to Penn Station. When I got home, Luigi had made us a plate of tomato sandwiches, the sandwiches of his youth.

They were wonderful. Ordinarily, I don't eat much in the morning and I don't think of tomatoes as breakfast food. Yet I wolfed down these sandwiches.

Luigi showed me how he had made them. He started with a thin slice of homemade white bread. The bread, he said, had to have some substance.

I soon saw why the bread has to have some backbone. It was mugged, perhaps massaged would be a better word, by a slice of tomato. Luigi cut a thin slice of tomato, then folded the slice in half, and pressed it into the slice of bread. He didn't let the juice merely drip onto the bread, he rubbed it in. His motion of the tomato working on the bread reminded me of the way a masseur works on tight back muscles. He was firm, not gentle.

Next, he discarded the slice of massaging-tomato and replaced it with two fresh slices of tomato. These were also thin. He positioned them on the bread.

The tomato slices were then sprinkled with a few drops of extra virgin olive oil, the finest grade. Luigi was partial to Italian olive oils. The only bottle of extra virgin olive oil we had was one from California. At first he was skeptical, but as he applied the drops to the sandwich, he nodded approval. The color and aroma of the American extra virgin olive oil met his Italian standards.

He sprinkled the slices of tomato with sea salt, and covered them with flecks of crushed black pepper. He salted moderately but peppered heavily. The sandwich, an open-face variety, was ready. The juice of the tomatoes, the texture of bread, the fruit flavor of the olive oil, and the bite of the pepper all came together.

Since that morning in the kitchen, I have been trying to replicate Luigi's tomato sandwich.

Sometimes I have come close. I have learned that the slices of the bread have to be thin, about as thick as a matchbook. I have learned that the more sandwiches you make, the more adept you become at rubbing tomato slices into thin slices of bread. And I have learned you can't try to cheap out on the olive oil and use a less-expensive grade. It has to be extra virgin olive oil; the tomato flavor suffers otherwise.

I also know that soon my tomato sandwiches are going to taste better. They might even surpass the sandwiches of Luigi, the master. When Luigi made his sandwiches in early June he used store-bought tomatoes. They were red, but not very juicy. That was all that was available then.

But when the tomatoes in my garden ripen, I get to make this sandwich using slices of dead-ripe, juice-laden, home-grown tomatoes.

Making the best of green tomatoes

ONE TRUTH ABOUT GREEN TOMATOES IS THAT THEY DON'T TASTE NEARLY AS good as their red-skinned relatives.

Another truth is that while "Fried Green Tomatoes" is a pretty good film, it is not a jump-up-and-say-hallelujah dish. Unless you fry the tomatoes in lard.

That's right, lard. You drop breaded slices of green tomatoes in a skillet of sizzling hog fat, and they come out tasting like a piece of heaven.

A related truth is that if you drop a slice of most anything — even tofu — in a skillet of sizzling hog fat, it will come out tasting on the up side of wonderful.

Because lard makes things taste so good, it is, of course, bad for us. It is not merely high in fat, it is off the charts. Just looking at lard probably clogs an artery or two.

I figure that the way things are going in the eating world, lard will soon be declared a controlled substance. That would mean friends of lard wouldn't be able to get a hunk of hog fat on the open market unless they could produce a note from a cardiologist.

Another dirty little secret about green tomatoes is that folks who sing the praises of other green-tomato dishes — like pie and relish — would never make these concoctions if they had to pay for the main ingredient, unripe tomatoes.

The motivating forces behind most green-tomato dishes are glut and guilt.

Let's take glut first. Most folks wouldn't mess with green tomatoes if they didn't have them coming out of their ears. There are always more green tomatoes on a plant than you expect. A plant could be dead longer than Huey Long, and it can still have more progeny than a jack rabbit. It happens every fall. The frost hits, the tomato plants die, and backyard gardeners go into trauma at the prospect of saying goodbye to the garden.

This is where the guilt comes in. I know, I have been there. You start by yanking the spindly plants out of the ground, then you end up caressing the plants' last offering of the season, the rock-hard green ovals known as green tomatoes.

Pretty soon you've got a bucket full of green tomatoes and a conscience nagging you to do something with them besides tossing them at telephone poles.

So you end up slicing them and putting them in a green-tomato pie — one of the few pies in creation that can sit unprotected in the kitchen overnight with no chance of being attacked.

Or you chop them up, add peppers and make a few thousand jars of off-color relish that you palm off as Christmas gifts to unsuspecting relatives.

These culinary attempts to embrace green tomatoes are noble. I applaud the change-of-season dinner-table rituals they inspire. But let's face it: Most green-tomato dishes are like the drawings your kid did in kindergarten. They give you pleasure because of the kinship involved, not the artistry.

I'm as guilty as the next green-tomato guy of fawning over these little baseballs. Instead of using them to practice my fastball, I want to take them home. They remind me of the juicy delights of summer.

So, as autumn descends, I gather my garden survivors, the green tomatoes, in my arms. I carry them to a warm kitchen and fry them in a warm skillet. Some will sizzle in hot olive oil. But, if no one is looking, I fry a batch or two in hissing hog fat.

Fried Green Tomatoes

Serves 4

Heat ⅛ inch of olive oil (or lard) in a cast-iron skillet. Slice 8 green tomatoes ¼ inch thick. Dip in stone-ground cornmeal blended with freshly ground black pepper, cayenne pepper and salt to taste.

Fry on medium-high heat about 5 minutes on each side until golden brown and crisp. Pat with paper towel to remove excess oil and serve immediately.

From "The Kitchen Garden Cookbook"
by Sylvia Thompson (Bantam, 1995)

Tomatoes and kids

DURING THE SERIOUS TOMATO-TENDING SEASON, I OFTEN THINK ABOUT THE parallels between raising tomatoes and raising kids. For starters, both efforts require seemingly endless amounts of work. There is always one more scheme, whether it is fertilizing a plant or a mind, that some expert somewhere has said you absolutely should be undertaking if you are serious about growth. I tend to believe that kid-raising and tomato-growing are pretty much on-the-job training experiences. You learn as you go.

That doesn't stop folks from telling you what you should be doing. Merely by attempting to bring kids and tomatoes into this world you automatically expose yourself to a hailstorm of advice. Everybody has an insight on proper development that must be shared.

More often than not, the theories conflict. The disciplinarians tell you that you should keep a tight rein on both kids and tomato plants, restricting them, directing their growth.

Meanwhile, the libertarians advise you to let nature work in an unfettered fashion. The child and the tomato plant should, they say, be allowed to roam.

I think of myself as a disciplinarian. But in quiet moments of reflection, I sometimes see that my kids and my tomato plants behave as if I were a pushover.

Which leads me to the matter of posture. Neither kids nor tomato plants want to stand up straight. In their early days, both tomato plants and kids tend to be spindly. They seem vulnerable to any ill wind. In fact, they are amazingly resilient, bouncing back much faster from any setback than we, their older keepers, thought was possible.

The other day, for example, as I struggled to correct the posture of a cherry tomato plant that had thrown itself across the garden, I was struck by how much the sprawling plant resembled a certain teen-ager stretched out on a sofa. Limbs were draped in all directions. The position looked wrong and uncomfortable to me. But correcting the posture of the teen-ager or the tomato plant seemed futile. As soon as I left the scene, both the tomato plant and the teen-ager resumed their original poses, and seemed perfectly happy.

Another similarity between tomatoes and kids is that they both grow in sudden, alarming bursts. Almost overnight they are poking out of pant legs, toppling tomato cages, tossing off old clothes and dead leaves. What is it, I wonder, that fuels such spurts? Is it all the expensive nutrients we feed them? Is it nature's timing? I tend to believe it is orneriness. Tomato plants and kids grow to keep us, their caretakers, guessing what will happen next.

Both tomatoes and kids are fond of water. Children are great fans of splashing in a pool, or running through a sprinkler, or aiming the hose nozzle so that it removes the top four inches of soil from the yard. Tomatoes, too, enjoy flowing water. No matter how sorry its appearance, a row of droopy tomato plants can, it seems, be revived by spending an afternoon under the garden hose.

I have also found that both tomato plants and kids respond well to threats. Experience has taught me that one way to hurry along slow-moving kids is to start the engine of the family car. Once kids realize the driver might actually make good on his threat to leave without them, they quickly get in gear, find those missing shoes, and get out the door and into the car.

With tomatoes, a proven way to hurry them along, to get reluctant ones to ripen, is to threaten to go on vacation. Just walk to the garden and announce, within earshot of the tomatoes, "We're going on vacation tomorrow." The next day, get in your car and drive away. Before your car gets two blocks from the garden, at least four tomatoes will have turned from pale green to fire-engine red.

There is little doubt that raising kids and tomatoes tests your fortitude. For endless hours, you cultivate and pamper them. You wait for some reward, for some sign of progress. Then, just when you are about to throw up your hands in disgust, something pleasant happens. You show up at school, for example, and hear a teacher singing the praises of your kind child, the same kid who at home regularly announces his deep-seated desire to beat his brother to a pulp. You show up at the garden and discover that a row of spindly tomato plants, a row you were going to replace with pumpkins, has miraculously come to fruition. It surprises you. It makes you feel proud. It makes you think your efforts were worth it.

If tradition holds, my garden will have failed to produce ripe tomatoes by the Fourth of July, thereby marking me, in the minds of some people, as a less-than-successful gardener. Moreover, I will also be a moral slacker, in the view of some, because my kids still enjoy the primal thrill of shooting off fireworks. I have even been known, in previous Julys, to slip over the border into Virginia with the kids and shoot off fireworks that aren't sold in Maryland.

Which proves, I guess, that I believe in talking the tight-reins talk, but in practice I cut both my progeny and my tomatoes a lot of slack.

Summertime — and the sipping is easy

ON LANGUID SUMMER AFTERNOONS WHEN THE SHIMMERING HEAT AND THE BIG lunches slow life down, I feel like making something cold and old-fashioned.

Last summer it was iced tea. I found a new, cold-water method of brewing tea. On days when I had time on my hands, I put 4 teaspoons of loose tea in a teapot and filled the pot with about a quart of cold water. I let the tea sit for three hours, then poured it in glasses filled with ice cubes. The result was a cold, refreshing tea that didn't have the bite of the teas I made with boiling water. It was also easier on the ice cubes.

This cold-brew method came from Jerry Railey, who once ran a barbecue stand in the Cross Street Market. When Railey was growing up in Elm City, a small town in North Carolina, one of his evening chores was putting loose tea in a cheesecloth and dropping it in a barrel filled with water. The mixture would sit overnight, in a cool spot. Come morning, the tea was ready. Sugar and ice were added when it was served.

This summer I got the urge to make lemonade. I looked around for old, rural recipes. I found two good ones in "Farm Recipes and Food Secrets From the Norske Nook" (Crown, 1993) This is a collection of the recipes of Helen Myhre, a farmer's wife who, in addition to cooking for her family, ran the Norske Nook cafe in Wisconsin for years.

Unlike so many of the cookbooks published today, this one does not shy away from big amounts of politically incorrect ingredients such as sugar and butter. The book, co-authored by Mona Vold, has sold well. As part of the book's promotion, Myhre appeared on David Letterman's show to try to teach the not-too-attentive comedian how to make a pie.

The restaurant, situated in Osseo, a town of 1,500 about 100 miles east of Minneapolis-St. Paul on Interstate 94, has long lines of customers even though Myhre sold it recently.

"On the farm," Myhre wrote in her book, "if we're busy, we eat those butter-filled recipes, not once, but six times a day, and we're still standing where the sun shines. Of course, maybe it's because we are so active!"

When I reached Myhre on the phone, she said she was getting ready to make one of her old favorites, lemonade in a 10-gallon milk can. That is a lot of lemonade, but she was expecting a big crowd. There was going to be a reunion of folks who went to a nearby rural school. The school, with the Norwegian name of Huskelhus, was where kids in grades one through eight had been taught. It had been around since 1872.

"We decided to have a picnic like we always did when we were kids," said Myhre, who is in her late 60s. "So we are going to have the lemonade in a milk can."

Back when she was a girl, lemonade was made in a milk can because the can was a big, sturdy vessel, she said. And in the days before refrigeration and ice cubes, if you cooled the metal can down with spring water, the lemonade would stay cold.

Making lemonade in a 10-gallon milk can is not hard, she said, and talked me through the procedure. In the bottom of a clean milk can, you mix the juice of 2 dozen oranges and 1½ dozen lemons with 6-10 cups of sugar. Some folks like the taste of 10 cups of sugar, she said. But the orange juice is also sweet, she added, so you can use a lesser amount of sugar, 6 cups or so, if you like. Then you fill the can about two-thirds full of cold spring water and "stir real good." Finally, you toss in a few lemon and orange rinds and let them float in the lemonade.

While the technique isn't tricky, she said, finding a milk can is. Now that milk is shipped in big tanker trucks, milk cans are scarce. But Myhre, whose husband ran a dairy farm, said she "grabbed a few cans a few years ago ... before everybody went to bulk shipping."

For folks who don't have milk cans, or don't want oranges in their lemonade, Myhre has another recipe.

This one calls for mixing the juice of 4 lemons with 1 cup of sugar in a 2-quart pitcher, then adding cold spring water until the pitcher is full.

This is the kind of lemonade her mother used to make on sizzling summer evenings when the family ate outside, Myhre recalled. "We would have sandwiches and lemonade. The grass would be crisp under your feet. And we would sit on a hillside and watch the sun go down. That was all we would need."

So that is what I am trying in the summer: farmer's wife lemonade. Since I don't have water from a cold spring, I am using tap water, and maybe I'll try some bottled water.

The kind of water you use to make lemonade is important, said Myhre, a fan of water from gurgling farm springs. When she and her husband moved off the farm and into town a few years ago, they moved off spring water and onto city water. "And," said Myhre, "I do miss our good water."

The signs of summer

IT IS A SIGN OF SUMMER WHEN YOUR COFFEE CHANGES COLOR. ON WARM afternoons you drop ice cubes in your coffee and add a shot of cream. The cream cloud descends on the ice cubes like an ocean wave rolling over rocks at the beach. The color of the coffee changes from black to mocha, and the personality of the drink changes from a hot, start-your-engine beverage to a cool, indulgent companion.

It is a sign of summer when you find yourself lingering in a neighborhood restaurant, Kelly's, in the 2100 block of Eastern Ave., on a Friday night waiting for your order of carryout crabs. You are not agitated at the delay. At Kelly's they steam crabs only a few nights a week, and they don't begin steaming your carryout order until you show up at the restaurant. The procedure insures that the crabs will still be hot when you get them home.

It is a sign of summer when your car smells like steamed crabs. On the drive from the crab house to your house, you turn off the car air conditioner, and keep the windows up, to keep your order of carryout crabs hot.

It is a sign of summer when later that night, your houseguest calls up his folks in Connecticut to tell them when he will be flying home and he can't resist teasing them by saying: "We had crabs tonight. Eat your heart out."

It is a sign of summer when you start eating whole tomatoes as if they were apples, picking them out of a bowl on the kitchen counter, taking a bite, sprinkling on a little salt, then eating more.

It is a sign of summer when you buy limes in bulk. Some are squeezed and go into marinades for fish. Some go into salsas. Some are used to make a limeade, an old-fashioned drink made of lime juice, sugar and water that never ceases to quench thirsts.

It is a sign of summer when the pantry's seemingly unending supply of canned tuna suddenly vanishes. Where has all the tuna gone? It has been stuffed into cored tomatoes and cantaloupes, culinary moves that can be successfully employed only in the summer, when the flesh of these tuna-holders is sweet enough to balance the tang of fish.

It is a sign of summer when peach cobbler expectations rise, when your 11-year-old comes running into the kitchen and grabs a bowl of sliced peaches from your hands, convinced he has been wronged. He suspects that peach cobbler has been made and that he has not been told. The kid sniffs at the bowl, discovers that it holds peaches and cream, and like a cop letting a speeder off with a warning, gives your bowl to you. "Just checking," he says.

It is a sign of summer when it is 10 o'clock at night and you are sitting in the back yard eating supper. June Bugs are dive-bombing the candles, you are polishing off those bits of grilled chicken; sliced tomatoes in olive oil; and summer squash that you sliced, brushed with olive oil, salted with sea salt, then grilled. You are feeling proud of yourself that you acted spontaneously earlier in the evening and rushed off to see the movie "Purple Noon" at The Charles, that had subtitles. You are sitting at the supper table trying to talk about filmmaking with your teen-age son, and you realize this will be a limited discussion. The kid has seen six or seven films this summer, you have seen only two.

Finally, it is a sign of summer when you start drawing up a list of things you must do — eat a crab cake at the Lexington Market, crack open a locally-grown watermelon, finish reading that novel — before this summer, the season of strong flavors and sweet freedoms, comes to a close.

Index of recipes: